. . . All These To Teach

C. A. ROBERTSON

And I will undertake all these to teach.
I doubt not but this populous city will
Yield many scholars.

Pericles, IV, 6, 196

Essays in honor of C. A. ROBERTSON

. . . All These To Teach

Edited by 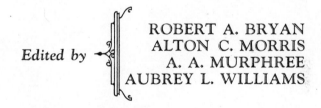 ROBERT A. BRYAN
ALTON C. MORRIS
A. A. MURPHREE
AUBREY L. WILLIAMS

University of Florida Press · Gainesville · 1965

A University of Florida Press Book

ALTON C. MORRIS
Professor of English
University of Florida

Charles Archibald Robertson

An Appreciation

HE ESSAYS IN THIS VOLUME, CONCEIVED AS A
salute to Professor C. A. Robertson upon his
retirement, are contributed by men who
have been associated with him as colleagues,
have served in the department under his
chairmanship, or are counted among his
other friends. They are offered as a tribute to his more than
forty years of service to humanistic studies at the University of
Florida and the South Atlantic Region.

Professor Robertson was nourished in a tradition that
placed stress upon Latin and Greek language and literature
and upon Shakespeare and the King James version of the Bible.
Determining at an early age to be a teacher, he devoted a lifetime to sharing his love of learning with students and colleagues alike. Born in Iamonia, near Tallahassee, Florida, he
attended secondary schools in that region. From the University
of Florida he earned a Bachelor of Arts degree in 1915, major-

ing in Greek, Latin, and English; and in 1919 he went on to the Master of Arts degree. He studied for the doctorate at Harvard University for two years and returned to the University of Florida as an assistant professor of English in 1923. Promoted to a professorship in 1928, he has held the position of head professor since 1946. For his interest in humane letters he was awarded the degree of Doctor of Literature by the University of the South in 1952. He served as president of the South Atlantic Modern Language Association, and has been elected to Phi Beta Kappa, Blue Key, and other honorary societies.

Professor Robertson's teaching of Shakespeare has been a memorable experience for thousands of students who took English 401-402 with him. Whether from farm or city, students left his class ennobled by the experience. His keen perception of human nature enabled him in presenting Shakespeare to give his students flashes of insight and moments of illumination into the nature of their own existence. Moreover, no student left his class without first acquiring a stock of quotable lines from Shakespeare. Many of his students, long after leaving the University, have sustained their relationship with this inspiring teacher.

From the outset of his career he was called to leadership. His nearly completed work at Harvard University was interrupted by the untimely death in 1927 of Dr. A. A. Murphree, then president of the University of Florida. The head of the Department of English at that time was elevated to the acting presidency, and Professor Robertson was recalled from Harvard to assume leadership of the English staff. As a chairman he made ceaseless efforts to bring into his department teacher-scholars of the highest caliber. His devotion to the department, his insistence upon quality instruction, and his loyalty to his staff have won for him the esteem of those whose privilege it has been to serve with him in building the department from one in which the M. A. degree was terminal to the present one which offers the Doctorate of Philosophy and post-doctoral fellowships.

One of Professor Robertson's most profound interests has been the University of Florida Library, which will reap the rewards of his vision for years to come. He championed library improvement not only in his own field but in all related areas. His zeal for finding funds, his perceptiveness in the value of proposed acquisitions, and his interest in a well-administered library have earned for him the gratitude of all students and faculty. As a member of the University Library Committee for several decades, he played an important role in the Library's growth from an institution containing possibly forty thousand books housed in a basement of one of the halls to its present building with over a million volumes.

He and his wife, Alleyne Redding Robertson, to whom he was married in 1926, have been host and hostess to many people of distinction in the humanities. Robert Frost in his annual visits to the University of Florida for over a decade shared the warm hospitality of the Robertson home, and Mr. Frost's lectures to the student body, sponsored by Professor Robertson, became a traditional event of the campus. In addition, the Department and the University have been favored by many visits from other literary men and women—a bounty to the University community made possible largely by the friendly relationships created with them by Professor and Mrs. Robertson. As a consequence of her warm regard for this department and its administration, the late Marjorie Kinnan Rawlings gave her manuscripts to the University of Florida Library and made the University of Florida residual beneficiary of her Cross Creek home.

Though Professor Robertson's primary love in literature has always been Shakespeare, he has had a lively interest in the whole range of English and American literary study. It is fitting, therefore, that the contents of this volume should exhibit a diversity of subject matter in keeping with his own wide range of interest in humane letters. Among the essays here presented the reader will find, in a chronological order of subject, topics ranging from linguistics to the Shakespearean drama, from the Middle English Digby play of Mary Magdalene to the letters of Elizabeth Madox Roberts.

The colleagues and friends of Professor Robertson, acknowledging his devotion to literature, his excellence as a teacher, his selflessness as a leader, offer this volume as a tribute to him. It may be said of him as was said of another great teacher: "He gave back as rain that which he received as mist." It is our hope that good fortune for many years ahead may

Furnish him with all the appertinents
Belonging to his honour. *(Henry V)*

Contents

ix

x

THOMAS PYLES
Professor of English
University of Florida

Inkhornisms, Fustian, & Current Vogue Words

BUCCINATE 'TO TRUMPET FORTH,' DIREPTITIOUS 'given to plundering,' *ineffrenate* 'unbridled,' *honorificabilitudinity* 'honor'—such lush creations of classically educated intellectuals and those who, like Shakespeare's Holofernes, aspired to be thought of as intellectuals had a considerable vogue in the Early Modern English period. Words like these were in the nature of caste-designators: their use indicated that one was "in," that one knew his way about in what were conceived to be the most exalted intellectual circles. Nevertheless, they were lambasted about as vigorously by the conservative folk of the time as the considerably less colorful and less flamboyant *finalize* has been in our own day.

Such words were derisively called *inkhorn terms*. The author of *The Arte of English Poesie* (1589) tells us that "*Irreuocable, irradiation, depopulation* and such like . . . were long

1

time despised for inkehorne termes."[1] They could not have been far removed from the so-called fustian eloquence of the time.

Education (1531), *chronology* (1593), and *contemplate* (1594),[2] however, must have seemed equally gaudy and tasteless to linguistic conservatives as those words just cited as having been "long time despised." They, like many other learned adaptations of the Early Modern period, were ultimately to enter ordinary usage; yet they were just as vulnerable as the archaisms cited at the very beginning of this paper, and must have been regarded with like abhorrence by those who wished above all things to keep the English language "pure," whatever that may mean. The conclusion is obvious: there is no way of predicting which words will catch on, which will die.

It is just as impossible to predict which of those words which have long been a part of our word stock will suddenly become vogue words. *Activate* and *priority* have been with us in an unobtrusive way for a very long time, only to become voguish in our own day. *Automation* has been with us for less than two decades, but it is likely to stay with us for a long time to come. In the history of vogue words, however, no man dare prophesy. On the other hand, fashion, to some extent governed (the voguish word here would be *conditioned*) by the political, economic, intellectual, and religious life of a people, to some extent purely whimsical, has driven out of use such mellifluous American words as *conbobberation*, *absquatulate*, *peedoodles*, and *hornswoggle*, all of which enjoyed a considerable vogue on the frontier in the more innocent days of our country; nowadays they are not heard even in the "adult" Westerns.

As I have pointed out elsewhere,[3] vogue words are, to use a voguish phrase in defining them, words which have prestige

1. Cited in the *OED*, s.v. *ink-horn*. *Inkhornism, inkhornist,* and *inkhornize* are also listed as from this period.
2. The dates of earliest known occurrences are those given in the *OED*.
3. "Subliminal Words Are Never Finalized," New York *Times Magazine,* June 15, 1958, pp. 16, 55, 57, 58. Some of the examples to be cited subsequently also occur in this article.

2

value. They invariably have a flavor of bright sophistication, of urbanity, of ultramodernity—in short, of know-how—and they are in the beginning employed for this very reason. Many in due time enter the general word stock, like *to contact*, which has survived the belaboring of teachers, who objected to it on the grounds that *contact* was "properly" a noun, despite the fact that there are many instances of such conversion of noun into verb in English. No really up-to-date purist winces at it nowadays; those who conceive it to be their mission to police the language have other supposed offenders against linguistic propriety to bludgeon. Some such words, as we have seen, disappear altogether. By the time either of these possibilities occurs, there is bound to be a new flowering among those who set the pace.

In the mid-teens of the present century, according to Sir Arthur Quiller-Couch in his chapter "On Jargon" in The *Art of Writing* (1916), English newspaper writers were excessively fond of such locutions as *psychological moment, obsess, recrudesce, envisage*, and *adumbrate*. Today not one of these is really fashionable, and only one calls for comment—*psychological moment*, used then as now in the sense 'most favorable time,' though this was not the meaning of the German *das psychologische Moment*, its ultimate source.[4] The mistranslation has been so long established and so freely used as to have become a mere cliché, though it is rapidly being supplanted by *moment of truth*.

An examination of the vogue words of the middle years of our century must inevitably tell us a great deal of the concerns and the mores of the period—its spiritual, intellectual, and

4. The French misunderstood it first, at the time of the Siege of Paris in 1870, when they encountered the phrase in a German journal in reference to the bombardment. In German *Moment* means 'momentum, impetus' when used as a neuter noun; only as a masculine does it mean 'moment of time.' According to the *OED*, the French mistranslation of *das psychologische Moment* as *moment psychologique* "has passed equally nonsensically into English journalese." (The relevant section of the *OED* was issued in 1909, a date which accords well with Quiller-Couch's statement.) This example I have used in a somewhat different connection in *The Origins and Development of the English Language* (New York, 1964), p. 311.

social aspirations and predilections. Just as the Renaissance rage for inkhornisms indicates the tremendous enthusiasm in those days for classical values—misguided though it certainly sometimes was—so does the current rash of vogue words taken from psychiatry and the so-called behavioral sciences indicate the values of our own world, ignoble as some of these may seem to those who live in ivory towers. It is likely that many of these words would be incomprehensible to one who died so recently as Franklin Delano Roosevelt, if we were able to resurrect him; and it is certain that under the same happy circumstances Calvin Coolidge would be completely in the dark as to the meaning of, say, *gimmick, name-dropping, psychosomatic, isometric,* and *moisturize.*

Just as *disposition, complexion, temper(ament), humor, choleric, melancholy, sanguine, phlegmatic,* and a number of other words taken from the voguish scientific and pseudo-scientific parlance of an earlier day indicate to us an intense concern with astrology and physiology, so future commentators on our own era will certainly note our vast preoccupation with mental aberration of one sort or another as this is reflected in our voguish use of the terminology of psychoanalysis and psychology. Practically always these lose any sharpness of definition when they pass into popular use and are employed in reference to widespread and more or less vaguely delimited traits of character. This has happened, for instance, to the psychoanalyst's *complex,* which in voguish use has come to designate little more than the sort of obsessing idea which has temporarily taken hold of many of us at some time or other in our lives without in the least upsetting the mental balance. The word has been highly progenitive; there are nowadays many complexes which Freud never dreamed of. It is similar with the word *psychology* itself, as in *sales psychology,* which apparently means something like 'ability to discern the mental processes of one's "prospects" in such a way as to persuade them to purchase from one what they have no need for and frequently cannot afford.'

As E. E. Ericson has shown, with many citations, *sadism* has come to mean simply cruelty, with no connotations of *psychopathia sexualis,* and *moron,* at least in the Chicago area in the

1930's and 1940's, was used, perhaps euphemistically, in the specialized sense 'sex degenerate'[5]—a usage most unfair to those actual morons whose name is legion and who do much of the uninspiring but nonetheless useful work of the world. It is doubtful that calling a person an *exhibitionist* is any longer actionable, inasmuch as the word has come to refer to a comparatively harmless human failing referred to less pretentiously as "showing off," and is so defined in recent dictionaries[6]—a far cry indeed from the Baron von Krafft-Ebing and Havelock Ellis. Other terms from psychiatry and social psychology which have passed into voguish usage include *behavior pattern* 'behavior,' *neurotic* 'nervous, worrisome,' *ambivalent* 'ambiguous, two-sided' (like *empathy*, a great favorite nowadays with literary critics), and *compulsive* 'habitual.' The last-cited word is doubtless used out of humanitarianism, as in *compulsive drinker*, with much the same sense as *alcoholic* 'one who likes to drink, does so habitually and usually over his capacity.' On the other hand, *insanity*, a more or less technical term, has come to be replaced by *mental illness*, but this is doubtless to be attributed to the same sort of tender feeling which calls a drunkard a compulsive drinker or an alcoholic. (It should be noted also that *sick* has acquired a specialized meaning 'insane,' so that one can tell only from context whether a *sick man* is crazy or merely dyspeptic.) It is similar with sociological *senior citizen*, beloved of politicians for 'aging and decrepit person,' and *juvenile delinquent* 'underbred and badly behaved adolescent.' No doubt such verbal subterfuges help to make life more bearable for decaying oldsters and the parents of naughty brats.

The voguish use of *image* seems to be an extension of its use in psychology for the phenomenon of experiencing anew some sensation with the original stimulus lacking. In really up-to-date speech much of this technical meaning, as we should

5. "New Meanings in Current English," in *Philologica:The Malone Anniversary Studies*, ed. Thomas A. Kirby and Henry Bosley Woolf (Baltimore, 1949), pp. 321-25.

6. The word is listed in the *OED* in the sense 'one who takes part in a performance,' with a single citation (1821). *Exhibitionism*, in the psychopathic sense, is entered only in the *Supplement* of 1933, the first citation being from 1908; but by the 1920's the figurative and general use had begun to occur.

expect, has been lost, and the word means simply the impression, true or false, which one is able to make upon others. Such an image is almost invariably *projected*, and would seem to be vastly more important than what a person or an institution really is. An interview with some very eminent members of the American Psychiatric Association around the time of the political conventions in 1960, syndicated by the Women's News Service,[7] disclosed that women, particularly those with weak husbands, wanted a "father image" as president. Dwight David Eisenhower, it was thought by the psychiatrists being interviewed, had projected just such an image,[8] whereas Mr. Nixon was "not quite old enough for a father image and not quite young enough to appeal to women as a boy," that is, presumably, as a son image. One pundit feared that Mr. Nixon's appearance on television, when with the aid of his family and the little dog Checkers he defended himself against slush fund charges, had affected him adversely, but added, in what must be considered a little gem of voguish diction, "However, I am not discounting the fact that the Nixon image can be repackaged before the next election." Mr. Kennedy's chances were not rated high by the psychiatric mahatmas. In what was probably the most inept prophecy of the year 1960, they agreed that, although there was no doubt of his appeal to women as "the image of their little boy," they "will not vote for him because they do not want a boy in the White House." Nowhere in the article, it should be noted, was there any reference to a husband image. But this omission may be attributable to the fact that the assembled magi were by and large speaking for the American homemaker (she used to be a "housewife"), for whom a mere husband cannot be expected to project much of an im-

7. Jacksonville *Florida Times-Union*, February 9, 1960, p. 10.

8. This fantasy was very widespread. Cf. Ralph McGill, "The Image of the President," in his column *Conscience of the South*, Gainesville (Fla.) *Sun*, February 24, 1964, p. 4: "They [poll takers] could explain that General Eisenhower was the father image for which all of us instinctively and psychologically seek . . . the universal father who knows best." President Johnson, however, has also built up an image, "not that of a comfortable and comforting father," but that "of a competent man who knows how to get things done." We shall see more of the Johnsonian projection later.

age—or, to put it in another way, almost equally voguish, hus-bandwise she is left cold. An eminent lady doctor put the cap on the interview when she remarked that "the man who will be the next president will have to be presented to women in the image of a salesman."

More recently, according to Ben A. Franklin in an article copyrighted by the New York *Times*, government historians have agreed that in the earliest days of his presidency, Lyndon B. Johnson "projected a very strong image."[9] We should all feel a great sense of security, inasmuch as it is only the image, the appearance, which seems to be really important. In "The Image of a Simple Man," *Time* reports an official White House "adviser" as declaring "I believe—and I'm sure he believes—that the best image for him now is that of a serious, able, competent man who understands the office of the presidency. . . ."[10]

The physical and biological sciences have supplied comparatively few vogue words. Nevertheless, the awesomeness of their mysteries, as well as the tremendous prestige which they enjoy in the lay mind, is indicated by the use of *lab(oratory)* in non-scientific contexts (for instance, *composition lab, writing lab*). The use of *potential* as a noun may come from physics; it is now very fashionable and may in time supplant *potentiality* altogether.[11] Medical terminology is widely used—and doubtless misused—but it is primarily in the employment of *allergy* for 'distaste,' as in *an allergy to learning, clinic* as in *reading clinic* and *high school football coaching clinic,* and *intern* for 'novice schoolteacher' that similar extensions and laxations may be observed. It is likely that *condition* as a euphemism for practically any sort of ailment originated with doctors: "You have a liver condition" is far less alarming to the victim than "You have cirrhosis of the liver."[12]

9. Gainesville (Fla.) *Sun*, December 4, 1963, p. 4.
10. March 27, 1964, p. 14.
11. Thus Charles Reid, music critic, in the London *Spectator* (March 6, 1964, p. 316): "For all the sudden throat trouble that marred her big coloratura number and made her duck a high note or two, Elizabeth Harwood is obviously a Zerbinetta of rare potential."
12. But *condition* as verb (*air-conditioned, flight-conditioned,* and the like) in the sense 'adapt' seems to have grown out of similar uses by psychologists and sociologists. To *recondition* means 'to repair' ("Let Us Re-

Charisma seems to have dribbled into vogue usage from theology; in very high-toned circles it is used as a synonym for *glamour*. It is impossible to account for the resuscitation of this rather rarefied word. The adjectival form *charismatic* was occasionally used by the tonier columnists in reference to the late President Kennedy. *Mystique*, with similarly metaphysical overtones, is even commoner in voguish use;[13] the craze for it is echoed in the title of a very popular book, *The Feminine Mystique*, by Betty Friedan. There has been a similar upsurge in the more or less figurative use of *viable*, and *methodology* has practically ousted the once fashionable *technique*, being frequently used to mean simply 'method of scholarly procedure.' *Climate*, which many of us have been so naïve as to associate primarily with the weather, has come to have a much more metaphysical meaning, as in "The preface of the document [issued by the Florida Legislative Investigations Committee and labeled "obscene and pornographic" by Dade County State's Attorney Richard Gerstein] said the report could be of value to all citizens, 'for every parent and every individual concerned with the moral climate of the state should be aware of the rise in homosexual activity noted here. . . .' "[14] *Time* has reported that, according to Senator Jacob Javits, "It is up to Latin American governments . . . to do more to improve the climate for business."[15] Finally, at the trial of Jack Ruby for the murder of the alleged assassin of President Kennedy, Judge Joe Brown "rejected a defense demand that all prospective jurors as well as spectators be searched for concealed weapons, on the

---

condition Your Shoes") and was probably born of the desire, laudable enough in a democracy, to dignify what might otherwise be thought of as humble work. A reconditioned car, as everyone is aware, is a second-hand one.

13. Thus Murray Krieger, "The Poet and His Work," *College English*, XXV (1964), 406: "Seeing the intimate relationships between the materials of the poem and the surrounding world which provides them, Spitzer refuses to engage in the mystique that cuts them off as 'not-words.' " Cf. the use by Henry C. Wolfe in the *Saturday Review* of March 21, 1964, p. 46: "Only his [Franz Josef's] sense of duty and his dynastic mystique sustained him."

14. Jacksonville *Florida Times-Union*, March 19, 1964, p. 22.

15. March 20, 1964, p. 29.

ground that there is a 'climate' in Dallas of fear and animosity."[16]

Though a few rare and cantankerous souls may object to such words and their uses as have been cited thus far, it cannot be denied that many of them have connotations and associations which make them at least interesting. The same cannot be claimed for a group of almost completely colorless words which are nonetheless very stylish: *media* (as in *advertising media, news media*), for instance, and the interchangeable *level* and *bracket* (as in *teen-age level, income bracket*). *Area* is also very fashionable: what used to be a field of study is now an *area of research* and, as everybody knows, the once humble kitchen has become the *food preparation area* and the dining room the *dining area* in all the swanker advertising media and, doubtless, in split-level Suburbia as well. The dedicated (another very voguish word) men and women who write the nation's advertising copy and those who read their "messages" over television and radio are arbiters of amazing potency.

The vogue words which we have hitherto been concerned with have been on the whole learned words, some of them flashily so, a few downright exotic. There is, however, an opposite tendency at work in the Land of the Free: a self-consciously coy use of native words in place of words which, though of learned origin, are perfectly familiar to most people: *analysis*, for instance, has been largely supplanted by *breakdown*, as *to analyze* has been supplanted by *to break down*.[17] Other examples of this particular tendency are *to spell out* 'to explain,' *to fill in* 'to furnish background information,' and *rundown* 'summary.' Furthermore, in really high-powered circles an appointment is never arranged; it is *set up*. A problem is not investigated thoroughly or completely, but *in depth* or *in its totality*. One's attitudes and points of view concerning it are put in the form of a *position paper*, whatever that form is.

16. UPI item from Dallas in the University of Florida *Alligator*, February 18, 1964, p. 1.
17. A "quaint result" of the craze for this word is cited by Sir Ernest Gowers in *Plain Words: Their ABC* (New York, 1954), p. 128: "Statistics have been issued of the population of the United States, broken down by age and sex."

Breakthroughs are much in evidence, practically all of them "major" or "revolutionary,"[18] and they may be achieved through the efforts of a *task force*, that is, two or more persons working on a single project, usually of industrial research, though the term has by now invaded the groves of Academe, ever on the alert for fertilization by industry.

Commenting on a plan for Protestant unity proposed a few years ago by the Reverend Doctor Eugene Carson Blake, chief administrative officer of the United Presbyterian Church, the Right Reverend James A. Pike, Bishop of California, said that it was "a great prophetic breakthrough." That Bishop Pike knows his way around in vogue talk is indicated by his ghostly pronouncement "I know of no event in American church history of greater overall significance,"[19] for to the man who has mastered this type of verbal communication *overall* is always to be preferred to *total, comprehensive, general,* or even *average*. Programs, plans, objectives, philosophies, pictures, views, and the like are practically always overall, just as surely as fundamentals are always basic. I note in passing that the sermon topic of the pastor of the First Methodist Church of Jacksonville, Florida, on December 6, 1959, was "The Big Break Through" and devoutly hope that God broke through somewhere in the course of the homily.[20]

Fashion alone would seem to be responsible for the widespread vogue of such self-consciously homely yet essentially newfangled expressions as *screen* 'examine with a view to classifying,' *pinpoint* 'determine exactly,' *undercut* 'take unfair advantage,' *fact-finding* 'investigative,' *cutback* 'reduction,' *kickback* 'enforced return of part of wages or commission,' *spot check* 'random verification,' *bottleneck* 'hindrance,' and *slant* 'represent with bias.' Changes in American sleeping habits may

18. I have cited a number of examples of these in " 'Task Force' Makes 'Breakthrough,' " *American Speech*, XXXV (1960), 155-56, including one in polyethylene wrapping proudly announced by the Scandia Packaging Machinery Company. *Breakthrough*, like *position paper* and *task force*, seems originally to have been a military term, though apparently a fairly recent one, since it is not listed in either the *OED* or the *OED Supplement* of 1933.

19. Jacksonville *Florida Times-Union*, December 5, 1960, p. 1.

20. *Ibid.*, December 5, 1960, p. 8.

well render the literal meaning of *featherbedding*, a voguish homespun metaphor meaning 'limitation of work to make more jobs,' as archaic as that of *chamber pot* and *nightcap* (except in the alcoholic sense). *Knowing* and *knowledgeable* are practically synonymous as vogue words, but somehow they lack the true homespun quality; there is about them a big-city slickness in contrast to the rural wholesomeness of *know-how*, with its pleasantly American connotations of horse-trading, whittling, wooden nutmegs, and tinkering. Truly homespun (and very fashionable nowadays) is the laying of *guidelines* instead of the setting up of criteria or the making of plans.

Thought and *thinking* have held their own for some time as voguishly homespun synonyms of *opinion*, and seem well on the way to displacing pseudo-learned *reaction* in the same sense. "Will you give me your thinking about [or *in regard to* or *in relation to*] this?" has come to be indicative of a sophistication even greater than that implied by "What is your reaction to this?" *Thought* in the answer would go far toward maintaining the same high tone, thus: "My thought is that it is not too out-standing,'[21] though one's diction would by no means be lacking in tone if one merely replied "I don't subscribe to it," "I won't buy it," or "I don't go along with it."

One of the most voguish of phrases nowadays is *way of life*, which may replace *philosophy* in its popular sense 'body of practical opinions,' *regimen* ("vegetarianism as a way of life"), or simply *life*, as in the statement some years back of a poltergeist-ridden housewife, then very much in the news, to Mr. Ed Murrow on his television program *Person to Person*: "We were just leading a normal, quiet way of life." Preceded by *American* or *democratic*, the phrase has inspiring connotations of patriotism, high living standards, technological progress, freedom, equalitarianism, and high ideals. *As of now* is preferred by stylish speakers to *now* or *at present*, though *presently* in the same sense has by no means gone out of fashion.[22]

---

21. *Too* as a simple intensive, replacing *very*, is quite widespread, as in "He didn't know too much about it."

22. *Presently* in the sense 'now' was widely current in older English. According to the *OED*, the growth of the blunted sense insisted upon by

Of one's choice is also widely heard, as in "Go to the church of your choice this Sunday," as if it really didn't matter, one being just as equal as another. It may be recollected at this point that the platform of the Democratic Party in 1960, as read over television by Mr. Chester Bowles, affirmed the right of "every qualified boy to go to the college of his choice." It is perhaps just as well that this was never taken literally, for it is unlikely that Harvard, to name a possible choice of many, would hold all the qualified boys who might choose it. But it all sounds fine, modern, and democratic, like the ubiquitous *regardless of race, creed, or color.*

Of voguish affixes *-ize* stood well to the front until a few years ago. A brand of condensed milk, for instance, was *instantized*; a certain hair-dressing *moisturized* the scalp; fountain pens of a certain brand were *genderized*, since it was obviously degrading to the national character for men and women to use the same style of writing implement; and T-2 tankers were *jumboized* by increasing their length. Though these may be for the most part ephemeral creations, they nevertheless indicate the vogue of the suffix. Other examples are *personalize, hospitalize, editorialize, accessorize, formalize,* and *glamorize,* with *finalize,*[23] the most successful of all, doubtless here to stay.

But it would seem, on the basis of my recent researches, that the adverbial suffix *-wise* has pushed far ahead of the verbal suffix *-ize*. Previously occurring only in a few words like *lengthwise* and *crosswise*, this suffix has proliferated, as they say, like mad. There is no point in illustrating its proliferations, amusing as some of them may be.

Adjectives in *-type* are an equally interesting development: there are, for instance, modern-type refrigerators, prescription-type formulas (for headache remedies), and city manager-type governments. A single documented example should suffice—a

---

certain present-day prescriptivists "was so imperceptible, that early examples, esp. before *c* 1650, are doubtful."

23. The tempest in teapot over this word is one of the most amusing phenomena of our times. Its inclusion in *Webster's Third* has apparently given many critics the notion that they are required to use the word.

reference to "Cesare Siepi, the glamour-type leading basso of the Metropolitan."[24]

Now that the New Testament has been made readily available to us in understandable present-day English, it is high time that certain important older literary and political monuments be put into a form of our language "understanded of the people," to use the old-fashioned, naïve morphology of the Book of Common Prayer. I have attempted to do this with our most important American national document—a position paper spelling out a somewhat antiquated-type American mystique—which must be almost unintelligible to the modern reader conditioned to the lucid prose of writers of advertising copy, press releases, book reviews, and the like. How inept, from our more enlightened point of view, were the founders of this great democracy, which in their simplicity they chose to call a republic, when they wrote such stuff as this: "We hold these truths to be self-evident, that all men are created equal, that they are endowed by their Creator with certain unalienable rights, that among these are Life, Liberty, and the pursuit of Happiness. . . . That whenever any Form of Government becomes destructive of these ends, it is the Right of the People to alter or to abolish it, and to institute new Government"—and so on. I conclude with a sample of my translation of this cumbersome and archaic language into the racy and voguish diction of our own day, in the hope that others may follow suit with similar important documents:

> Our thinking as of now is to the effect that prioritywise these facts are basic and fundamental and definitely in no need of spelling out in depth: that one man should not be placed in a lower bracket than any other man, regardless of race, creed, or color, due to the fact that God the Father Image has implemented all men with certain human-type rights, among these being a democratic way of life and the right to indulge in the group recreational pleasures of their choice so long as approval of these pleasures has been finalized by responsible-type top-level coordinators; that if, after making a careful breakdown, it becomes possible to pin-

24. Jacksonville *Florida Times-Union*, January 8, 1961, p. 75.

point the fact that any administrative setup in any area whatsoever, high-level or low-level, is dedicated to a philosophy that will activate a climate of opinion conducive to a cutback in these aims and objectives, then it is the right of all freedom-oriented personnel to condition themselves revolutionwise for a major breakthrough. . . .

ROBERT H. BOWERS

Professor of English
University of Florida

The Tavern Scene in the Middle English Digby Play of Mary Magdalene

N THE PRESENT PAPER I SHALL DISCUSS WHAT seems to me an artistic failure in the representation of the striking "seduction-in-a-tavern" scene in the late Middle English Digby play of Mary Magdalene, which employs aureate diction and sensibility when both the subject matter and rhetorical decorum (Chaucer's "The wordes mote be cosin to the deede") would seem to call for a colloquial style. Naturally I hope that this discussion may contribute an iota towards a more precise awareness of the manifold and often unsolved problems of style and sensibility in ME literature.

I

These problems involve such annoying and persistent matters as the question of a poet's conception of the relation of form and content, of his "intention," or his "sincerity"—is he

15

speaking in jest or earnest?—and of his grasp of Ciceronian invention and structure.

After discussing what he regarded as confusions in the structure and tone, in the total composition, of Deschamps' *Le Miroir de mariage,* Johan Huizinga stated that: "To distinguish clearly the serious element from pose and playfulness is a problem that crops up in connection with nearly all the manifestations of the mentality of the Middle Ages."[1] (Huizinga was not immediately concerned with mere verbal irony where the meaning is often the reverse of the literal significance of the words employed but with a failure in imaginative ordering, in Ciceronian invention, not with mere rhetorical ordering according to Ciceronian disposition.)

This statement is akin to a favorite principle of C. S. Lewis, who said of Langland that he "hardly makes his poetry into a poem"; of Skelton that he "is not a *writer* at all. In a poem by Skelton anything may happen, and Skelton has no more notion than you what it will be. That is his charm; the charm of the amateur."[2] And a similar assessment is evident in Dryden's famous denomination of Chaucer as a "rough diamond," who "writes not always of a piece, but sometimes mingles trivial things with those of greater moment."[3] This insight has been rehabilitated and applied recently to "The Knight's Tale" and "The Clerk's Tale" in a brilliant monograph by Elizabeth Salter, who observes that: "Chaucer is often a curiously erratic artist. Able to build up to superb dramatic climaxes, he is liable to follow them with comment unsuitable, even banal . . . he can shift position and style so rapidly that we may be persuaded of a quite illusory logic or consistency."[4] Josephine W.

1. *The Waning of the Middle Ages* (London, 1924), p. 217.
2. *The Allegory of Love* (Oxford, 1938), p. 161; *English Literature in the Sixteenth Century* (Oxford, 1954), p. 97.
3. Preface to *Fables, Ancient and Modern* of 1700 (*Dryden's Poetical Works,* ed. G. R. Noyes, p. 746). Dryden's observations must be respected, not only because he had a fine critical mind but also because as a translator of several of Chaucer's tales he had earned the intimate knowledge of another poet's work that only the labor of translation can afford.
4. *Chaucer: The Knight's Tale and The Clerk's Tale* (Great Neck, N. Y., 1961), p. 67; her pp. 66-70 should be read in their entirety. James J. Murphy, "A New Look at Chaucer and the Rhetoricians," *RES,* n.s.,

Bennett noted that Spenser's *Faerie Queene* is a very difficult work to classify or to "make generalizations about," because Spenser was "uncertain of his models at the start of his great work."[5]

Helen Gardner, dealing with the problem of Satan in *Paradise Lost*, a famous crux that has plagued Milton scholarship since the time of Blake, has written: "The *subject* [my italics] demanded an 'infernal Serpent'; instead Milton has given us 'a lost Archangel.' There would be no difficulty if Satan were simply an Iago; the difficulty arises because he is a Macbeth."[6] And no amount of ingenious argument can dispel the stubborn fact that Shakespeare's so-called problem comedies, such as *All's Well that Ends Well*, have often seemed artistic failures to sympathetic and open-minded critics mainly because the subjects were intractable, and would not submit to the proposed imaginative treatment. Obviously such difficulties are more apparent in an extended, ambitious composition than in a short one.

Before considering the ME Digby play I shall provide a rough sketch of the three major rhetorical styles, the high, middle, and low, as late ME writers practiced them.[7] I use the term

XV (1964), 1-21, has sharply challenged the older assumption, first urged by Manley, and fully documented by Veré L. Rubel, *Poetic Diction in the English Renaissance* (New York, 1941), pp. 14-30, that Chaucer was enthralled by "rethorike."

5. "Genre, Milieu, and the 'Epic-Romance,'" in *English Institute Essays for 1951* (New York, 1952), pp. 108-9.

6. "Milton's 'Satan' and the Theme of Damnation in Elizabethan Tragedy," in *Essays and Studies of the English Association* (Oxford, 1948), I, 66.

7. I am unaware of any systematic treatment of the three styles (*tenue, medium, grande*) in ME literature: there are many useful but scattered references in such handbooks as Charles S. Baldwin, *Medieval Rhetoric and Poetic* (New York, 1928); J. W. H. Atkins, *English Literary Criticism: The Medieval Phase* (Cambridge, 1943); Ernst R. Curtius, *European Literature and the Latin Middle Ages* (London, 1953). The editorial prefaces to Early English Text Society editions of individual authors are valuable, but they are seldom comparative in nature. Walter F. Schirmer, *John Lydgate* (London, 1961), pp. 70 ff., is useful on Lydgate's aureate, elevated style; but perhaps the best analysis is still that of Eleanor P. Hammond, *English Verse Between Chaucer and Surrey* (Durham, N. C., 1927), pp. 77 ff. J. P. Oakden, *Alliterative Poetry in Middle English* (Manchester, 1930-35), II, 175 ff., 392 ff., is useful but R. J. Menner's Preface to his edition of *Purity* (New Haven, 1920) is more pointed. Coleridge's

"style" in an inclusive sense, to embrace the problem of the relation between form and content mentioned above; and I assume, without further ado, that no theories of Coleridge about organic artistry had entered the head of a ME poet for whom art meant the deliberate treatment of subject matter on formal, rhetorical principles and the deliberate use of adornment, of metaphor and simile.

Of course, the concept of style, like that of genre, must always remain a crude critical tool since it can do no justice whatsoever to the uniqueness and self-sufficiency of any first-class work of art; it works best with second-class art that does not attempt to comprehend inner contradictions and complexities.[8] Furthermore, it is difficult to locate examples of a "pure" style, except in short compositions directed by a laudatory or abusive purpose.

And the interspersion of comic elements in serious profane and sacred art is a frequent medieval aesthetic practice (ludicra seriis miscere) unknown to Senecan tragedy or the classical epic such as the *Aeneid* which are elevated throughout.

---

famous chapter on the "natural" style (*Biographia Literaria*, xix) considers Chaucer's *Troilus* v.603-37, and reinforces the principle: "ars est celare artem." A. J. Bliss, in his edition of *Sir Launfal* (Edinburgh, 1960), treats ME romances, such as *Havelok* and *The Tale of Gamelyn*, written for a peasant audience (pp. 42-46).

There is an admirable account of Elizabethan practice (which generally aligned heroic topics with the high style, satire and pastoral with the low, and love lyrics with the middle) in Maurice Evans, *English Poetry in the Sixteenth Century* (London, 1955), pp. 31-46. The flamboyant and naturalistic styles in Franco-Burgundian literature and art of the waning Middle Ages have been studied by Huizinga (*op. cit.*), *passim*; Erich Auerbach, *Mimesis* (Princeton, 1953), Chap. X; Erwin Panofsky, *Early Netherlandish Painting* (Cambridge, Mass., 1953), *passim*.

8. One burden of Charles Muscatine's *Chaucer and the French Tradition* (Berkeley, 1957), esp. pp. 222-23, 237-47, is Chaucer's use in his mature work of a mixed style, where juxtapositions, tensions, and counterpoints abound, with stunning results. Nevill Coghill, "God's Wenches and the Light that Spoke," in *English & Medieval Studies presented to J. R. R. Tolkien*, ed. Norman Davis and C. L. Wrenn (London, 1962), pp. 200-218, discusses the fusion of the comic and the sublime in Langland's style. Dunbar's most recent editor, James Kinsley, says that *The Tretis of the tua mariit Wemen and the Wedo*, "juxtaposing the language of romance and the vernacular of the streets, is a grand linguistic joke" (*Poems*, Oxford, 1958, p. xv).

II

Under a monarchy such as that of Richard II or Henry VI it is understandable that a poet should think of a high style as appropriate for representing aristocratic sensibility, a middle style for bourgeois sensibility, and a low style for rude peasants or urban workers. This is mainly a sociological consideration. Under monarchy, too, most poetry is occasional and laudatory, written expressly to celebrate a triumphant or solemn occasion, a marriage or a death, in the life of king or noble under whose patronage and protection most poets wrote. At this point it is worth noting that of the three major rhetorical genres: judicial; political; panegyric or demonstrative, the third, also often called the epideictic, had by far the strongest influence on medieval poetry since its principal objective was eulogy. On the other hand religious writing could veer from elevated praise of a martyr, from theological analyses for other theologians, to a simple sermon for the laity. Generalizations as to the function of styles are hazardous, but they must be risked: I would say, then, that the high style is essentially laudatory, ceremonial, retrospective, and sentimental; that the middle style is explanatory or expository, or politely conversational; and that the low style is colloquial, naturalistic, immediate, and unadorned. Some illustrations may validate these claims. (In the quotations that follow, the ME thorn is represented by *th*; and the arabic numeral *3* has been used to designate the ME yogh.)

i

(a) The high style of secular, baronial poetry is most evident in descriptive passages of knightly magnificence, not always the conversational lines, such as the following from *Wynnere and Wastoure* (ll. 90-98, ed. Gollancz, Oxford, 1920):

This kynge was comliche clade in kirtill and mantill,
Bery-brown as his berde, brouderde with fewlys,
Fawkons of fyne golde, flakerande with wynges,
And ichone bare in ble, blewe als me thoghte,
A grete gartare of ynde gerede ful riche.
Full gayly was that grete lorde girde in the myddis,
A brighte belte of ble, broudirde with fewles,

With drakes & with dukkes, daderande tham semede,
For ferdnes of fawcons fete, lesse fawked thay were.

(b) The aureate style employed in religious devotion is illustrated in such poems as Lydgate's *Ballade at the Reverence of Our Lady* (*EETS ES* No. 107, p. 258):

O ruby, rubifyed in the passyoun
All of thi sone, among haue us in mynde,
O stedfast dyamaunt of duracyoun . . .
O gloriois viole, O vitre inviolate! . . .
O precyous perle, with-outyn ony pere,
Cokyl with gold dew from aboue ireyned. . . .

The coining of sonorous polysyllabic French and Latin terms comprehensible mainly to humanists seems strained; but we must remember that many of Lydgate's neologisms have enriched the language: e.g., abuse, avaricious, capacity, credulity, deception, terrible, passionate, incredible, etc., while many others, such as hiems (winter), bravy (prize), reclinatory (couch), oppilate (blocked), facundious (eloquent), diverticle (inn), may be regarded as failures although in their day they may have seemed both strange and delightful to those who enjoyed solving etymological challenges.

(c) Dunbar's *Golden Targe* (*Poems*, ed. Kinsley, Oxford, 1958) evidences the straining for the elegance presumably achieved by aureate poets of old:

Discrive I wald, bot quho coud wele endyte
How all the feldis wyth thai lilies quhite
Depaynt war brycht, quhilk to the hevyn did glete?
Noucht thou, Omer, als fair as thou coud wryte,
For all thine ornate stillis so perfyte;
Nor yit thou Tullius, quhois lippis suete
Off rethorike did in to termes flete:
Your aureate tongis both bene all to lyte
For to compile that paradise complete.   (ll. 64-72)

Dunbar's subsequent apostrophe to Chaucer demonstrates the fact that Chaucer was generally regarded as an aureate poet in the fifteenth century, not as the poet of the *Canterbury Tales*:

20

O reverend Chaucere, rose of rethoris all,
As in oure tong ane flour imperiall
That raise in Britane evir, quho redis rycht
Thou beris of makaris the tryumph riall;
Thy fresch anamalit termes celicall
This mater coud illumynit full brycht: (ll. 253-58)

ii

(a) The middle style, less ornate, more natural, is shown
in the following expository lines from Hoccleve's polite, conventional society poem *Letter of Cupid* (ed. Skeat, *Chaucerian
and Other Pieces*, Oxford, 1897):

Of twelve apostels oon a traitour was;
The remenant yit gode were and trewe.
Than, if it happe men fynde, per cas,
Oo woman fals, swich good is for t'eschewe,
And deme nat that they ben alle untrewe.
I see wel mennes owne falsenesse
Hem causeth wommen for to trusten lesse.   (ll. 162-68)

(b) In expository or didactic prose, as in this passage from
Usk's *Testament of Love*, II.xi (ed. Skeat, *Chaucerian and
Other Pieces*, p. 87), where some ethical terminology must be
employed:

Every soule of reson hath two thinges of stering lyf, oon
in vertue, and another in the bodily workinge; and whan
the soule is the maister over the body, than is a man maister
of himselfe. And a man, to be maister over him-selfe, liveth
in vertu and in goodnesse, and as reson of vertue techeth.
So the soule and the body, worching vertue togider, liven
resonable lyf. . . .

(c) In a typical sermon (Harley MS. 2276, fol. 34ᵛ), wherein the anonymous writer is most concerned to explicate clearly
for a presumably lay audience:

The first vertu is stilnesse from iangelyng of idul speche;
the second vertu is inward biholdyng of heuenli thyngs
aȝens foule thouȝtis an idel; the third vertu is bisi wakyng

of mynd in prayers aʒens slumberyng of thouʒt, as thouʒ
we slepten whan we witen not what we blaberen; the
fourthe is fastyng or ellis discreet abstynence aʒen takyng
of mete and drynke ouer mesure and aʒens grete stiryngs to
leccherie. . . .

iii

(a) The most audible voicing of the low style is the vivid
speech of sweating humanity, as in the anger of a crafty pub-
keeper in *Piers Plowman* (ed. Skeat) B, xix.394-99:

'ʒe bawe!' quod a brewere I wil nouʒt be reuled,
Bi Iesu! for al ʒowre ianglynge with spiritus iusticie
Ne after Conscience, by Cryste whil I can selle
Bothe dregges and draffe and drawe for that is my kynde,
And nouʒte hakke after holynesse holde thi tonge,
    Conscience!

Or in the Cain of the Towneley Cycle (Pageant No. 2) (*EETS
ES* No. 71, ll. 30-33) who swears and acts like a rough Yorkshire
ploughman as he curses his mare to better effort:

Yit, shrew, yit, pull on a thraw!
What! it semys for me ye stand none aw!
    I say, donnyng, go fare!
    A, ha! god gif the soro & care!

(b) The low style is evident in a metrical romance such as
the ME *King Horn*, stripped of ornament, where the interest
centers on overt action and rapid narration, uninterrupted by
any probing of human motivations or feelings. (The next three
quotations are from W. H. French and C. B. Hale, *Middle English Metrical Romances*, New York, 1930.) Fykenhild the slan-
derer speaks:

Aylmar, ihc the warne,
Horn the wule berne:
Ihc herde whar he sede,
And his swerd forth leide,
To bringe the of lyue
And take Rymenhild to wyue.   (ll. 689-94)

In the ME *Gamelyn*, composed perhaps for a peasant audience, where nobles are treated with disrespect rather than resentment, or where they are endowed with the rude brutality that might have met with peasant approval:

> Gamelyn ouertook the porter and his teene wrak,
> And gert him in the nekke that the bon tobrak,
> And took him by that oon arm and threw him in a welle,
> Seuen fadmen it was deep as i haue herd telle   (ll. 303-6)

In mock-heroic parody such as the ME *Tournament of Tottenham*, which ridicules chivalry:

> Ther was clynkyng of cart-sadellys and clatteryng of cannes;
> Of fele frekis in the feld, brokyn were ther fannes;
> Of sum were the hedys brokyn, of sum the brayn-panes;
> And yll ware it be sum or thay went thens.   (ll. 163-66)

III

John Lydgate's *The Life of Our Lady*, commissioned by Henry V and composed between 1409 and 1411, the first of ten verse hagiographies which he wrote, set a new emphasis on the writing of saints' legends.[9] His ambition was epic—the work runs to 6,000 lines; his invocation, elevated epithets, learned etymologies and references, ejaculations on the part of the fictitious narrator, and so forth, are designed to appeal to a cultured audience. Older ME collections of saints' lives, perhaps compiled for church use, are generally unadorned and non-literary in character.[10] Notable poetic emulators of Lydgate in this new genre, who wrote for aristocratic patrons during the reign of Henry VI, were Osbern Bokenham (1392-1447), an Augustinian monk of Stoke Clare, who wrote *Legends of Holly Women* (*EETS OS* No. 206); John Capgrave (1393-1464), Pro-

9. See Walter F. Schirmer, *John Lydgate* (London, 1961), pp. 149-72; on the Lydgate canon, see Henry N. MacCracken, *EETS ES* No. 107, pp. xi-lviii; Schirmer, pp. 264 ff. Lydgate's *Life of Our Lady* was recently edited by J. A. Lauritis, R. A. Klinefelter, and V. F. Gallagher, for the Duquesne University Press (Pittsburgh, Pa., 1961).

10. See prefaces to Karl Horstmann, *Altenglische Legenden* (Heilbronn, 1881); *Early South English Legendary* (*EETS OS* No. 87); *South English Legendary* (*EETS OS* Nos. 235, 236, 244).

vincial of the Augustinian friars in 1456, who wrote a *Legend of St. Catherine* (*EETS OS* No. 100); and Henry Bradshaw (d. 1513), a Benedictine monk of Chester, who wrote a *Life of St. Werburge* (*EETS OS* No. 88). Hagiography, of course, is animated by a commemorative, laudatory impulse; it is retrospective, uncritical, sentimental, and nostalgic.[11] It was often used as propaganda, to make converts, to elevate holy poverty, to celebrate martyrdom. An aureate, devotional style is here appropriate, and accords with rhetorical decorum since its mode is deictic rather than elenctic. Hagiography presents a simplified romantic memorial: it denies error and dilemma in its memorialized hero, it glosses over lightly the complexities and confusions of human motivations and feelings—the proper subjects of history and secular biography. It is, therefore, the opposite of a dramatic style that explores and exploits the confusions of human motivations, the immediacy, the stress of the human condition. But the anonymous author of the Digby play of Mary Magdalene, enthralled no doubt by the Lydgate tradition, uses the aureate style appropriate for retrospective narration, instead of a dramatic style appropriate to the presentation of present, immediate action, and hence violates rhetorical decorum.

IV

Since Mary Magdalene was the patron saint of sinners and penitents, her career was a favorite topic for the medieval hagiographers of Western Europe who were engaged in pastoral propaganda.[12] Next to the Virgin Mary she was probably

11. On hagiography in general see René Aigrain, *L'Hagiographie: ses sources, ses methodes, son histoire* (Paris, 1953); Hippolyte Delehaye, S.J., *Les Légendes hagiographiques* (Brussels, 1905); John M. Mecklin, *The Passing of the Saint: A Study of a Cultural Type* (Chicago, 1941). On English material see Gordon H. Gerould, *Saints' Legends* (New York, 1916); Charles W. Jones, *Saints' Lives and Chronicles in Early England* (Ithaca, 1947); Helen C. White, *Tudor Books of Saints and Martyrs* (Madison, Wis., 1963), pp. 3-30. Some modern critics apparently feel that it is impossible to write a credible saint's legend, that the effort to make characters more human *and* more religious is irreconcilable: e. g., Edward A. Block, "Chaucer's *Man of Law's Tale*," *PMLA*, LXVIII (1953), 616. Any effort to counter this view would demand a long digression.

12. See Helen Garth, *St. Mary Magdalene in Medieval Literature* (Baltimore, 1950).

the most popular saint—for the following essential reasons: first, her career illustrated vividly the actual process of moral redemption;[13] secondly, according to Scripture (Mark xvi.9), she was the first person to see Jesus after the Resurrection.[14] Although Mary appears as an important character in many ME lives of Our Savior and in the extant ME Corpus Christi dramatic cycles, there is only one surviving ME play, the so-called Digby play, written sometime during the reign of Edward IV, which is devoted entirely to her legendary biography.[15] It is a long, rambling, episodic play of 2,144 lines, with some 52 separate scenes and over 60 characters, which narrates rather than dramatizes her long involved career. The accounts of her career had grown to excessive length through apocryphal accretions which hagiographers had appended.[16] These accretions are fully

13. The account of Mary in John Mirk's *Festial*, a collection of ME homilies fashioned for the use of preachers about 1400, sets forth the orthodox view: ". . . that was soo holy a womon, that our Lorde Ihesu Crist aftyr his modyr louyd her most of all woymen . . . that dyde penawnce for her synnes and soo recouered aȝayn the grace by doyng of penaunce and repentyng that scho had lost by lust of flesch and sore synnyng" (*EETS ES* No. 96, p. 203).

14. ME accounts explain the First Appearance on the basis of her great love for Jesus: e.g., *Stanzaic Life of Christ, EETS OS* No. 166, 1. 7552: "by-cause ho lufd so tenderly"; *Speculum Sacerdotale, EETS OS* No. 200, p. 172/22.

15. *EETS ES* No. 70 (1896): All subsequent citations are taken from this edition, wherein the text is based on Digby MS. 131 at the Bodleian, the unique copy. Arnold Williams, *The Drama of Medieval England* (East Lansing, Mich., 1961), p. 166, describes the play as adumbrating the romantic drama of the Elizabethan age, "The sort which Shakespeare gives us in *Pericles* . . . with a vast variety of incident and character, time covering thirty or forty years and action crossing and recrossing the Mediterranean." The first section of the play is of the mystery cycle type: Tiberius Caesar, Herod, and Pilate introduce themselves in traditional, ranting set-speeches. Then Mary's sad story is narrated: her inheritance from her wealthy father Cyrus of Bethany; her sin and repentance; her washing of Our Savior's feet in the house of Simon the Leper; the death and raising of her brother Lazarus; and finally her experiences at the Resurrection. The second part is pure miracle and fictitious legend; it narrates Mary's career as an apostle and her conversion of the heathen King and Queen of Marseilles after some spectacular miracles; the consequent pilgrimage to the Holy Land of these converts; then Mary's retirement into the wilderness and her saintly death.

16. Hagiographers, intent on edification, speculated beyond the confines of Scripture or prior accounts of saints, on the basis of "ethical

assembled in that great repository of saints' lives designed for popular education rather than for liturgical use, the *Legenda Aurea* of the Dominican Provincial of Lombardy, Jacobus de Voragine (d. 1298), that served as the most immediate source used by the Digby author, and was well known in the England of Henry VII because of Caxton's translation with the title *The Golden Legend* (1483).

Crucial to the import of Mary's conversion is the occasion and reason for the lapse into sin of this wealthy sister of Lazarus and Martha. On these points Scripture is silent, hence the Digby author invents two scenes to provide motivation: first, that of the allegorical figures, the World, the Flesh and the Devil, gleefully plotting her downfall in the older clumsy manner of externalized morality used in such morality plays as *The Castle of Perseverance* (c. 1420?)[17]; and second, a seduction scene in a tavern. Both of these scenes are unique in medieval accounts of Mary: some hagiographers imagined that she had turned to a life of debauchery in utter despair after Jesus supposedly prevented her proposed marriage to John the Baptist.[18] Although the tavern episode is striking, and is probably the earliest tavern seduction scene in English literature, it has received no careful consideration by historians of the English drama.

---

truth," which is akin to the "feigned speeches" based on probability that historians such as Thucydides fabricated for politicians to deliver. There was Gospel authority for such activity since John xx.30 states, "Multa quidem et alia signa fecit Jesus in conspectu discipulorum suorum, quae non sunt scripta in libro hoc," a ME equivalent of which appears in the *Meditacyuns on the Soper of Our Lorde* (*EETS OS* No. 60, 1875), ll. 967-68: "The euangelystes telle nat of thys doing,/ For they myȝte nat wryte alle thyng." In practice hagiographers often took considerable liberty with their material, often introducing long digressions to vent a particular interest: e.g., the pro-feminist author of the ME *Southern Passion* (*EETS OS* No. 169, 1927, ll. 1925-90) interrupts his account of Mary Magdalene to defend eloquently the reputations of women against ale-house slanderers and sundry boasters and liars.

17. See W. R. Mackensie, *The English Moralities from the Point of View of Allegory* (Boston, 1914), pp. 34-36; Charles Muscatine, "The Emergence of Psychological Allegory in Old French Romance," *PMLA*, LXVIII (1953), 1160-82, provides indispensable background for the allegorical tradition.

18. See the ME *South English Legendary* (*EETS OS* No. 235, 1956), ll. 302-16.

Prior to the action at the tavern, Lady Lechery has been deputized by the World, the Flesh, and the Devil to lead Mary into temptation. And Mary, in agonized despair at the death of her father whom she loved dearly, proves a pliable victim, allowing Lady Lechery to entice her into the putative gaiety of tavern frequenting as a way of drowning her sorrow. It is important to note that Mary is corrupted before she enters the tavern. The action starts with an identification and expository speech by the proprietor, who boasts that he operates the best tavern in town (i.e., Jerusalem), and advertises his choice stock of wines (N.B., not beer!) imported from France and Spain (ll. 470-80). Apart from the obvious anachronisms, we can see that the author is presenting an upper-class London tavern similar to a modern Bavarian *weinstube*: this is no working-class alehouse such as that operated by Betty the Alewife and frequented by Gluttony in *Piers Plowman* (B.v.306), or hinted at in the scenes of seamy London life in such Tudor interludes based on the Prodigal Son theme as *Hyckescorner* (*c.* 1513) or *Mundus et Infans* (*c.* 1508). Hence Tucker Brooke's description of the scene as one of "low realism" is certainly mistaken.[19] Then the ladies enter, and Lady Lechery, who has already put Mary into the proper frame of mind for a night on the town, orders a bottle of the best which they sip while they eagerly await the prospect of male companionship, like most unattached ladies in a tavern.

Shortly thereafter, a gallant called Curiosity enters the acting area, and loudly proclaims that he is not in trade, not a member of the scorned merchant class, but rather that he is a natty man-about-town in search of an accessible barmaid. He then describes the elegance of his garb and smugly brags of his sexual conquests. Then Lady Lechery prompts Mary to ask the taverner to invite the young gallant to have a drink with them, and the taverner is happy to oblige. Immediately Curiosity

19. C. F. Tucker Brooke, *The Tudor Drama* (Boston, 1911), p. 33. There are few more confusing and useless critical terms than that of "realism" since it confuses sociology with art—it should be jettisoned. It is far more instructive to ask if an artist's intention has been realized, if form and content coalesce in the aesthetic object.

starts a bold flirtation, calls Mary a daisy's eye, and rolls off the
following aureate apostrophe to her:

> Splendaunt of colour, most of femynynte,
> Your sofreyn coloures set with synseryte!
> Conseder my loue into yower alye,
> Or elles I am smet with peynnes of perplexite!   (ll. 516-19)

In his own style he is as articulate and facile as that bold soph-
ister, Christopher Marlowe's Leander. Mary pretends to be
both startled and shocked, and protests in false modesty: "Why
sir, wene ye that I were a kelle?" (l. 520). But Curiosity brushes
aside her initial protest and continues like the poised, experienced gallant that he is. They dance, partake of some sops in
wine; and then Curiosity pointedly invites her to retire elsewhere. Delighted, Mary accepts with alacrity; and they go off
stage hand in hand, leaving Lady Lechery to fend for herself.
Thus is Mary's downfall signalized.

I repeat that this is not a scene of "low realism," nor is the
tavern like that operated by Skelton's Eleanor Rumming of
Leatherhead or Shakespeare's Mistress Quickly of Eastcheap.
The main characters all talk in aureate language, far from the
colloquialism or immediacy of even upper-class speech: Lady
Lechery, when she first tempts Mary, prior to the scene just
described, speaks affected, aureate language:

> Heyl lady most laudabyll of alyauns!
> Heyl, oryent as the sonne in his reflexite!
> Bryter than the bornyd is your bemys o bewte!
>
> (ll. 440-41, 444)

There is no effort or desire on the part of the author to indi-
vidualize his main characters by their speech. Yet he is perfectly
aware of a kind of sociological decorum since he can switch to
a low style when, in a later episode, the seasick cabin boy
speaks:

> I tell yow plenly beforn;
> for swyche a cramp on me sett is,
> I am a poynt to fare the worse;
> I ly and wryng tyll I pysse. . . .   (ll. 1406-9)

28

Or, when the rude, "Mohammedan" altar boy Hawkyn insults the "Mohammedan" priest:

> whan women comme to here thi sermon,
> pratly with hem I can houkkyn,
> with Kyrchon and fayer Maryon.
> they love me better than ʒe. . . .   (ll. 1159-62)

to whom the priest retorts:

> I xall whyp the tyll thi ars xall belle!   (l. 1169)

Lydgate, too, that great master of Lancastrian enameled aureate verse, can switch to the low style when "rude vpplandische people" are to be ridiculed for the snobbish delight of aristocrats, as in the *Mumming at Hertford* (*c.* 1430?; *EETS OS* No. 192, p. 676):

> For Obbe the Reeve, that goothe heere al to-forne,
> He pleynethe sore his mariage is not meete,
> For his wyff, Beatryce Bittersweete,
> Cast vpon him an hougly cheer ful rowghe,
> Whane he komethe home ful wery from the ploughe,
> With hungry stomake deed and pale of cheere
> In hope to fynde redy his dynier;
> Thanne sittethe Beautryce bolling at the nale,
> As she gyvethe of him no maner tale;
> For she al day, with hir iowsy nolle,
> Hathe for the collyk pouped in the bolle.   (ll. 30-40)

So it is perfectly clear as to what the Digby author was attempting. He was observing sociological decorum in his depiction of the seduction scene in tailoring speech to the social status of his main characters. He must follow decorum because he was depicting the life of a saint. But he is trying to write drama, the presentation of an immediate, present happening rather than a retrospective, nostalgic narrative of past events. And it seems to me that this inability to grasp the limitations of genre is what causes the trouble—in other words he is confusing didactic with mimetic. For in the Digby tavern scene, the visual action happens far too quickly for any adequate motivation to be developed;[20] in retrospective narration the author can state, and his audience will accept, "this is what happened, this is what 'olde bookes tallen us,' and we can only guess the reasons why"—questions of possibility and probability are not urgent. Furthermore, in the Digby tavern scene there is no real dialogue, no real drama, no direct discourse where one character stands face to face with another character in any clash of will. So the characters are never fully realized. Also the subsequent repentance of Mary comes very abruptly with no preparation or retardation, after a short admonitory speech by a Good Angel that represents her conscience (ll. 588-601). We are reading narration, or "closet-drama," rather than authentic drama. In addition, one feels that the aureate language and the posturing of the main characters are almost calculated euphemisms, society devices employed by the author to keep vitality at a safe distance far from the manor, and to avoid serious consideration of the human condition. The action is not like that of the Towneley Cycle, which "specializes in the high comic which changes into the high tragic before your very eyes."[21]

An instructive contrast to the texture of the Digby play is offered by Bokenham's narrative—not dramatic—account of Mary Magdalene in his *English Legendys of Hooly Wummen* (*EETS OS*, No. 206), written in 1445 at the express request of Lady Bourchier, sister to the then Duke of York. His verse account is aureate and aristocratic: he writes a "literary" work for the sensibility of aristocrats which is successful because it is coherent and "of a piece." He states on several occasions that he aspires to what he takes to be the "sweet and sententious" elevated rhetoric of his masters: Chaucer, Gower, Lydgate. He prides himself on his aureate diction and his sonorous, polysyllabic rhymes, such as "acusacyoun/ excusacyoun" (ll. 5559-60); "proteccyoun/ remyssoun" (ll. 6308-9); "inspyracoun/ habytacoun" (ll. 6154-55). Tactfully he avoids any description of Mary's lapse such as that attempted by the Digby author, and

20. Sister Mary John of Carmel Chauvin, *The Role of Mary Magdalene in Medieval Drama* (Washington, D. C., 1951), notes the uncomplicated psychology in the Digby play, and remarks of Mary that "she is at the author's mercy" (p. 44).

21. Arnold Williams (*op. cit.*), p. 128.

hence avoids problems of probability as he skips quickly over the distressing episodes in the life of his heroine; he has no desire to denigrate her,[22]

> For al hir youth in dislauynesse
> Of hir body so vnshamefastly
> She dispendyd & in synfulnesse . . .
> That Marie the synnere thei dede hir name
>
> (ll. 5402-4, 5408)

in order to compose a long, lachrymose aria of contrition for her to deliver. He deals with the sentimental, with the exterior of events, with externals held at an aesthetic and hence moral distance. He must, because he is writing hagiography, and he does not confuse didactic with mimetic. Euphemism and omission obliterate human problems in Bokenham's version; his aesthetic can only represent an aristocratic view of life. The aureate style,[23] even at its best, is undramatic because it is retrospective and commemorative; it is incapable of representing dramatic process since it deliberately eschews the problematical side of human experience. It achieves success in Lydgate's epithalamium *The Temple of Glas* (*c.* 1402?), or in Dunbar's enameled *Golden Targe* (*c.* 1508),[24] in representing static, timeless visions of unquestioned symbolic and aristocratic values. It was a natural mode of expression of an aristocratic society that wanted to think of itself as magnanimous and chivalric as it strove through conspicuous pomp and pageantry to define and assert itself against the relentless economic forces that were changing Europe into a commercial world.[25]

22. On Bokenham, see H. S. Bennett, *Six Medieval Men & Women* (Cambridge, 1955), pp. 94-99. Other ME hagiographies of Mary Magdalene likewise skip quickly over distressing episodes: e.g., *Early South English Legendary*, *EETS OS* No. 87 (1887), p. 462/54, states without elaboration: "Manie riche men hir lei3en bi." Robert Southwell's *Marie Magdalens Funeral Teares* (1591) completely omits her gaudy past.

23. See J. C. Mendenhall, *Aureate Terms* (Lancaster, Pa., 1919).

24. See Denton Fox, "Dunbar's *The Golden Targe*," *ELH*, XXVI (1959), 311-34.

25. See R. L. Kilgour, *The Decline of Chivalry* (Cambridge, Mass., 1937); A. B. Ferguson, *The Indian Summer of English Chivalry* (Durham, N. C., 1960); Robert Withington, *English Pageantry* (Cambridge, Mass., 1918), Vol. I.

But an aesthetic that is retrospective and narrative cannot readily accommodate the immediacy of drama. The Digby author has not solved the relation of form and content; and it would be pointless to raise a question of his "sincerity." No doubt he felt he had solved the relation, but a solution appears only when form and content coalesce in the aesthetic object. In this connection Wellek and Warren have written: "As for 'sincerity' in a poem: the term seems almost meaningless. A sincere expression of what? Of the supposed emotional state out of which it came? . . . Or a sincere expression of the poem, i.e., the linguistic construct shaping in the author's mind as he writes? Surely, it will have to be the last: the poem is a sincere expression of the poem."[26]

The most charitable thing that one could observe of the Digby author would be that he wrote "closet-drama"—no doubt with the best of intentions.[27]

26. *Theory of Literature* (New York, 1949), p. 215.
27. At the conclusion of the Digby play, the allegorical character Epilogue, as he begs indulgence, states: "I desire the redars to be my frynd" (l. 2143). If this assertion is by the author and is not the addition of a later scribe, it suggests that the author had readers as well as spectators in mind, and was accordingly composing "closet-drama."

FRANK A. DOGGETT

Principal
Duncan U. Fletcher High School
Jacksonville Beach, Florida

Repetitions of a Young Prince
A Note on Thematic Recurrence in *Hamlet*

LD FAMILIAR THINGS LIKE *Hamlet* BECOME loosened in their setting of sequential happenings. In time we take for granted the order of succession of events and, in pondering, move freely from one occurrence to another, backward and forward or about. In this way, all of the play has a kind of simultaneous existence. When we consider the occurrences out of their set order, we may see other arrangements than the usual one of narrative sequence. To some extent this may have been true even for Shakespeare's audience, if the evidence can be trusted that *Hamlet* is a rewriting of a popular old play by Thomas Kyd. In the case of *Hamlet* these other patterns or relationships of its components (apart from the order of its plot) suggest a representation of ideas in the play, and new import enters the play's happenings when they jostle each other in the freedom of meditation. Then by comparing the implications of similar events,

33

by observing the relation of one element to another of denial, fulfillment, recurrence, we can detect the true complexity of its structure. Considerable attention has been given to the repetition of major themes in Elizabethan subplots and the similarities among events in a given Shakespearean play. There is no novelty in pointing to thematic recurrence in Shakespeare. But *Hamlet* is an exceptional case in this regard, and I hope to show here that the amount and variety of repetition of certain of its components deserve special attention, and that these recurrences constitute a characteristic configuration of its action.[1]

When we discuss action as a configuration, we consider it apart from its functional character, but not entirely. Most commonly it is seen as behavior with its main function a cause-and-effect progression that indicates motive and defines character. However, dramatic elements have other functions; the emblematic function, for one, is the subject of much critical study, with action seen as a representation of moral, theological, political, social abstractions. As for the function of the recurrent elements in *Hamlet*—at least they contribute to the rich, intricately woven effect that could not be given alone by the almost episodic succession of the basic dramatic units of the play. These basic units are consonant in themselves, but the unity of this play must arise from another principle of organization than the mere progression of these units. For we must remember that one of *Hamlet*'s imperfections, the one most often mentioned, is an inconsistency in behavior and motivation, a lack of complete accord among the parts of the narrative.

The basic unit of *Hamlet*'s narrative is a unit of action briefer usually than the purely mechanical scene divisions that are the conveniences of its staging. These units are units of tone as well as of incident and each unit surrounds a center of concern, with the tone an accordance of the responses among the speakers, one to another, and of the attitudes they indicate toward their subject of discourse. Thus these basic units of the

1. Francis Fergusson discusses analogous action in *Hamlet* from a different point of view in Chap. 4 of *The Idea of a Theater* (Garden City, N. Y., 1953).

play in its presented order are integral and successive spans of feeling and action.

Span of feeling and action is obvious in such plain units as the audiences of the King with Voltimand and Cornelius, or Hamlet with Osric, or with Rosencrantz and Guildenstern. The change from one span to another is usually not as clearly indicated as it is when Hamlet breaks off his ridicule of Polonius with "for look where my abridgement comes" to greet the players, or even as in the same scene where, following the exit of everyone but Hamlet, he meditates with "O what a rogue and peasant slave am I," and prefaces it by the announcement, "Now I am alone."[2] But slides or preparatory shifts in mood usually move us from one span of feeling to another—for instance, the deepened tone of Claudius' cry of conscience, as preparation for "To be or not to be."

Sometimes the unit is single in tone, as in Hamlet's triumphant exultation after the King has fled the scene of the Gonzago play, or again it mixes two feelings, such as Hamlet's mockery of Polonius with his death wishes in the fishmonger dialogue. Mostly the span of feeling is brief, and the pulse of the play is quickened by the shifting emotional quality. Nearly always the tonal quality is indicated by a phrase whose implications we can link to the meaning. We can sense this immediately when Francisco, in the first scene, says as though in anticipation of fear and of the visit of fear and death: "'tis bitter cold/ and I am sick at heart." The association with fear and death can be felt here, as in the second scene with Hamlet's "The air bites shrewdly; it is very cold." In various phrases the tone is set even in units that lack the definite emotional cast of the ghost scenes. Remember the King's "With one auspicious and one dropping eye,/ With mirth in funeral and with dirge in marriage,/ In equal scale weighing delight and dole," and you can sense the ambivalent aspect of this unit in which he accedes unwillingly to Laertes' request for leave, and adjures Hamlet to give up his mourning. The characteristic tone is implied in the family scene of Laertes' leavetaking with the

2. In all quotations the text used is the Variorum edition edited by H. H. Furness (Philadelphia, 1905).

key phrase: "do not sleep,/ but let me hear from you." My explanation here is gross, but the tonal phrases work deeply and subtly in the context.

The spans of feeling, one to another, are relevant no matter how abrupt the change of action, scene, character. The tone of the King's solitary and stern warning to England after urging Rosencrantz and Guildenstern to hurry aboard the ship with Hamlet, "Do it England:/ For like the hectic in my blood he rages," is appropriate to the next span or unit, composed of Hamlet's interview with Fortinbras' captain and his soliloquy ending "O! from this time forth,/ My thoughts be bloody, or be nothing worth." When the character of one span of feeling might appear unrelated to the preceding one there is a preface to provide juncture of feeling. Ophelia's first distraught entrance coheres to the tone of the soliloquy mentioned above by means of the Queen's immediate rejection and refusal, "I will not speak with her."

Thus we have coherence maintained in several ways through the use of certain functional phrases or sentences, some of which provide transitions from one unit of action to another, or prepare for the shift in tone, or point up the quality of tone. Some phrases may perform all of these functions: such a multiple use can be seen in the opening sentence of Act V when the first clown asks his many-pointed query, "Is she to be buried in Christian burial that wilfully seeks her own salvation?" This is a transitional sentence whose implications suggest much of the flavor of the span of action and feeling that it introduces and that Ophelia's funeral procession terminates. This question of the First Clown reaches back into the preceding span with the reminder that Ophelia died through her failure to seek willfully her own preservation (or salvation). The misuse of the term "salvation," its identification by mistake with its antonym "destruction," connotes by the ineptness of wrong usage, as well as by the meaning of the two words confused, the idea of ultimate human defeat that is the persistent, recurrent topic of the dialogue of this span. The defeat of intention by mortality is the major implication of this reverberating question; and politician, courtier, lawyer, jester, Lady

36

Worm, and Alexander and Caesar in Hamlet's enumeration of them answer its literal sense affirmatively; for all that lie buried in Christian burial willfully sought their own salvation (in the sense of preservation from destruction). This implication suffuses the whole dialogue of the gravediggers and Hamlet and Horatio, and the lament for Yorick especially reinforces it. There is also a barb aimed here at the Puritans, who willfully and personally seek their own redemption (or salvation) instead of receiving atonement through the church. But this set verbal thrust takes us out of the play and into history, and the other implications are more pertinent to the unity of feeling of the span.

The problem of finding adequate transitions from one span of feeling to another is sometimes more than a mere phrase or sentence can handle. With the next span, the one comprising Hamlet's and Laertes' struggle in the grave, there is such a sudden change of tone that the transitional element becomes especially important. Hamlet prepares for the juncture by his meditation on Alexander before giving the actual transition itself, the quatrain, "Imperious Caesar, dead and turn'd to clay." The link is completed by simple association as Hamlet ends the one span and opens the next with "here comes the King."

Part of the deep, inner unity of *Hamlet* is created undoubtedly by the coherence of these spans of action and feeling and the relevance of their succession. A study of such coherence and relevance would be both feasible and interesting, but would still be only a study of the consecutiveness of the play. And the structure of *Hamlet* is not only subtly continuous, but complex and interrelated. Many elements of the basic units of tone and feeling are repeated. Strong similarities in tone are obvious in the two verbal bouts that Hamlet has with Rosencrantz and Guildenstern, and the two occasions of his bitter and bawdy words with Ophelia, or the King's two official audiences with his emissaries to Norway, or the two appearances of the Ghost on the platform before the castle, and many other such corresponding dramatic units. There is so much recurrence like this, and of other kinds too, that the principle of recurrence itself seems essential to the structure of *Hamlet*.

In a sense, recurrence is a representation of the basic event. Shakespeare begins his play with disclosure of the accomplished murder, and he knows that its twin act, revenge, will close it. The total dramatic concept is duplication, murder and murder in revenge, and the creative act weaves various details of duplication in event and idea in every part of the narrative. Even the basic theme of murder and revenge is repeated. Old Hamlet is murdered, his murderer is disclosed by the King's ghost to Hamlet, who accomplishes his revenge; old Polonius is murdered, his murder is disclosed by the King to Laertes, who accomplishes his revenge. Hamlet, whose father has been murdered, feigns madness (or his reason has been shaken, if you prefer); Ophelia, whose father has been killed, exhibits her madness, also, to the court. Both have lost their beloved, in that Ophelia returns Hamlet's letters and he is separated from her by his madness, as well as by the instructions of her family.

Shakespeare points to the duplication of the basic plot when he has Hamlet say of Laertes, "For by the image of my cause, I see/ The portraiture of his." But duplication in *Hamlet* is more than a mere matter of the analogous subsidiary plots sometimes found in other Elizabethan plays (as in *Lear*, for instance) and often noted by critics. The instances of duplication already given are few and plain, and more intricate interweavings are needed to show recurrence as the intrinsic design of the play. At random: Laertes warns Ophelia; then, too, Polonius cautions her; Hamlet kills the father, then repeats the action by killing the son. There is Hamlet's letter to Horatio, followed by his letter to Claudius; there is Claudius' letter asking England to kill Hamlet, and Hamlet's letter (with the old king's seal) demanding instant death for Rosencrantz and Guildenstern. Then Polonius is buried with scant ceremony, and Ophelia with "maimed rites."

Double within double, repetition of concept and act, minor detail, and large action, Hamlet is a complexity of echoes: the cannon at the disclosure of old Hamlet's murder, and the cannon at the final scene when the revenge is accomplished; the two processions of Fortinbras' party; Laertes' poison, the King's poison, both for Hamlet, and each receiving his own poison.

38

Hamlet's uncle has gained the Danish crown, Fortinbras' uncle the Norwegian crown; old Hamlet smites the Polack, and so does young Fortinbras, both with small cause—one "even for an eggshell," the other in "an angry parle." Then, of course, there is the murder of Hamlet's father, told by the Ghost, and, mirror to mirror, its duplication in the Gonzago play and the dumb show. Also, there is Hamlet's dumb show of madness to Ophelia in her closet, preceding his acted madness to the court. The Gonzago play itself is a mirror of a real event; for it, as Hamlet says, "is the image of a murder done in Vienna." The pattern of duality is displayed in even the small moments of the play. Horatio has come from Wittenberg and so have Rosencrantz and Guildenstern; Laertes sets sail hurried by Polonius, and Hamlet is hurried aboard ship by Claudius. Rosencrantz and Guildenstern are sent by Claudius with a message to England imputing blame ("with ho! such bugs and goblins in my life"), thus imposing pretended faults on Hamlet; Reynaldo goes to France with instructions from Polonius to defame Laertes "and there put on him/ What forgeries you please." All these twin events make us remember with some amusement that *Hamlet* itself is a duplication of an older play.[3]

But the list is growing longer than necessary. You can add to it at will, and the addition will intensify the feeling of the

3. To show that many more instances could be given than those mentioned above and to avoid turning the body of this paper into a list, additional examples of recurrence are relegated to this footnote. Hamlet "tents" the King by describing his crime through the agency of the Gonzago play; he "tents" the Queen too when he recounts her sins to her in the bedroom scene, and both cry for light and help. We enjoy Polonius' affected speech and Hamlet's mockery as we do Osric's affected speech and Hamlet's mockery. Early in the play Claudius sends a mission to Norway to prevent danger from young Fortinbras, and later he sends to England to prevent danger, to himself from Hamlet. We could list as duplications the King's adviser, Polonius, and Hamlet's confidant, Horatio; Ophelia's two flower scenes, one at the court, the other in the brook; the two families (Claudius, Gertrude, Hamlet—and Polonius, Ophelia, Laertes); Ophelia's funeral procession, Hamlet's body borne away in the "rites of War"; old Hamlet's single combat with old Fortinbras, young Hamlet's duel with Laertes. Both Hamlets win, but both die, both poisoned by Claudius ("the king, the king's to blame," Laertes says): the King communing with his conscience twice, just before "To be or not to be" and later in his attempt at prayer.

play's wonderful complexity of parallelism. There is even a
mirror implied beyond the actual play repeating all that has
taken place. At the end, Horatio announces that he will tell
the whole story, "speak to the yet unknowing world/ How
these things came about."

Duplication in *Hamlet* ranges from plain similitude to likeness that implies comparison in meaning and feeling, to metaphoric action. The implications are fainter in some instances
than others. The King seems like a child frightened in the dark,
as he calls "Give me some light: away." Again, like a child, he
will not face at the end what he knows has happened: "O!
yet defend me, friends: I am but hurt." We can see the implications as metaphor a little better in such a parallel as this:
Claudius pours poison into old Hamlet's ear to destroy him;
later he puts talk of poison into Laertes' ear, to Laertes' even-
tual undoing. True metaphoric action occurs when Hamlet
and Laertes fight in or beside the grave, surrounded by the
court. The implications of this scene emerge when it is mir-
rored in their final combat, with the grave as the environment
of one contention and the resolution of the other. With likeness of this kind the Queen's beautiful image of the "golden
couplets" comes to mind:

> Anon, as patient as the female dove,
> When that her golden couplets are disclos'd
> His silence will sit drooping.

And one should mention here that even this image with its
brooding dove is an echo of:

> There's something in his soul
> O'er which his melancholy sits on brood
> And I do doubt the hatch and disclose of it
> Will be some danger.

Hamlet's leap into the grave is a metaphoric one and his combat with Laertes is metaphoric too as well as a pre-enactment
of his duel with Laertes at the end. When we anticipate the
poisoned tip of Laertes' sword and Hamlet's death by that tip
we are reminded of Hercules wrestling with Death by the tomb
of Alcestis. This points up amusingly, for those who remember

them, Hamlet's words at the close of the incident: "Let Hercules himself do what he may,/ The cat will mew and dog will have his day." Orestes, however, is usually given as Hamlet's mythic analogue.

A unit of action like this struggle in the grave can be taken as *behavior*, just as we conceive in our judging minds the specific deed of a living specific person. But this struggle can also be considered as a demonstrative one, can be seen as *representing* a concept and thus making that concept a part of the overt event itself. Action, in such a case, is an illustration of an idea. *Hamlet* is a mixture of two kinds of narrative: the indication of character by appropriate behavior and the representation of moral concepts by illustrative action. The dramatization of idea through action in *Hamlet* is subtly interfused with that of psychologically "natural" behavior, and obvious allegorical action is avoided. But often it is on the verge of the symbolic. Thus Laertes, like a personification in a morality play, acts out his error in pride and extravagance of grief, and just as he does in his scenes with Polonius and Osric, Hamlet opposes himself to exaggeration and the pride of mannerism. "But sure the bravery of his grief did put me/ Into a towering passion."

To see literature as a vehicle for moral concepts, as Sidney does in the *Defense of Poesy*, and to find in action a representation of idea, as early criticism naturally and easily does with its abstractions, Despair, Anger, Sorrow (with the capitals), is to understand some action in the way a Renaissance audience probably did. Englishmen of an earlier day met everywhere the dramatization of religious and monarchical idea, and in more ways than the occasions of the Anglican service or ceremonies of government. The presentation of idea by dramatization was as implicit in the uses of the theater as in the forms of civic observances. Shakespeare manifests the abstract by the action of his plays as naturally and variously as he would any latent impulse of his age. Evident enough is simple abstract personification, and less evident a range of this use of action running from almost symbolic forms to mere indicative moral behavior. The ideas represented are seldom single and parallel like those in a morality play: often as in *Hamlet*, they are doubtful, scarcely realized, or if realized, then only through analogies.

Such a subtle but insistent, certainly a possible, representation of idea exists in the very configuration of recurrent themes in this play. By the recurrence of action *Hamlet* represents the duality of murder and revenge. Although such representation is never indicated and never rises to a conscious level, yet it is part of the play's underlying shaping matrix, and the relationship between recurrent action and the idea of revenge is a possibility that exists and is significant. Extension of this representation to the concept of moral retribution is natural and easy, especially since the play itself is so much concerned with retribution (example: "To be or not to be," or Claudius' soliloquy, "Oh, my offense is rank.") The moral concept here is contained in the form of the action, by duplication, recurrence, duality, like a very image of the idea. The form of the action of *Hamlet* represents the play's basic idea by its configuration. The effect even of irony when action is controverted or refuted by other action, as when assertions or intentions are turned upon themselves, is a frequent and essential device of the play that contributes to this configuration. In the principle of action that is ironic we find analogies to the concept expressed several times in *Hamlet* that moral forces exist beyond the range of accident and will, that our intentions do not determine our occurrences. In a similar way the occurrences of the play that involve dissimulation represent the persistent idea of a hidden evil beneath the fair appearance, like the King's secret murder.[4] Dissimulation is action with the real ill intent lurking beneath that displayed. The prevalence of dissimulation sets forth this concept of inner imperfection (even like original sin). Dissimulation like Hamlet's madness or the pretenses of good will for Hamlet by the King and his partisans involves a large part of the action, and contains the idea of hidden wrong as though by a likeness of the act itself. Ideas become represented by the form of action through permeation of the idea into the plan of

4. Caroline Spurgeon in *Shakespeare's Imagery* (Cambridge, 1939) pointed out the profusion of images in *Hamlet* concerned with hidden and interior sickness, and since then the idea of hidden evil as a basic theme has become a part of the customary interpretation of the play.

the play. These forms are natural shapes in view of the essential character of the moral concepts to the play, natural developments, although not necessarily conscious ones, of the idea that literature is a vehicle for moral ideas. The representational concept of action is, in a way, allied to the old idea that a man is as he is at a given moment in time. Remember Claudius at his prayers, and hence holding the virtue of that moment, that virtue frustrating Hamlet's opportunity for revenge. Much of the ambiguous character of *Hamlet* is due to this mixture of the representational and psychological modes of moral narrative.

When we consider action as an element in form and see the repetition of action as structural and often metaphoric, we can follow certain implications beyond their structural basis and find, in many cases, action becoming irony. Since *Hamlet* was an old play rewritten, the events were quite familiar, and then, too, the consequences of murder in a revenge play were already known. An audience for *Hamlet* always expects what is going to happen, and in that sense, all the action is simultaneous. We see each event in the light of the other events relevant to it; that relevance is often ironic and untoward. Hamlet's conscious spoken irony, like "Thrift, thrift, Horatio! The funeral baked-meats/ Did coldly furnish forth the marriage tables," is not what is meant here, but the irony that consequent events create in our minds when we know a statement or an act will be controverted. The irony in *Hamlet* is contrapuntal; action answers or returns upon the implications of simple statements and deeds, and both occur in the mind at once. The King says that because of Hamlet's "gentle and unforc'd accord" the cannon will roar each time he drinks a health. Here we know the character of the health he and the Queen will drink at the end, and the cannonade that speaks "to the heavens" near the end echoes ironically upon the earlier round of healths. At the beginning, the King assures Hamlet with "Be as ourself in Denmark," and we know that Hamlet, too, will murder, and that they both will die at the hand of avengers. Duality as a configuration of the play carries over thus into its ironic effects. Of course, there is no lack of the familiar irony of comment, like that of Hamlet and the baked-meats just mentioned, or his later "is thy union here" as he forces the King to drink the poisoned cup containing the pearl, the "union" with "follow my mother," or the gentle irony of Ophelia's proffer of her moralizing flowers.

Rich and complex as *Hamlet* is, we find everywhere the more immediate kind of irony in which the contrary implications lie in the language itself. The vessel that will hold the poisoned wine the King prepares for Hamlet is a chalice; the word "chalice" contains the suggestion of the wine of spiritual life. Laertes will anoint his sword with poison and the idea of consecration for holy purposes lies within the word "anoint." Another kind of simple verbal irony occurs in those lines having multiple meaning, with one carrying on the current overt meaning and another playing upon the moral life of the action. Remembering that Elizabethans punned on the word "die," using its other sense (for them) of the sexual act, the hidden meaning of the Queen's observation on our common mortality and Hamlet's dry agreement becomes a subtle by-play anticipating Hamlet's scolding and her defense later in her closet.

> Thou knowest 'tis common; all that lives must die,
> Passing through nature to eternity.
> *Hamlet*: Ay, Madam, it is common.

Of course the Queen is not supposed to be aware of the hidden meaning here; this meaning is evident only to Hamlet—and to the audience.

Irony resembles duplicate action in that it involves a form of completion. There is a duality here, in that we have a statement or an act and we later have its controversion. For instance, when Laertes and Polonius warn Ophelia to beware of Hamlet, "Be wary then; best safety lies in fear," we know that their caution is for her only, yet that Hamlet will be the undoing of them all. Polonius' famous advice to Laertes is controverted by Laertes' very nature, and by the later actions of both of them. "Give every man thine ear, but few thy voice" amuses us when we think of Polonius' loquacity, but is deepened in view of his fatal eavesdropping and cry for help. The

44

King's good wishes to Laertes when he takes his leave, "Take thy fair hour, Laertes; time be thine," can be taken in two ways—as part of the direct action and in the light of the short time left to him, and his known fate. The end is an ironic reversion of the human intentions of the beginning, for the guard and watch kept for Fortinbras on the platform before the castle bring about the meeting there of Hamlet and the Ghost and the subsequent chain of events that opens the throne of Denmark to the Norwegian.

There are many occasions when subsequent action is a controversion of simple statement. Two instances with tragic implications are Hamlet's remark about his father a short time before he sees his ghost. "He was a man, take him for all in all/ I shall not look upon his like again," and his unconscious wish that both he and Claudius had died early enough to die virtuously, "Would I had met my dearest foe in heaven."

Irony, thematic recurrence, and metaphoric action are not simply and separately present, but woven and mingled. Exploring any one instance of these three further, one soon comes upon the others. Taking a plain duplicate action and then turning it one way and another to see its ironic and metaphoric aspects, we note that the two women in the play, Ophelia and the Queen, suffer accidental, self-inflicted deaths, one by water and the other by wine. Ophelia, image of the archetypal Persephone, is "as one incapable of her own distress"; her fate is a synecdoche for her nature; she sinks among her symbolic flowers into the brook, pulled under by the figurative drinking of her garments, "Till that her garments heavy with their drink/ Pulled the poor wretch from her melodious lay to muddy death." As for the Queen, she drinks the poisoned cup prepared by Claudius, drinks it with an unconsciously ironic health to her son. "The Queen carouses to thy fortune, Hamlet," she says, and we hear it with all the implications of her other carousings in mind, and the meaning of the word beyond simple drinking, and knowing Hamlet's fortune, too.

Duplication, controversion, comparison make a pattern of action for *Hamlet* that is the play's essential configuration. For a revenge play that inner form is congruous and appropriate;

for revenge is the duplication of murder as well as its controversion, and the irony of murder for the murderer is that his
fate as victim is made by his act as murderer. The killing of
Polonius, while seeming an archetypal action like that of the
sacrificial victim at the spilling of whose blood the dead come
(here the Ghost),[5] is not only a duplicate action but a pivotal
point in the form of the play by which the narrative is divided
into two parts, physically as well as by the sense and feel of the
action before and after. We have seen that each death has its
duplicate action: Claudius for old Hamlet (and Polonius for
him, too); the Queen for Ophelia, and Hamlet for Laertes.
When we follow the complex pattern of form of *Hamlet*'s action, we see its horizontal succession of spans of feeling, pacing
a sort of narrative rhythm, and harmonized one to another by
slides or transitions of tone. We follow the form into its vertical
structure of duplications and mirrors of event and concept, of
ironic eventualities deepened by metaphoric action, and we find
at last the complex nature of *Hamlet* and its inner plan of narrative. Its rich language, too, belongs with its involved structure, its diversity of styles, its implications, one behind another,
its mixture of feelings like "the gaiety transfiguring all that
dread." Considering form in *Hamlet* is like considering pattern
in apparently simple, natural things or forces like leaves or the
recurrences of weather.

5. As in Book XI of the *Odyssey*.

T. WALTER HERBERT
Professor of English
University of Florida

A Study of Meaning in *Antony & Cleopatra*

HOUGH SHAKESPEARE'S PLAYS RESPOND TO MANY modes of inquiry and understanding, it is comfortable to employ a mode congenial with men's minds as they functioned in the decades nearest the death of Queen Elizabeth I. An Elizabethan felt that the macrocosm gave meaning to the microcosm, and vice versa. He also found for each part of his body, for his own existence in the world, for every stream and hillock of his island, this mode of meaning: each part of each whole has a meaning because of its relationships to other parts, and each part contributes a share of meaning to its proper whole and derives meaning from its whole.

Antony and Cleopatra has a meaning for us proportional to our knowledge of history and our own time if we perceive it as a microcosm alluding to the great world Shakespeare lived in and the great world we live in. This paper only glances at that kind of meaning. Principally it is an essay to phrase meanings

47

arising from relationships between part and part and between part and whole in *Antony and Cleopatra.**

An Elizabethan familiar with the doctrine of four humors out of which a personality is constructed would not be astonished at a doctrine of four dramatic constituents out of which a living play is constructed. These may be called setting, action, poetry, and characters, corresponding to what in life are environment, events, speech, and people. We may ask of each element in each constituent what it means, and look for an answer in how it shapes and modifies other elements and constituents and how it yields to their pressures. This process, though it depends upon analysis, resembles not so much dissection as an affectionate study of the physiology of a notably live person. If the process is successful, the meaning we state in answer to our question will ring true to the play as it comes direct to our perceptions.

SETTING

Antony and Cleopatra is often as remarkable for what it is not as for what it is. *Hamlet, Macbeth,* and *Lear* are set in a universe where the major characters are conscious of the great forces of nature, of destiny, of God, so that by virtue of their setting these plays involve serious inquiries into the quality of the cosmos. *Antony and Cleopatra* is earth-bound. Whenever there is reference to anything off the surface, it is an earthly metaphor, as when Cleopatra renounces her resemblance to the changeable moon; or it is a metaphor for transcendent human passion, as when, severally, Antony and Cleopatra both claim to be compounded of air and fire as against earth and water; or it is evocative of superstitious awe, as when the strange subterranean noises are interpreted as earth omens of Antony's fall; or it is fortune-telling without philosophic overtones; or it is a vision of an after-life luxurious with amorous possibilities; it is never as persuasively cosmic as even the star-crossed loving of Romeo and Juliet.

*People understand dramatic structure in a variety of ways. See Thomas B. Stroup, "The Structure of *Antony and Cleopatra*," in James G. McManaway (ed.), *Shakespeare 400: Essays by American Scholars on the Anniversary of the Poet's Birth* (New York, 1964), pp. 289-98.

But if the goddess of Antony's world treads on the ground it is a ground for spacious parade. Measure out the perimeter of Antony's world. Rome, Syria, and Alexandria stand at the borders, and Shakespeare insists upon the magnitude in Antony's vaulting phrase about "the wide Arch/ Of the raing'd Empire" and in Caesar's Homeric list of the dominions preparing under Antony for war. Shakespeare learned his lesson from Marlowe, whose Tamburlaine also strode over a world made enormous by scenes set far apart and by the recitation of high resounding place names. In Shakespeare as in Marlowe a vast empire makes a fit geometry for a tremendous conqueror.

This horizontal world that great Antony dominated in his great days had shape as well as magnitude; it had what we may call polarity. Rome, city of the north and west, and Cleopatra's Alexandria, city of the south and east, are capable of giving a local habitation to contrasted forces. Shakespeare makes them do that.

Alexandria was a home for gay and irresponsible play. There were pranks, as when Cleopatra discovered Antony cheating at a fishing contest and had a diver put a salt fish on his line. There were indecorous contests between Antony and men of low station, in which order was sacrificed to fun. There was an early form of pub crawling. There was gluttonous and wasteful eating, that the rumor of it was a legend in Rome. And there was such drinking that when the lords of creation drank themselves to dullness on Pompey's ship, Enobarbus found it not yet an Alexandrian feast.

Rome meant purposeful business. In Rome even the games between such great ones as Antony and Octavius were not for fun but for prestige. There was little drinking in Rome. When Shakespeare wanted to show us the Romans reeling he put them on a ship near Misenum, a hundred miles away. In Rome there was planning for the business of empire. In Rome there was blunt, straightforward speech between Caesar and Antony. In Rome Antony was capable of making reasonable answers—even concessions—in arriving at a sane basis for action. And in Rome Octavius was at his characteristic best: calmly evaluating the chances for concerted action with Antony, or finding reasons for waging the war that was to leave him absolute emperor.

The quality we call "Roman" is of course a quality of the people that Shakespeare caused to inhabit Rome, and those people are often elsewhere than in the imperial city. We do not define setting solely as inanimate place. Since we take setting to be the dramatic equivalent of all those things that in life we call environment, we may regard the Roman setting as extending as far as Roman modes of thought and action extend in the play. We bear in mind that Rome the empire was historically an extension of Rome the city; one might be born a Roman citizen without ever having dwelt in Italy, and he might live a consciously Roman mode of life surrounded by people who retained the patterns their forefathers evolved before the legions came. Shakespeare knew this well, and would have known it had he read only the New Testament.

In *Antony and Cleopatra* it is not the hills and buildings, the Tiber and the vineyards of Rome that call for Antony's loyalty. Shakespeare has Octavius and the soldiers make a point of it that Antony was the right Roman Antony far from the city, in barbarous places where he showed his hardihood by eating and drinking repulsive things and his potent drive by bursting with his heart the buckles of his breastplate. It was the Roman mode of life that Antony belonged to, and it never leaves off demanding his allegiance.

The setting of our play also includes a way of life that belongs only to Egypt, only to Alexandria, and only where Cleopatra is physically present. Her way of life is thus localized, whereas the Roman way, though very purely represented by Caesar in Rome, invests nearly all the Romans whether in Rome, Parthia, Syria, Misenum, or Egypt.

Setting is tightly bound up with every other aspect of the play, for in terms of setting the action can be called the resultant of the two pulls on Antony, in terms of setting every character finds his quality, and in terms of setting the playful or gorgeous speech of Egypt is set over against the smutty or straightforward speech of the Romans.

In the first scene the warrior business of Rome and its contrast with the amorous play of Egypt is spoken twice: once by the Roman Philo in the remarkable speech which ends describing

> The triple pillar of the world transform'd
> Into a Strumpets Foole,

and once also by an Antony at the moment fully given over to Egypt, clipped in Cleopatra's arms:

> Let Rome in Tyber melt, and the wide Arch
> Of the raing'd Empire fall: Heere is my space,
> Kingdomes are clay.

Cleopatra is always conscious that Antony feels his Roman obligations, and until she has seen his ruin at Actium knows that she is constantly threatened by his Roman loyalties, she and the gay life that belongs to her. She phrases her apprehension:

> He was dispos'd to mirth, but on the sodaine
> A Romane thought hath strooke him.

Equally well Antony knows the two forces pulling at him. After first protesting that the nobleness of life for him is to embrace Cleopatra, he presently acknowledges the demands of his Roman allegiance:

> These strong Egyptian Fetters I must breake,
> Or loose my selfe in dotage.

Antony and his followers recognize that his disaster is a departure from his original self, and this personal view is dramatic and just. But when these Romans are concerned with Antony's true self they are talking about his Roman self. That is the reason we are talking about his catastrophe in connection with setting. After Actium, Canidius says,

> Had our Generall
> Bin what he knew himselfe, it had gone well.

Antony says: "I have fled my selfe," "I have lost command," "I have offended Reputation," and in so saying he was talking of himself as Roman, not as one who with Cleopatra could say

> Eternity was in our Lippes, and Eyes,
> Blisse in our browes bent: none our parts so poore,
> But was a race of Heaven.

When Antony came to die, at first he sought to invite death at the hands of a creature, as Cleopatra later did, thus faintly confirming in an action what he had earlier said, that she had conquered him utterly at Actium. He acknowledges himself "no more a Soldier" as he divests himself of his Roman armor. He contemplates death with a mind bent on Cleopatra. At this moment the name of his body servant becomes a pun. He calls "Eros" as if calling on his god as he summons one sworn to obey him:

> Eros! I come my Queene. Eros! Stay for me,
> Where Soules do couch on Flowers, wee'l hand in hand,
> And with our sprightly Port make the Ghostes gaze.

But when Eros turns out to be of Roman temper, Antony tries for a like Roman death. And though he botches the job, he finally claims to have behaved like a Roman, describing himself bombastically as

> A Roman, by a Roman
> Valiantly vanquish'd.

Finally, beginning about the time of Antony's death Cleopatra takes a Roman resolution in her hands and, strangely blending elements peculiar to herself as a daughter of the East, lives up to the decision announced when she says:

> Wee'l bury him: And then, what's brave, what's Noble,
> Let's doo't after the high Roman fashion,
> And make death proud to take us.

Not only does she take heart, not only does she act with force; she comports herself no longer like a cow in June but with shrewdness, rationality, and wariness quite comparable to Caesar's. In the gorgeous fabric of her spirit there is a strand that makes her as it were the last effective soldier in Antony's Roman warfaring. Addressing the asp, she says,

> Oh could'st thou speake,
> That I might heare thee call great Caesar Asse, unpolicied.

Shakespeare varies his poetry depending upon whether the speaker is of Rome or of Cleopatra's Egypt. In the mouth of Charmian, Cleopatra is "a Lasse unparallel'd," "a Princesse Descended of so many Royal Kings." In the mouth of Roman Philo she is a gypsy, a strumpet, Pompey calls her "Egypts Widdow," Agrippa calls her "Royall Wench," Caesar calls her whore. Enobarbus describes her most extensively, and always with earthy admiration, but Enobarbus is not associated with the biases of either Rome or Egypt. It is in Antony's words that Cleopatra gets her widest selection of epithets. When he is her naturalized thrall she is "wrangling Queene: Whom every thing becomes," she is his "Serpent of old Nile," "my Chucke," she is his "precious Queene," she is "Egypt," she is "Love," she is "Lady." But when he is concerned with the Roman business of his life she is a boggler, "a Morsell, cold upon Dead Caesars Trencher," she is a gypsy, the "false Soul of Egypt," she is "thou Spell," and "the Witch."

This variation of epithet is paralleled by the contrasting ways in which Roman and Egyptian speak about loving. The Egyptians are as earthy as the Romans, but they are playful, as when Cleopatra recalls her days with Julius Caesar as her salad days or when Charmian and Iras are having their fortunes told; or they are exultingly passionate, as when Cleopatra speaks of "the Lovers pinch,/ Which hurts, and is desir'd" or of the kiss which is her heaven to have. The Roman way to speak of loving is coarse or brutal, as when Agrippa speaks of Julius Caesar's nights in Cleopatra's arms saying, "He ploughed her and she cropt," or when Philo speaks of Antony's heart as of no use now but to fan a gypsy's lust. The Romans make a distinction between love itself and love as an element in marriage. A Roman speaking of marriage is neither coarse nor playful nor passionate but sober and concerned with alliances and the creation of a family to which a steady loyalty belongs. Thus speak Octavius and Octavia and Lepidus, and also at times Antony, though of course when he speaks of Fulvia, Antony speaks of a wife who was a clog and a shrew. But Antony on the subject of loving runs the whole gamut of passion, play, smut, and family duty.

There is a quality belonging to the language of the Romans in all matters, a quality that distinguishes them from Cleopatra and her group. We have already glanced at it as blunt and straightforward and businesslike and rational. Enobarbus customarily speaks like the other Romans because he is rational. But in Enobarbus rationality goes the full distance and is high wit. He watches the great campaigns of the Romans and perceives it to be armed theft. He watches the Richard-like tragic posturing of Antony and reduces it from high to low pathos. He watches the superb loving of Antony and sees that in a middle-aged man desire is getting the better of reason and judgment. And he watches the dissolution of Antony's generalship and prudently, wittily, bides his time. When he actually deserts Antony he also deserts his wit, so that Enobarbus in Caesar's camp makes but one jest, then plunges into an eloquence of remorse as romantic and humorless as Wolsey. At that point the language of the whole play, released from Enobarbus' wit, goes headlong into passionate enthusiasm whenever Antony speaks, or Cleopatra, and it is often thus gorgeous in the mouths of those about these principals. Even plodding Caesar at the end is sporadically eloquent over the so famous lovers.

This triumph of a mode of poetry which the play associates with the gaudy passions of Cleopatra coincides with the transition of dramatic dominance from Antony to Cleopatra. Antony sets the key with his supplication for death at Eros' hands. But this Alexandrian mode Cleopatra soon takes over as her proper music. "Oh Sunne," she says, seeing wounded Antony,

> Burne the great sphere thou mov'st in, darkling stand
> The varrying shore o' th' world. O Antony, Antony, Antony.

This is language unreined by reason, and unpunctured by Enobarbus' wit. So it is when she says at Antony's death,

> Young Boyes and Gyrles
> Are levell now with men: The oddes is gone,
> And there is nothing left remarkeable
> Beneath the visiting Moone.

54

And so it is when with her final regal chord she asserts at once her passionate itch, her love for Antony, her consent to death, and her authority over every other force in the play except the mere power to kill—and even that she shares:

> Give me my Robe, put on my Crowne, I have
> Immortall longings in me.

The poetry of Egypt, if not her armies! But shortly Caesar enters and the coda is in the matter-of-fact cadences of Rome, only a little touched by Eastern color.

POETRY

We have already noticed that in *Antony and Cleopatra* contrasting modes of speech distinguish the Roman from the Egyptian, and we have watched how the Roman mode is almost overwhelmed by the Egyptian at the time when the departure of Enobarbus from Antony throws Cleopatra into the ascendant. Hence we have noticed how Shakespeare uses two tunes of poetry to reinforce the dramatic statement of his setting.

This play belongs among those with a dominant poetic texture: the sonorous eloquence of *Othello*, the lofty pathos of *Richard II*, the tempestuous agonizing of *Lear*, or the delicate melodiousness of *The Tempest*.

The passages most often remembered from *Antony and Cleopatra*, I suppose, are the description of Cleopatra on Cydnus recited by an amused Enobarbus to the gawking Romans, the first ringing speech of Antony about Rome in Tiber melting for all he cares, and the speeches of Cleopatra at Antony's death, "The Crowne o' th' earth doth melt," and at her own death, "Give me my Robe, put on my Crowne." These and gorgeous or voluptuous speeches like them are invariably focused on the person or spirit of Cleopatra, so that although the pivot of action is always Antony, it is Cleopatra who gives substance to the dominant song.

It is impossible adequately to describe this poetry, of course, but it is just as impossible not to recognize it. At the outset it has only obvious meanings, but when it sounds in work-a-day Rome in the mouth of Enobarbus, it sounds in an interesting situation. Antony has left Cleopatra, and by marrying Octavia has reduced Cleopatra to the status of a girl in a foreign port. At such a moment one might expect that the music to describe Cleopatra would be at least tinged with pity, probably with contempt, especially if the sophisticated Enobarbus is to speak. What he says is

> The Barge she sat in, like a burnisht Throne
> Burnt on the water.

The leitmotiv of Cleopatra's music strikes sharp and clear and sweet in the harsher sounds of Rome. Presently when Enobarbus, to the comment that Antony must now leave Cleopatra, responds, "Never he will not," he is simply repeating what the poetry has already in its own way told us.

That the characteristic rapturous poetry associated with Cleopatra should acquire the flavor of victory is not at all strange if we look at the conspicuous passages, for these come at moments when Cleopatra is represented as somehow superior to very weighty considerations. As if to nail down his point tight, Shakespeare prefaces the Enobarbus speech with a phrase of Maecenas, "She's a most triumphant Lady, if report be square to her." The sense of victoriousness in the Cleopatra music comes into its dramatic own in the latter acts when Antony is conquered by her and later when she matches her own decision against Caesar's. For Cleopatra defeated by an army still manages to turn the final moment into a triumph that Caesar himself concedes. Shakespeare puts her music in the mouth of Antony and astringent Enobarbus as tokens of her glory. In the last scene he bends even Caesar's tongue briefly to her song. It is a strange poetic trick, for Shakespeare in several consecutive speeches makes Caesar speak in two modes alternately: one flat and prosy, like a coroner, the other, when Caesar thinks of her spirit, vaulting poetry:

> If they had swallow'd poyson, 'twould appeare
> By externall swelling: but she lookes like sleepe,
> As she would catch another Anthony
> In her strong toyle of Grace.

56

Cleopatra's music stands in contrast with the sturdy sounds of the Romans, but a dominant mode of imagery sets her in vivid contrast with Antony. Whereas the most frequently recurring denominator in Antony's imagery—and that includes what is said about him as well as what he says of himself—is separation, the characteristic most common in Cleopatra's is putting things harmoniously together.

A wealth of phrases suggest the cracking of bonds within Antony and between him and factors in his world. In the first scene Philo says of Antony that sometimes "he is not Antony." In the second Antony says, "These strong Egyptian Fetters I must breake." In the third Antony says,

> The strong necessity of Time, commands
> Our Services a-while: but my full heart
> Remaines in use with you.

In the fourth Caesar, speaking of Antony's departure from his ancient virile Roman ways, says of him that he "Is not more manlike/ Then Cleopatra." The fifth scene is Cleopatra's, but in the sixth Pompey prays, about Antony, "That sleepe and feeding may prorogue his Honour." In the seventh scene Caesar, speaking of the Roman broils while Antony has been in Egypt, says, "you were the word of warre," meaning that divisions came about because of loyalties to Antony. In the eighth scene Antony, speaking his first word to his new wife Octavia, says,

> The world, and my great office, will
> Sometimes divide me from your bosome.

Let us here arbitrarily stop the parade of scenes and recall a most terrible image for a general. After watching at Actium, Scarus says that Antony clapped on his sea-wing when Cleopatra turned tail

> and (like a doting Mallard)
> Leaving the fight in heighth, flyes after her.

In contrast with this steady theme of division, Cleopatra, who disintegrated the emperor, comes to us in images of embraces, harmony, and things uniting. It is very strange, belonging as it does to a woman who knew that to hold Antony she must cross his moods.

The difference is illustrated in Antony's first big speech, where the empire is envisioned falling to pieces while he and Cleopatra embrace. It is illustrated also in Enobarbus' description of Cleopatra on the Cydnus, where the people leave Antony and go to Cleopatra: Antony,

> Enthron'd i' th' Market-place, did sit alone,
> Whistling to th' ayre: which but for vacancie,
> Had gone to gaze on Cleopatra too,
> And made a gap in Nature.

Sometimes Cleopatra's attractiveness is absurdly firm. After Actium, Antony brushes aside Cleopatra's disclaimer of responsibility for his behavior:

> Egypt, thou knew'st too well,
> My heart was to thy Rudder tyed by th' strings,
> And thou should'st stowe me after.

Sometimes the harmoniousness is a kind of special morality for her, as when Enobarbus says that "vildest things/ Become themselves in her." Even in Cleopatra's last metaphor death wields no scythe, but she, at length in imagery a complete woman, has her aspic baby at her breast, "who sucks the nurse asleep." As a final instance, notice one of the cases where for Cleopatra a superficial metaphor of separation overlies a concept of coming together, for she looks at death as a way to join amorously with Antony. She addresses the asp:

> Come thou mortal wretch,
> With thy sharpe teeth this knot intrinsicate,
> Of life at once untye.

Whatever referent we may conjure up as the physical basis of the metaphor, the untying of the knot is to release her, that she may embrace Antony as her husband.

I have dwelt on this conspicuous contrasting imagery mainly for noticing its bearing on what happens to the major characters. Antony's destruction is measured by his splitting himself

away from the Roman pattern which he once admirably ex-
emplified, and Cleopatra's glory is finally revealed when we
recognize that the qualities that made her a temptress still exist
in the same woman who meets her moment of disaster with an
equivalent to the high Roman dignity and a capacity for love
not wholly defined by gaiety and perishable flesh.

ACTION

Antony and Cleopatra is bound to disappoint critics who
must find an Aristotelian ethos or an equivalent to Christian
theology or a high assertion of accepted values lurking in the
action of tragedy. No great self-revelation ever came to Antony
except the obvious fact that he had behaved as no general ever
should, and no revelation came to Cleopatra because she was
never without knowledge of herself. Indeed if one perversely
insists upon looking for the great classical statements of tragedy
in the action of *Antony and Cleopatra* he will come closer to
finding their repudiation than their exemplification. But of
course the play is not a repudiation, and it does stir the heart
as only great tragedy ever does, and it is perfectly clear that
Shakespeare was neither Ben Jonson nor John Dryden to rub
Aristotle like a rabbit's foot.

Antony and Cleopatra has something in common with the
medieval conventions of the fall of princes and the wheel of
fortune. Witness indeed the parallel histrionics in falling Antony and falling Richard II. *Antony and Cleopatra* also invokes
the powerful dramatic appeal of the great Morality theme,
wherein good forces contest evil forces for the soul of man. But
in *Antony and Cleopatra* the excellent tags of *good* and *bad* do
not fit: computer-minded Caesar does not resemble a good
angel and neither does Cleopatra. For present purposes we are
perhaps better off if we refrain from allocating the action to a
category.

When the play opens Antony is in Egypt rejoicing in the
fruits of campaigns that have proven him the greatest soldier
in the world, the major fruit being possession of incomparably
the most remarkable daughter of Venus in the history of imagination in circumstances well adapted to the enjoyment of her

conversation. Already present are the forces that render this peerless conjunction of man and situation intolerable. His Roman soldiers have noticed that he has let passion warp his attention away from the royal occupation of war. He despises the Roman duty that justifies his presence in Egypt, but an endangered Rome is urgently calling him back to his soldiership.

When Antony once vacillates from his announced determination to remain with Cleopatra the pattern of the action is sketched and set in motion. Of course in this first vacillation, which carries him to Rome, he looks to everyone in the play like a man of power throwing off the temporary fetters of a casual affair made credible up to this point by a shrewish wife. Shakespeare is at pains to paint a picture of Cleopatra and her lascivious court so persuasively charming as to make Antony's departure appear a thing to be accomplished only by a man of conscience and serious purpose. But then Shakespeare goes the simple enticement and the simple alternative of this voluptuous gaiety one better. He lets the Roman duty dictate the physical action of the general but causes Cleopatra to exact from him a denial of whole-hearted performance:

> Thou residing heere, goes yet with mee;
> And I hence fleeting, heere remaine with thee.

Antony's initial action is thus not a renunciation of Cleopatra and her passionate life but something more complicated. Though Antony believes he is to have both worlds, the coarse realism of the Roman soldiers' comment upon him suggests that he is not really big enough. As the play goes forward, his effort to master irreconcilable opposites becomes the dominant question which event after event brings to test.

The weight of Antony in Rome is tremendous in every large issue. Lepidus bends all his effort to making Caesar content with Antony, and Caesar so far complies that he gives his beloved sister to be Antony's wife. The mere presence of Antony, without show of arms, quells the revolt of Pompey. Antony in Rome proves to have power vast enough to justify his pre-eminent position, and only in inconsequential games does Caesar have the advantage over him.

60

But Shakespeare makes Antony commit the unspeakable folly of following a summary of these childish contests with the assertion that he can at once do the Roman deed and live the Egyptian life:

> I will to Egypte:
> And though I make this marriage for my peace,
> I' th' East my pleasure lies.

He puts the East in his main clause. Soon thereafter Octavia's unhappy confession that she is divided in heart between Antony and Caesar is prologue to a division in Antony, for Antony divided from Caesar is Antony divided from the business of Rome and his quality as an emperor. This is a fact not even a war can demonstrate to Antony.

War can, however, demonstrate the fact to us, and the demonstration is rapid. Every common soldier knows better than Antony, the greatest general in the world, how to counter Caesar's onslaught, and Enobarbus sourly itemizes his lapses of judgment. Antony has been hooked like a fish by Cleopatra. In relinquishing the stern primacy of his Roman allegiance he has tossed away the Roman good sense. Instead of using his hitherto invincible army to shock Caesar back on his fleet heels, he relies, of all things, on the Egyptian navy with Cleopatra in the flagship. This is the dramatic way of saying what we can feebly say in prose, that Antony now fights like an Egyptian and not like a Roman, fights with his passion instead of his prudence, uses Cleopatra instead of his veteran infantrymen as his instrument of war. Actium makes evident that Antony cannot have both worlds, that he has chosen the world of Cleopatra, and that as a member of her gaudy world he is bound to go down before the swift ships and disciplined purposes of Rome.

But this is only a part of Antony. His Roman generalship and judgment are a dead sacrifice to Cleopatra. But his Roman memory, his Roman love of fighting, his Roman loyalty to his troops, are only partly gone. The latter days of Antony fulfill the nature of the initial event in the action. He vacillates and starts now in one direction and now in another: he offers treasure to his soldiers and has a gaudy night with Cleopatra, he outmaneuvers Caesar one day and on another ridiculously offers to fight Caesar singlehanded, he tries to make his followers cry and then tries to make them laugh and revel, he glories in the occupation of war like a Roman and has Cleopatra squire him into his armor, he whips Thyreus for familiarity with Cleopatra and blames her for treachery. And of course finally he tries to die like Cleopatra, then tries to die like a Roman, then tries to bid Cleopatra come down to him, then allows himself to be drawn up to her, and so on till the end.

Spoken thus barely, the final days of Antony sound weak to the point of effeminacy, and thus indeed the events paint him. But the play is more than action, and Antony never appears wholly petty.

The action of the play as it touches Cleopatra is less molding than revealing. Until the very end this versatile, mercurial woman appears to vacillate even in her loyalties. But in no real action does she ever waver from her characteristic self nor does any act support her words of parley with Caesar and his emissaries, words which imply a question of her devotion to Antony. Consequently the apparent contrast with Antony—first vacillation and then firmness—seems less a progressive development than an often surprising revelation of a constant though variously expressive character.

Cleopatra is really without weapons, save herself, at any time. Single she captures Antony. When he dies warning her to trust only Proculeius, she, better fitted than he for single combat, responds that she will trust only her own hands and resolution. Single she seeks to make terms with Caesar, betrayed by her own treasurer. And single she defeats Caesar by accomplishing her own death. This single, unaided quality in her action is in contrast with the real strength of the Romans, which was nourished by group disciplines and decisions whose corollaries one can accurately predict.

CHARACTERIZATION

At every point, in language, setting, and action, we have been concerned not only with the matter at immediate issue but also with its capacity to breathe distinctive life into the figures of Antony and Cleopatra. Characters also characterize one another in persuasive ways. And when they come vividly alive they make us invest with deep momentousness the worlds they inhabit and the actions they perform.

In *Antony and Cleopatra* characters describe one another. Both Antony and Cleopatra are seen and described differently by different people, and hence arises their lifelikeness, their substance in several dimensions.

Antony, as we have noticed, is to the Romans at first a great general misusing his powers. The Roman leaders presently describe him more and more contemptuously until he becomes simply an "old Ruffian" to Caesar. But when Antony is at the lowest in the estimation of the great Romans he is by the loyal soldier, by conscience-stricken Enobarbus, and finally by Cleopatra, described in glowing, heroic terms. Thus when Antony lies unheroically a corpse Cleopatra speaks to Dolabella:

I dreampt there was an Emperor Anthony.
O such another sleepe, that I might see
But such another man. . . .
His face was as the Heav'ns, and therein stucke
A Sunne and Moone, which kept their course, & lighted
The little o' th' earth. . . .
His legges bestrid the Ocean his rear'd arme
Crested the world:

and so on. Speeches like this belie the evidence of the action and help to leave us with the total picture of an Antony who does base things but in a manner extravagantly noble.

Reactions as well as words characterize a man. To the early Antony everybody except Cleopatra and Enobarbus is in varying degrees obsequious, and kings jump to serve him. To the later Antony a mere messenger can be impudent, and whatever else may be said about Eros' refusal to kill his master, his disobedience belittles Antony's authority.

Antony develops away from oneness and dominance, but even as weakness and distintegration proceed, he retains massiveness. Enobarbus' word for him is right: an old lion dying. This magnitude has many consequences, but surely the main one has to do with Cleopatra.

Cleopatra alone, so says the structure of the play, had the power to destroy Antony. Not great Caesar could do that unless Cleopatra had made Antony not himself. The magnitude of Antony thus confers a magnitude on Cleopatra, and her maintenance of that magnitude even in his disintegration and defeat is the condition upon which her final devotion to Antony achieves the proportions of the grandest of all recorded passions in woman.

Cleopatra's personality never suffers any loss. She and time crack Antony but nothing withers her. The range of her influence narrows until at the end, fleetingly, only Charmian remains her subject. But the voice we first heard quipping with the Emperor over the limits on love was the same witty voice that protests Iras' haste to the ghostly arms of Antony. The woman who toyed with the moods of passionate Antony at the beginning was the same—shall we say hypocritical, or versatile— woman who talks earnestly with earnest Caesar near the end and then comments, "He words me Gyrles, he words me." The strategist who watched her chances with an Antony struck by a Roman thought was the same strategist who sizes up Proculeius, Dolabella, and Caesar, and finds a way to act royally at a time when materially she is but a slave in her own tomb.

This indestructibility and vitality in Cleopatra's bountiful personality are just as germane to the splendor potential in human beings and to the terror residing in their relations to the world as are the concepts in *Lear* and *Macbeth*. Granted that the greater tragedies touch us nearer our hearts' homes. Cleopatra stands for the juice of Egypt's grape, for wasteful feasts, for revelry in authentic gaiety, and for all the wayward and unreasoned tempers of vivacious women as well as for amorous flesh spiced by happy wit. The proper adversary of these is the planning, rational, purposeful power-building of Caesar's ilk. I do not for a moment mean to imply that the play morally approves what Cleopatra stands for. But Cleopatra says that these qualities can be linked to an ultimate heroism just as surely as Goneril and Regan say that malice can usurp the prerogatives of responsible authority. Cakes and ale!

This intemperate and infinitely various queen, cruel, gaudy, witty, and superficially soft, must be persuasively presented so as to make convincing the proposition that a notorious lecher with endless opportunity for the gratification of his appetite in any land, that a man of power capable of denying his appetite for the sake of honor, that an emperor of Rome should find in one woman the wild fascination Antony finds in Cleopatra. Cleopatra must incorporate in herself qualities which make her persuasively the embodiment of an Eastern life splendid enough to compete with well-known Rome for a Roman's allegiance. And she has to make credible the outpouring from one mouth of the various modulations of the poetic tune which is hers.

Enobarbus is a character whose vitality is more than sufficient for the commentator's role commonly assigned him. He does indeed fulfill that function, calling the acts of Antony and Cleopatra by their right names and naming inevitable events as they are about to happen. As the sardonic truth-teller of the play he can prevent us from ever accepting the evaluations of those Romans who hold Cleopatra in contempt. As the loyal follower of Antony he contributes to the illusion of an Antony worthy to be followed, and when at last he deserts, the play shows us a general to whom a recognizable token of total disaster has come. When Antony then deals generously with Enobarbus and Enobarbus responds, the praise of what remains magnanimous in Antony comes from lips which the most cynical of us has come to trust.

This is where Enobarbus' function stops. He does not contribute one event to the action, and he is a contributor to neither the temper of the Egyptian nor the quality of the Roman way of life. This is where Enobarbus' function stops, I say, but most of us find Enobarbus so intrinsically delightful that we are at times tempted to say that he justifies all the rest of the pother because it gives him scope for his exhilarating wit. But it is a wicked temptation. Shakespeare has invented a character who at the moment of his death can reassure skeptical us that two figures of fantastic romance are personages of substance and grandeur. And precisely their substance and grandeur confer importance upon the tragic action.

Antony and Cleopatra, then, is a tragedy of tremendous

figures: an Antony whose legs bestride the ocean and a Cleopatra whose body servant could call her "O Eastern Star." The petty figure is as great a man as Caesar Augustus, who in order to establish the great Roman era of peace had to descend upon sun-drenched Egypt like winter and put a period to tumultuous passions unfit for his business-like and orderly world.

41958

CLIFFORD P. LYONS
Kenan Professor of English
University of North Carolina

The Hector-Achilles Encounters in Shakespeare's *Troilus & Cressida*

N SHAKESPEARE's *Troilus and Cressida* THE battle scenes (V.iv-x) present the fury of a disillusioned Troilus, aware of Cressida's affair with Diomedes, and the death of Hector, murderously slain by Achilles and his Myrmidons. Aroused finally to action by Patroclus' death, Achilles enters seeking Hector:[1]

Enter Achilles.

Achilles.   Where is this Hector?
Come, come, thou boy-queller, show me thy face;
Know what it is to meet Achilles angry;
Hector! where's Hector? I will none but Hector.

(V.v.44-47)

1. The reference text is *Troilus and Cressida*, ed. J. Dover Wilson and Alice Walker, New Shakespeare (Cambridge, 1957). Other editions consulted: *Troilus and Cressida*, ed. Harold N. Hillebrand and T. W. Baldwin, New Variorum (Philadelphia, 1953); *Troilus and Cressida, First*

67

In Scene vi Achilles enters to Hector, who is already on stage (I have omitted editorial stage directions, giving only the two of the substantive texts, the Quarto, 1609, and Folio, 1623):

Enter Achilles.

Achilles. Now do I see thee; ha! have at thee, Hector!
Hector. Pause, if thou wilt.
Achilles. I do disdain thy courtesy, proud Trojan.   15
Be happy that my arms are out of use;
My rest and negligence befriends thee now,
But thou anon shalt hear of me again;
Till when, go seek thy fortune.   *Exit.*
Hector.   Fare thee well.
I would have been much more a fresher man,   20
Had I expected thee.   (V.vi.13-21)

Theobald was puzzled. In a letter to Warburton, March 6, 1729/30, he wrote: "I cannot understand what our Poet means here: Achilles is on the point of attacking Hector; Hector bids him take breath; Achilles will not accept of the courtesy; yet pretends to be restive, and leaves Hector with a threat that he will be up with him anon."[2] Presson, in his interesting comparative study of sources, interprets the incident thus: "The first armed encounter between Achilles and Hector does not develop into a combat. Though Achilles is in the field to avenge Patroclus' death by slaying Hector, he foregoes the fight, out of weariness. Hector feels that he himself isn't as fresh as he should be to match arms against Achilles."[3] One conjectures that what, in part, may have misled Presson in this dubious reading of the lines, and puzzled Theobald, is the absence of stage directions in the substantive texts other than *Enter Achilles* and

---

Quarto, 1609, Shakespeare Quartos in Collotype Facsimile, No. 8 (London, 1952); *Mr. William Shakespeares Comedies, Histories, & Tragedies, A facsimile edition prepared by Helge Kokeritz* (New Haven, 1954). In the essay all editorial stage directions are in brackets. The substantive stage directions, unbracketed, are those in the Folio; they are occasionally more full than those in Quarto, but otherwise practically the same.

2. Letter printed in John Nichols, *Illustrations of the Literary History of the Eighteenth Century* (London, 1817), II, 543.

3. Robert K. Presson, *Shakespeare's Troilus and Cressida* (Madison, 1953), p. 74.

Exit. Baldwin's terse comment (Variorum, p. 303) is to the point: "The poet means that a fight takes place between lines [13 and 14]." Almost all eighteenth-century editors, from Rowe, 1709, to Rann, 1789, added a stage direction indicating a fight after Achilles' initial challenge to Hector. It is curious, as Baldwin notes, that subsequent editors (i.e., prior to Variorum, 1953) added no stage direction at this point. In the New Shakespeare, however, Alice Walker (as does Virgil Whitaker in his 1958 Pelican Shakespeare edition) reinstates the Rowe stage direction, which one may justify by citing "Have at thee" (Diomedes to Troilus, V.iv.22) and "have at you both" (Troilus to Diomedes and Ajax, V.vi.II), in each instance signaling an attack and combat. It is the purpose of this brief essay, however, to show the likelihood of significant action in additon to [*They fight*].

It is a commonplace that Shakespeare's plays are dramatic scripts written for performance on a stage, although implications of this fact may be easily overlooked or underestimated by editors, critics, and general readers. It will also be readily acknowledged that stage directions of our substantive texts are, on the whole, incomplete guides to essential supplementary and clarifying acting and staging. Nearly all editors have recognized this to some extent. By inferences from relevant evidence, it is often possible, I believe, to reconstruct, with a high degree of probability, missing stage action. In the instances here considered there is evidence: in the dialogue of the Hector-Achilles encounters; in the larger context of the play; in sources Shakespeare knew, Lydgate and Caxton, principally the latter; in Heywood's *Iron Age, Part I*; and Dryden's adaptation of Shakespeare's play.[4] I shall present and discuss relevant

4. *Lydgate's Troy Book*, ed. Henry Bergen, EETS, Extra Ser., CIII: Part I, Bk. III (London, 1908); William Caxton, *The Recuyell of the Historyes of Troy*, ed. H. O. Sommer (London, 1894). Selected passages from Lydgate, ed. Bergen, and Caxton, ed. Sommer, are reprinted in the Variorum, pp. 424-47. Thomas Heywood, *The Iron Age, Part I, Dramatic Works*, ed. R. H. Shepherd (London, 1874), Vol. III; John Dryden, *Troilus and Cressida, Dramatic Works*, ed. Montague Summers (London, 1932), Vol. V. Since the lines are not numbered in the Heywood and Dryden plays, I supplement act and scene references with page numbers of the editions cited. On the question whether in date of composition

evidence for elaborating stage directions for each of the two encounters, and then give the text of each encounter with amplified and additional editorial stage directions, concluding with brief comment on the significance of these scenes for themes of the play.

THE SECOND ENCOUNTER

Before exploring further the first encounter (in V.vi) it is, I think, instructive to consider the second encounter (V.viii), which is fatal to Hector. In Scene vii Achilles orders his Myrmidons to attend him in search for Hector, to conserve their strength until they find him, to encircle Hector with their weapons and to use them in "fellest manner."

Enter Achilles with Myrmidons.
Achilles. Come here about me, you my Myrmidons;
Mark what I say. Attend me where I wheel;
Strike not a stroke, but keep yourselves in breath,
And when I have the bloody Hector found
Empale him with your weapons round about;
In fellest manner execute your arms.
Follow me, sirs, and my proceedings eye;
It is decreed Hector the great must die.   (V.vii.1-8)

In Scene vi (lines 27-31) Hector sees and covets the armor of a Greek, who flees in fear with Hector in pursuit: "I'll hunt thee for thy hide." One is tempted to conjecture that in Scene viii Hector, by the drawing aside of rear curtains, is 'discovered' standing over the dead body of the Greek in sumptuous armor.

Hector. Most putrified core, so fair without,
Thy goodly armour thus has cost thy life.   (V.vii.1-2)

Although Caxton does not, Lydgate vigorously condemns this covetous act, and asserts Hector's death to be a consequence of

Heywood's *Iron Age* precedes or follows Shakespeare's play, see E. K. Chambers, *William Shakespeare* (Oxford, 1930), I, 448-49. If, as Chambers believes, Shakespeare's play influenced Heywood's, then the staging evidence in Heywood has added significance. In any case, however, the parallels are illuminating.

the reprehensible deed (Bergen, Bk. III, lines 5325 ff.). The dramatic effect is not pleasant—even though Hector presumably kills the Greek in fair fight—and reminds us that while Hector is the most estimable character in this dark drama, he somewhat compromises his code of conduct in this episode; as, more importantly, he compromises his ethical reasoning in the great Trojan debate (II.ii) when he agrees to continue a war which by his own standards he knows to be a bad cause. Since the encounters discussed contrast the shameful conduct of Achilles with the honorable code of Hector, it is appropriate to recognize that Shakespeare's Hector is not a faultless hero.

Here is the episode (all of Scene viii) with the Folio stage directions (unbracketed) and Alice Walker's editorial stage directions (bracketed), which are representative of editorial tradition. After the two opening lines quoted above, Hector continues:

Now is my day's work done. I'll take good breath.
Rest, sword; thou hast thy fill of blood and death.
                                        [*Disarms.*]
          Enter Achilles and his Myrmidons.
Achilles. Look, Hector, how the sun begins to set,
How ugly night comes breathing at his heels;
Even with the vail and darkening of the sun,
To close the day up, Hector's life is done.
Hector. I am unarmed; forego this vantage, Greek.
Achilles. Strike, fellows, strike; this is the man I seek.   10
                                        [*Hector falls.*]
So, Ilion, fall thou next! now, Troy, sink down!
Here lies thy heart, thy sinews, and thy bone.
On, Myrmidons, and cry you all amain
'Achilles hath the mighty Hector Slain.'   *Retreat.*
                                        [*Retreat sounded.*]
Hark! a retire upon our Grecian part.
Myrmidon. The Trojan trumpets sound the like, my lord.
Achilles. The dragon wing of night o'erspreads the earth,
And stickler-like the armies separates.
My half-supped sword that frankly would have fed,
Pleased with this dainty bait, thus goes to bed.   20
                                        [*Sheathes his sword.*]

Come, tie his body to my horse's tail;
Along the field I will the Trojan trail.
        Sound Retreat. Shout. [*They go; retreat sounded.*]

I shall discuss in succession these stage directions and the evidence for making them more complete. [*Disarms*] is clearly called for by "Rest, sword" (line 4) and "I am unarmed" (line 9). We are justified in elaborating *disarms* to indicate that Hector is utterly defenseless (as Troilus is in Caxton, see below).

We should add to *Enter Achilles and his Myrmidons* the following: [*who surround Hector with threatening spears*]. In Scene vii Achilles instructs the Myrmidons: "Empale him with your weapons round about;/ In fellest manner execute your arms" (lines 5-6). There is no indication in the text what weapons the Myrmidons carry. It is reasonable to assume spears or spear-like arms. In Heywood's *Iron Age* (IV.i) the Myrmidons are armed with "steele polaxes." Spears are, of course, common in Caxton and Lydgate, as are spears, pikes, partisans, and halberds in Shakespeare.[5] Achilles taunts the helpless Hector hedged in with spears. The Trojan exclaims against this dishonorable attack: "I am unarmed; forego this vantage, Greek." But Achilles cries: "Strike, fellows, strike," and they thrust him through, using their arms "in fellest manner."

The stage direction [*Hector falls*] is obviously just. He falls, certainly, but it is likely that there is more to the action than that. Does Achilles also use his sword against the fallen Hector? In Caxton, Achilles, alone, slays Hector: "Hector had taken a very noble baron of Greece, that was queintly and richly armed, and for to leade him out of the hoste at his ease, had caste his shielde behinde him at his backe, and had left his breast discovered: and as he was in this point, and tooke none heede of Achilles, he came privily unto him, and thrust his speare within his bodie, and Hector fell downe dead to the grounde" (Sommer, Bk. III, Chap. xvii).

It is clear that in dramatizing the death of Hector, Shake-

5. It may be noted that in the drawing attributed to Henry Peacham, 1595 (reproduced in Chambers, I, 312), the attendants of Titus Andronicus are armed with both partisans and swords.

speare drew rather on Caxton's account of the death of Troilus, slain by Achilles with the aid of his Myrmidons:

> After these things the nineteenth battel began with great slaughter, and afore that Achilles entered into the battaile, he assembled his Mirmidones, and praied them that they would intend to none other thing, but to inclose Troylus, and to hold them without flying till hee came, and that he would not be farre from them. . . . Then the Mirmidones . . . thrusted in among the Troyans, and recovered the field. And as they held them together, and sought no man but Troylus, they found him, that hee fought strongly, and was inclosed on all partes. . . . And he was all alone among them, and had no man to succour him, they slew his horse, and hurt him in many places, and plucked off his head his helme, and his coife of iron, and he defended him in the best manner he could. Then came on Achilles, when he saw Troylus all naked, and ran upon him in a rage, and smote off his head and cast it under the feete of his horse, and tooke the body and bound it to the taile of his horse, and so drew it after him throughout the host. . . . Certes, if anie nobleness had been in Achilles, he would not have doone this villanie. (Sommer, Bk. III, Chap. xxii)

Certain points of difference from Shakespeare are apparent; there are, too, obvious similarities and suggestive details. Troilus is stripped of all defenses, his helmet off, "naked" to Achilles' attack, who kills him, but not before the Myrmidons have already "hurt him in many places." The tradition which these two Caxton accounts represent supports the textual evidence that Shakespeare's Achilles has a hand in the slaying of Hector.

Heywood's treatment of the incident is instructive.

> *Enter Achilles with his guard of Mermidons.*
> *Achilles.* Come cast your selves into a ring of terrour,
> About this warlike Prince, by whom I bleede.
>
> . . . .
>
> *Achilles.* For eminent death, you of my warlike guard,
> My Mermidons, for slaughters most renown'd,
> Now sworne to my designments, your steele polaxes,
> Fixe all at once, and girt him round with wounds.

> *Hector.* Dishonourable Greeke, Hector nere dealt
> On base advantage, or ever lift his sword
> Over a quaking foe, but as a spoyle
> Unworthy us, still left him to his feare:
>
> . . . .
>
> And shall I now be slayne by treachery?
> *Achilles.* Tell him your answer on your weapons points,
> Upon him my brave souldiers.

After some defiant words by Hector we have the stage direction: *Alarum. Hector fals slayne by the Mermidons, then Achilles wounds him with his Launce. (Iron Age,* IV.i; Shepherd, pp. 321-22)

In Dryden's play says Achilles to his Myrmidons:

> Make hast, my Soldiers: give me this days pains,
> For my dead friend: strike every hand *with mine,*
> Till Hector breathless, on the ground we lay!
>
> (V.ii; Summers, p. 100; my italics)

Shakespeare's lines (19-20) support the conjecture:

> My half-supped sword that frankly would have fed,
> Pleased with this dainty bait, thus goes to bed.

The implication is clear that Achilles has used his sword: though hungry for fighting it is satisfied with "this dainty bait." (Alice Walker, ed. cit., glosses 'bait' as 'refreshment' or 'snack.') Achilles' sword has 'fed on' Hector. The scene of ruthless brutality concludes with the Myrmidons dragging the murdered hero off stage, shouting the 'triumph' of Achilles.[6]

6. Reynolds quotes from Edmund Gayton's *Festivious Notes upon Don Quixote* (1654) an interesting account of audience reaction, possibly to a performance of *The Iron Age*: "Our *Don* is not so much transported with *Belianis* his Blowes as a passionate Butcher of our Nation was, who being at the Play, called *the Greeks and the Trojans,* and seeing *Hector* over-powered by *Mirmydons,* got upon the Stage, and with his good Battoone tooke the true *Trojans* part so stoutly, that he routed the *Greeks,* and rayled upon them loudly for a company of cowardly slaves to assault one man with so many odds. He strooke moreover such an especiall acquaintance with *Hector,* that for a long time *Hector* could not obtaine leave of him to be kill'd, that the Play might go on; and the cudgelled *Mirmydons* durst not enter againe, till *Hector,* having prevailed upon his

THE FIRST ENCOUNTER

Now to return to the first encounter (V.vi.13-21) and consider what the editorial stage directions should indicate more than [*They fight*]. We recognize at once the contrast between the vicious behavior of Achilles in the scene just discussed and the sporting courtesy of Hector in this earlier scene.

Hector. Pause, if thou wilt.
Achilles. I do disdain thy courtesy, proud Trojan.

In Heywood's play, when Hector is surrounded by the Myrmidons he protests to Achilles:

Hector. Dishonourable Greeke, Hector nere dealt
On base advantage, or ever lift his sword
Over a quaking foe, but as a spoyle
Unworthy us, still left him to his feare:
Nor on the man, whom singly I strucke downe,
Have I redoubled blowes, my valour still
Opposed against a standing enemy.
Thee have I twice unhorst, and when I might
Have slaine thee groveling, left thee to the field.
(*Iron Age*, IV.i; Shepherd, p. 321)

Hector scorns base advantage, his valor always opposed against a standing enemy.

Shakespeare's play emphasizes again and again the honorable code of Hector. Just before the Ajax-Hector duel, Ulysses contrasts Hector and Troilus, who is, he says:

Manly as Hector, but more dangerous;
For Hector in his blaze of wrath subscribes
To tender objects [i.e., makes concessions to the
defenseless], but he in heat of action
Is more vindicative than jealous love.   (IV.v.104-7)

In the sportful combat between Ajax and Hector (lines 113-16), although there are no substantive stage directions except at the beginning *Alarum* and at the end *trumpets cease*, we may reasonably infer that Hector is both master and merciful;

---

unexpected second, return'd him over the Stage againe into the yard from whence he came." See George Reynolds, *The Staging of Elizabethan Plays at the Red Bull Theater, 1605-1625* (London, 1940), p. 10.

for Ajax says when his kinsman embraces him and does him honor:

> *Ajax.*   I thank thee, Hector.
> Thou art too gentle and too free a man.
> I came to kill thee, cousin, and bear hence
> A great addition earned in thy death.   (IV.v.138-41)

Dryden so interprets the action of the Hector-Ajax episode. This is his interesting stage direction:

> *Fight equal at first, then Ajax has Hector at disadvantage; at last Hector closes, Ajax falls on one knee, Hector stands over him but strikes not, and Ajax rises.* (IV.ii; Summers, p. 80)

Later in Scene v, Shakespeare's Nestor says to Hector:

> *Nestor.* I have, thou gallant Trojan, seen thee oft,
> Labouring for destiny, make cruel way
> Through ranks of Greekish youth; and I have seen thee,
> As hot as Perseus, spur thy Phrygian steed,
> And seen thee scorning forfeits and subduements
> When thou hast hung thy advanced sword i'th'air,
> Not letting it decline on the declined,
> That I have said to some my standers-by
> 'Lo, Jupiter is yonder, dealing life!'
> And I have seen thee pause and take thy breath
> When that a ring of Greeks hath hemmed thee in,
> Like an Olympian wrestling.   (IV.v.183-94)

In V.iii, the Scene immediately preceding the battle sequence, Hector advises Troilus to disarm and to refrain from wars until his youthful sinews grow stronger. Troilus responds:

> *Troilus.* Brother, you have a vice of mercy in you,
> Which better fits a lion than a man.
> *Hector.* What vice is that? Good Troilus, chide me for it.
> *Troilus.* When many times the captive Grecian falls,
> Even in the fan and wind of your fair sword,
> You bid them rise and live.
> *Hector.* O, 'tis fair play.
> *Troilus.*   Fool's play, by heaven, Hector.

Hector. How now! how now!
Troilus.   For th' love of all the gods,
Let's leave the hermit pity with our mother;
And when we have our armours buckled on,
The venomed vengeance ride upon our swords,
Spur them to ruthful work, rein them from ruth!
Hector. Fie, savage, fie!   (V.iii.37-49)

We should not neglect the cumulative, climactic effects which Shakespeare artfully contrives. It is reasonably clear that in Act V, Scene vi, after Achilles challenges and attacks Hector, there is staged a spirited fight. Then Hector has Achilles down and at his mercy, but will not take advantage of a fallen opponent, offering him a chance to "pause," to rise and rest before continuing. Says Achilles, "I do disdain thy courtesy," showing contempt for Hector and his code; but he takes advantage of the pause to discontinue the combat, pleading his unexercised fighting condition, which clearly suggests that he has been getting the worst of it. "Fare thee well," says the courteous Hector to Achilles, who goes off—to find his helpful Myrmidons. Hector's words are a tribute to Achilles' prowess; it has been a hard fight: "I would have been much more a fresher man,/ Had I expected thee."

Here, then, are the two encounters between Hector and Achilles, with more complete stage directions, which do not run counter to, but rather add to and expand those of the substantive texts and representative editions:

I. (V.vi.13-21)   *Enter Achilles.*
    Achilles. Now do I see thee; ha! have at thee, Hector!
              [*They fight fiercely for a time on even terms; then*
              Hector is master, driving Achilles to his knees;
              but he lowers his sword and steps back.]
    Hector. Pause, if thou wilt.   [*Achilles slowly rises.*]
    Achilles. I do disdain thy courtesy, proud Trojan.
    Be happy that my arms are out of use;
    My rest and negligence befriends thee now,
    But thou anon shalt hear of me again;
    Till when, go seek thy fortune.   *Exit.*
              [*Hector cries after Achilles as he goes off stage.*]

Hector.   Fare thee well.
          [*Then, breathing hard, leaning on his sword.*]
I would have been much more a fresher man,
Had I expected thee.

II. (V.viii)   *Enter Hector*

Hector. Most putrefied core, so fair without,
Thy goodly armour thus has cost thy life.
Now is my day's work done. I'll take good breath.
          [*He lays aside his sword, and then his shield and
          helmet.*]
Rest, sword, thou hast thy fill of blood and death.
          *Enter Achilles and his Myrmidons, [who surround
          the completely defenseless Hector with threatening
          weapons.*]
Achilles. Look, Hector, how the sun begins to set,
How ugly night comes breathing at his heels;
Even with the vail and darkening of the sun,
To close the day up, Hector's life is done.
Hector. I am unarmed; forego this vantage, Greek.
Achilles. Strike, fellows, strike; this is the man I seek.
          [*Hector falls, thrust through by many spears.
          Achilles then plunges his sword into the dying
          Hector.*]
So, Ilion, fall thou next! Now, Troy, sink down!
Here lies thy heart, thy sinews, and thy bone.
          [*Flourishing his bloody sword.*]
On, Myrmidons, and cry you all amain
'Achilles hath the mighty Hector slain.'
          Retreat [*sounded, off stage.*]
Hark! a retire upon our Grecian part.
          [*Retreat sounded, off stage from opposite side.*]
Myrmidon. The Trojan trumpets sound the like, my lord.
Achilles. The dragon wing of night o'erspreads the earth,
And stickler-like the armies separates.
My half-supped sword that frankly would have fed,
Pleased with this dainty bait, thus goes to bed.
          [*Sheathes his sword.*]
Come, tie his body to my horse's tail;
Along the field I will the Trojan trail.
          [*As again off-stage trumpets*] *Sound Retreat* [*the*

Myrmidons drag off Hector's body, and] Shout
[Hector's death and Achilles' triumph.]

Theobald, in his letter to Warburton, gave just reasons for puzzlement; without the accompanying stage action the dramatic script is incomplete. By a consideration of all relevant evidence we can, with a high degree of probability, reconstruct the missing parts of the context in both the first and second encounters between the Trojan and Greek champions, and in so doing help make clear the heightened dramatized contrast between the code of Hector and the vindictive ruthlessness of Achilles.

"Fie, savage, fie," says Hector in response to Troilus' advocacy of pitiless, venomed vengeance. It is pertinent to note that here and in the battle scenes, the attitudes and standards of Troilus are more akin to those of Achilles than to those of Hector. And we are reminded of Hector's thematic lines to Paris and Troilus in the Trojan debate, when he chides them for their arguments against returning Helen to her rightful husband:[7]

The reasons you allege do more conduce
To the hot passion of distempered blood
Than to make up a free determination
'Twixt right and wrong: for pleasure and revenge
Have ears more deaf than adders to the voice
Of any true decision.   (II.ii.168-73)

Earlier in the same scene Hector asks Troilus:

          . . . is your blood
So madly hot that no discourse of reason,
Nor fear of bad success in a bad cause,
Can qualify the same?   (II.ii.115-18)

When considering themes of *Troilus and Cressida* we may observe that in these final battle scenes Shakespeare gives us a Troilus raging in vengeful fury, and in the death of Hector a savage outcome of a bad cause.

7. For my study of staging and theme in this play, with the emphasis on Troilus, see "The Trysting Scenes in *Troilus and Cressida*," *Shakespearean Essays*, ed. Alwin Thaler and Norman Sanders, *Tennessee Studies in Literature*, Special Number: 2 (Knoxville, 1964).

A. C. SPRAGUE
Professor Emeritus of English
Bryn Mawr College

A *Macbeth* of Few Words

T THE BEGINNING OF THE NINETEENTH CEN-
tury, dramatic performances in London were
much restricted. The monopoly bestowed
upon D'Avenant and Killigrew at the Restoration still remained in force. Legitimate
plays, Shakespeare's plays, for instance, and
the "old comedies," were in theory confined to the patent theaters: they belonged to Drury Lane, to Covent Garden, and
through part of the year to the Haymarket. The flourishing
minor theaters supplied their repertories as best they could
with dramatic fare of other sorts, "burlettas" and the like.
There was little agreement as to just what a burletta was,
though songs were associated with it, and such spoken dialogue
as it contained was likely to be accompanied by music.[1]

1. See especially Ernest Bradley Watson, *Sheridan to Robertson*,
(Cambridge, Mass., 1926), Chapter 2, and Dewey Ganzel, "Patent Wrongs
and Patent Theatres," *PMLA*, LXXVI (1961), 384 ff.

Early in 1809 the Royal Circus (better known as the Surrey) came under the management of Robert William Elliston, the illustrious, the *great* Elliston of two of Lamb's happiest essays. On June 15 *The Beggar's Opera* was presented, with its dialogue "reduced to the common standard of the Circus recitative."[2] *Macbeth*, a Ballet of Music and Action, was advertised in the *Times* on August 30.[3] It was then promised that "an anxious and industrious effort" would be made "to illustrate the scenes, machinery, imagery, and descriptions, as delivered to us in that play by the immortal Shakespeare. A greater part of the Compositions of Matthew Lock will be preserved. The new Overture and other Music by Dr. Busby. . . . The Ballet prepared for representation by Mr. Cross." Thomas Busby was a composer of some prominence who had written the music for Holcroft's famous melodrama *A Tale of Mystery*, and J. C. Cross was stage manager at the Royal Circus. He had just published in two volumes, *Circusiana, Or A Collection of the Most Famous Ballets, Spectacles, Melo-dramas, &c. Performed at the Royal Circus, St. George's Fields*. A very spectacular *Cora; Or, The Virgin of the Sun* from Kotzebue is among these, but nothing from Shakespeare.

Macbeth, given at the Circus on August 31, was noticed next day in both the *Times* and the *Morning Post*. "Much as we might have been inclined to condemn the experiment," the *Times* reviewer writes, "we were really most agreeably surprised at the event. The performance, as far as action went, was uncommonly expressive and clear; and the incantations of the witches, from being given in scenery the most appropriate (we must say) we ever saw, boasted a more grand and imposing effect than we ever before witnessed. In fact, the whole was produced with that attention to costume, scenic splendour, decoration and embellishment, that the greatest admirer of our immortal bard could but regret his divine language was precluded." The same sense of relief, as if the reviewer had been

2. *The Monthly Mirror*, June, 1809.
3. On August 24, *The Morning Advertiser* has: "ELLISTON is about to bring out SHAKESPEARE's *Macbeth*, at the Circus, as a *burletta!* *Hamlet* we expect to see transformed into a *farce*, and a *ballet* made of *King Lear*."

expecting something much worse, is discernible in the *Morning Post*. "Whatever might be the opinion of the most captious of SHAKSPEARE's admirers previous to the drawing up of the curtain, they retired pleased with the efforts of all concerned at the close of the performance. Never did a performance more progressively rise in fascinating an audience, and proving to conviction, that an attention to scenic display, embellishment, and decoration, is one of the necessary supports of the Drama. We never witnessed a piece upon the whole so well got up."

Several further performances were given in September before a final one, honoring Elliston, on the twenty-seventh, when the bill included *The Beggar's Opera* and "a new comic pantomime," and Elliston in addition to playing both Macbeth and Macheath recited Collins's "Ode on the Passions." On this occasion, the house from an early hour was "filled in every part" and "the boxes contained many of the nobility."[4]

Copies of the 1809 *Macbeth* are of extreme rarity. The one on which the present text is based, bound with several other plays, was obtained in a Boston bookshop in 1961. A second copy, identified by Dr. Stanley Wells of the Shakespeare Institute, is in the Birmingham Reference Library. I know of no others. Perhaps as a consequence of its scarcity, the burletta has been almost wholly forgotten, passing unmentioned in Genest, in Jaggard's *Shakespeare Bibliography*, and Nicoll's *History of Early Nineteenth Century Drama*. Its recovery, that of a Shakespearean acting version amusing in itself and typical of its time, should not be without interest to historians of the English stage.

4. *The Times*, September 30, 1809. Lord William Pitt Lennox states that he once saw " 'Macbeth' acted as a burletta at the Royal Circus, with a pianoforte accompaniment" (*Plays, Players, and Playhouses*, London, 1881, I, 131; I am indebted to my friend Mr. Malcolm Morley for this reference).

THE
HISTORY,
MURDERS, LIFE, and DEATH
OF
Macbeth:

And a **FULL DESCRIPTION** of the

SCENERY, ACTION, CHORUSES, and CHARACTERS

OF THE

BALLET
OF
MUSIC and ACTION,

OF THAT NAME,

As performed, with enthusiastic Applause, to over-flowing Houses, a Number of Nights, at the

ROYAL CIRCUS,
St. GEORGE's FIELDS, London,

WITH THE

OCCASIONAL ADDRESS,

Spoken by Mr. Elliston ;

And every Information, to simplify the Plot ; and enable the Visitors of the Circus, to comprehend this matchless Piece of *Pantomimic* and *Choral* Performance.

London:
Printed by T. Page, Black Friars Road,

For **STEVENS & Co.** St. George's Circulating Library, Borough Road: and W. **KEMMISH**, King Street, Borough,

T. Hughes, Ludgate-Hill ; N. & J. Muggeridge, and Wilmott and Hill, Borough ; Perks, St. Martin's Lane; Elliot, Shadwell ; Walker, Holborn ; Evans, Gerrard-Street, Soho; Broom, Drury-Lane, Barfoot, Norton-Falgate ; &c. &o.

Price only 6d.

CHARACTERS.

SCOTCH.

MACBETH	Mr. Elliston.
DUNCAN, King of Scotland	Mr. James.
MALCOLM, his Heir, ⎰ his Sons	Mr. Taylor.
DONALBAINE, ⎱	Master Hatton.
MACDUFF	Mr. Gomery.
BANQUO	Mr. Makeen.
FLEANCE, his Son	Miss C. Giroux.
ROSSE	Mr. Cooke.
SEYTON	Mr. Rivolta.
LENOX	Mr. Jefferies.
PHYSICIAN	Mr. Ellar.
OFFICER	Mr. Isaacs.
CHAMBERLAINS	Messrs. H. Elliston & Mezzia.
GENTLEMEN	———Day, Thomson, &c.
	Mrs. Hatton.
LADY MACBETH	Mrs. Makeen.
LADY MACDUFF	Miss Evans.
GENTLEWOMAN	Mesdames Slader, James, Wilmot, Stacey, &c.
LADIES	

ENGLISH.

EDWARD THE CONFESSOR, (King of England)	Mr. Payne.
SIWARD, (a General)	Mr. James.
YOUNG SIWARD	Mr. Giroux.

WITCHES, &c.

WIERD SISTERS   Mess. Johannot, Slader, and I. Taylor.
HECATE   Mr. S. Slader.
CHORAL WITCHES   Mess. Williamson, J. Williams, Dickinson, Greenard, Burden, Macartey, Tett, Tett, Junior, Giroux, &c.; Mesdames Sarrat, Parkinson, May; Misses Stubb, Green, Goodchild, Taylor, two Girouxs, &c.
APPARITIONS, (raised by the Wierd Sisters), Mr. E. James, Master Hatton, and Miss C. Giroux.
SPRIGHTS, Misses Adunice, Moseley, Hart, O'Brian, and Mortram.

OCCASIONAL ADDRESS,

Spoken by Mr. Elliston.

With nature, and the energies of man,
The reign of poesy and song began;
The passions' language with the passions sprung,
And in each clime the muse her raptures sung.
With epic numbers early Greece was fir'd,
While love the tender elegy inspir'd;
The joyful Pæan swell'd upon the gale,
And simple pastoral charm'd the silent vale.
But chief the drama's sweet delusion stole
The captive sense, and rapt the yielding soul.
To Aeschylus, majestic as severe,
Enlighten'd Athens lent the astonish'd ear;
Euripides dissolv'd with softest art,
And lofty Sophocles sublim'd the heart;
While Aristophanes the poignant lay
Of satire woke—and vice was laugh'd away.
Italia heard and felt the vivid strain,
And arch Thalia spread her frolic reign;
Stern Rome relax'd at Platus' comic fire,
And in chaste Terence hail'd Menander's lyre.
        Then sunk the stage—ordain'd in after-times
To rise again and bless more distant climes.
Spain Vega saw relume the tragic flame,
And Caldron's wit ensur'd immortal fame;
Gallia the gay Moliere true humour taught,
And bold Corneille the classic furor caught.
Fair Albion too the scenic harp essay'd,
And Johnson's learned sock her skill display'd;
But, O! for numbers equal to the theme,
While fancy hovers over Avon's stream!
Shakespeare arose;—Full-orb'd *then* genius shone,
The ancient stars all blaz'd again in one
Superior luminary! form'd to light
The world of Man; to usher to the sight
The dark, close windings of the mind, and show
The bosom's secret transport, secret woe;
Its depths explore, and bid his searching ray
On all the hidden springs of action play.

O'er wild imagination's rich domain,
He held a glorious, undisputed reign;
The regions of existence all too poor,
He seiz'd *her* treasures, and created more,
Sprites, goblins, witches, at his bidding rise,
And new-form'd beings dance before his eyes;
All to his magic circle he could bend,
The subject bosom pacify or rend;
Rejoice, alarm, opposing thought dethrone,
And rule us by the wonders of his own.
   Faithful to nature and the drama's law,
From this great source our promis'd scenes we draw
MACBETH, the regicide MACBETH, pourtray—
His ruthless consort and her direful sway.
Though not indulg'd with fullest pow'rs of speech
The poet's object we aspire to reach;
The emphatic gesture, eloquence of eye,
Scenes, music, every energy we try,
To make your hearts for murder'd Banquo melt;
And feel for Duncan as brave Malcolm felt;
To prove we keep our duties full in view,
And what we must not *say*, resolve to *do;*
Convinc'd that you will deem our zeal sincere,
Since more by *deeds* than *words* it will appear.

———

Every department under the direction and inspection of Mr. Elliston.

Reduced to a Ballet by Mr. Cross; the music principally the composition of the late Matthew Locke; the overture by Dr. Busby, as well as other introductory Music, and performed with the assistance, and under the direction of Mr. Sanderson, leader of the band.

The Scenery by Messrs. Greenwood, Marchbanks, Mortram, Williams, &c.

The banquet prepared by Mr. A. Johnson.

The dresses executed and designed by Mrs. Brett, Mrs. Williams, Misses Smiths, &c.

Property Man, Mr. C. Sutton and Property Woman, Mrs. Freelove.

The dances by Mr. Giroux.

Scene, principally in Scotland, with the exception of—scenes, which are in England. Time sixteen years at least, and by some historians twenty one years.

The Play originally written by the immortal Shakespeare, in 1606, and performed in the reign of James II. founded on the records of Buchanan and Boetheus, Scottish Historians.

The Ballet in three Acts.

THE

HISTORY, &c.

OF

MACBETH.

Sweyno, King of Norway, having invaded the dominions of Duncan, King of Scotland, was joined by the rebellious Thane (or Lord) of Cawdor; Duncan dispatched his generals Macbeth and Banquo against him, who obliged him to evacuate the kingdom, and take the Thane of Cawdor prisoner; Duncan being informed of which, he bestows his forfeited honours on Macbeth.

At that time there were three witches (called the Wierd Sisters), in Scotland, who being envious of the numerous virtues of Duncan, determined to compass his destruction. They choose Macbeth as their instrument, whom they meet as he is returning, and greet him Thane of Glamis and Cawdor, as well as king that shall be: and at the same time greet Banquo as the father of kings, but inform him he shall never be one. Macbeth is shortly after informed that he is Thane of Glamis, by his father's death, and Thane of Cawdor, by the king's creation. Of this he writes to Lady Macbeth, whose ambition immediately aspires to the throne; which purpose is forwarded by Duncan declaring his intention of sojourning at Macbeth's castle: which he does with his train, including his sons Malcolm and Donalbaine. During this time Macbeth pushed on by his wife, murders him in bed, and so contrives that the suspicion alights on the grooms, whom he stabs to strengthen it. The witches meet and rejoice over the deed, and determine to urge him on further to his destruction. Malcolm fleeing to England, Macbeth seizes the crown, and orders a solemn banquet, to which he invites Banquo, who promises to come, but having a short journey to perform, Macbeth has him way laid and murdered, but his son Fleance (who is with him him) escapes.

Banquo's Ghost disturbs the harmony of the Banquet, and Macbeth determines, in consequence, to seek the Weired Sisters, and know more of his fate; but being previously informed that Macduff, (the Thane of Fife) has refused his attendance, he orders his Castle to be surprised, and his wife and children murdered, which is done. The Witches raised three Spirits; the first warns him to beware of Macduff; the second that he shall never be conquered by man of woman born; and the third not to fear till Birnam Forest comes to Dunsinane. The witches also shew a long line of Kings of Banquo's race. In the mean time, Edward the Confessor, to whose Court Malcolm, (the rightful heir) and Macduff have fled, gives them a succour of 10,000 men, headed by Siward, the English General, who march against Macbeth, and coming to Birnam wood, the soldiers each take a bough, and with them march to Dunsinane. Macbeth desperately defends his castle, in the midst of which Lady Macbeth, being very much distressed in mind and body, dies. Macbeth hearing that Birnam wood is coming is much alarmed, but still determines to fight for his Crown—he kills young Siward—but at length meeting Macduff, he attacks him, but boasts that he can never be conquered by man of woman born, when Macduff informs him, that he was untimely ripped from his mother's womb. Macbeth then despairs of success, and falls by the hand of Macduff, and Malcolm becomes King of Scotland.

MACBETH,
A BALLET OF ACTION.

ACT THE FIRST.

SCENE I.

Open Country.

Thunder and Lightning—enter the Wiered Sisters.
1st Witch. When shall we three meet again,
    In thunder, lightning, or in rain?
2nd Witch. When the hurley-burley's done;
    When the battle's lost or won.
3rd Witch. That will be 'ere set of sun.
1st Witch. Where the place?
2nd Witch. Upon the heath.
3rd Witch. There to meet with—
1st Witch. Whom?
2nd Witch. Macbeth.   [*Noise of a Cat.*
1st Witch. I come, gray-malkin.   [*Noise of a Toad.*
2nd Witch. Paddock calls.
1st Witch. Anon.
    All. Fair is foul, and foul is fair,
Hover through the fog and filthy air.   [*Thunder and lightning, exeunt.*]

SCENE II.

A hall in Duncan's Palace.

Duncan, (king of Scotland,) Malcolm, and Donalbaine enter with their attendants, soldiers bearing banner.—A wounded soldier, borne by his companion, appears, who announces Macbeth to be victorious—Macduff enters, and announces the "traitorous Thane of Cawdor to be prisoner."—Duncan orders Macbeth to receive his honors.

SCENE III.

A blasted heath.—Enter the Wierd Sisters.

1st Witch. Where hast thou been, sister?
2nd Witch. Killing swine.
3rd Witch. Sister, where thou?

1st Witch. A sailor's wife had chesnuts in her lap,
And mounch'd, and mounch'd, and mounch'd:—
                    "Give me," quoth I.
"Aroint, thee witch!" the rump-fed ronyon cries;
Her husband to Aleppo's gone, master o'the Tiger:
        But in a sieve I'll thither sail,
        And like a rat without a tail,
        I'll do, I'll do, and I'll do—
2nd Witch. I'll give thee wind.
1st Witch. Thou art kind.
3rd Witch. And I another.
1st Witch. I, myself, have all the other.
(The sound of Macbeth's troop approaching, is heard, and are seen at a
                    distance.)
3rd Witch. A drum, a drum;
        Macbeth doth come.
All. The Wierd Sisters hand in hand,
        Posters of the sea and land
        Thus to go about, about;
        Thrice to thine, thrice to mine,
        And thrice again to make up nine;
        Peace! the charm's wound up.

Macbeth and Banquo with the Army enter, with grand martial music,
bearing banners—Macbeth exclaims "halt" which Banquo repeats—they observe the weather. The Wierd Sisters enter: Macbeth and Banquo appear
confounded at their appearance, and demand their business: to which they
reply—

1st Witch. All hail, Macbeth! hail to thee, Thane of Glamis.
2nd Witch. All hail, Macbeth! hail to thee, Thane of Cawdor.
3rd Witch. All hail, Macbeth! hail to thee, that shalt be king hereafter.

Macbeth revolves their salutation in his mind, and Banquo makes
enquiries of them; to which they answer—

1st Witch. Hail!
2nd Witch. Hail!
3rd Witch. Hail!
1st Witch. Lesser than Macbeth, and greater.
2nd Witch. Not so happy, yet happier.
3rd Witch. Thou shalt get kings, though thou be none—so all hail,
Macbeth and Banquo!
1st Witch. Banquo and Macbeth, all hail!

Wierd Sisters disappear.—A messenger enters, bearing a banner, on
which is written, *"By Sinel's death, Macbeth is Thane of Glamis."* Shortly
after enters Macduff, with a banner, on which is *"Duncan doth create
Macbeth Thane of Cawdor;"* he invests Macbeth with his new honors—
Macbeth ruminates, and manifests his surprise at this fulfilment of a
prophecy of the Wierd Sisters—he then orders his troops to "march" which
Banquo reiterates.   [*Exeunt omnes.*

90

SCENE IV.

A room in the castle of Macbeth.

Lady Macbeth enters and reads the following letter, at various parts of which, she manifests her pleasure and surprise:

"They met me in the day of success, and I have learned by the perfectest report, they have more in them than mortal knowledge. When I burned in desire to question them further, they made themselves air, into which they vanished. Whiles I stood wrapt in wonder of it, came missives from the king, who all hailed me by the titles of *Glamis and of Cawdor;* by which titles before, these Wierd Sisters saluted me, and referred me to the coming on of time, with *hail, king that shalt be!* This have I thought good to deliver thee, my dearest partner of greatness, that thou mightest not lose the dues of rejoicing, by being ignorant of what greatness is promised thee. Lay to thy heart, farewel."

A messenger arrives and desires her to *"prepare for the king's reception;"* Macbeth enters, they embrace, and congratuate each other on their meeting; at length she says—

L. Macb. Thus to behold thee Cawdor, hope imparts.

Macb. My dearest love, Duncan comes here to-night.

L. Macb. But when departs?

Macb. To-morrow, love, as is his fixed decree.

L. Macb. O never, never, shall sun that morrow see.

Lady Macbeth then appears to work him up to some desperate deed.

[*Exeunt.*

SCENE V.

Outside of Macbeth's castle.

Enter Duncan, Malcolm, Donalbaine, Macduff, Banquo, Fleance, &c.; Lady Macbeth enters from the door to welcome Duncan; soon after Macbeth follows. Duncan then addresses those around him:

Duncan. Sons, kinsmen, Thanes, to each and all be it known,
We will establish our estate upon our eldest son,
Malcolm; whom we name hereafter Prince of Cumberland,
Which honor, not unaccompanied, must him invest;
But signs of nobleness on all the rest,
Like little stars shall shine.

Macbeth enters and receives the king. They all enter the castle, Macduff last, very sternly, which Macbeth observes—he then follows.

SCENE VI.

The same as scene four.

Pages pass with refreshment. Enter Macbeth, who appears revolving somewhat in his mind; (a chorus of sprites) Lady Macbeth enters and says—

L. Macb. The King has supped, doomed by your hand to bleed;
The daggers of his grooms must do the deed. (The chorus of sprites continues.)

[*Exeunt deeply affected.*

SCENE VII.

Interior of the castle, two flights of stairs at the back of the stage, and two wings on each side.

Duncan, Malcolm, and Donalbaine enter, to retire for the night, with attendants, led by Lady Macbeth—Duncan retires to the right—Lady Macbeth lights Malcolm, and Donalbaine up the stairs—Banquo and Fleance then appears, and Macbeth enters musing, and starts at beholding them—Banquo gives Macbeth a ring, they part affectionately—Macbeth then shews them to a chamber to the left. [*This part is very solemnly and strikingly performed without music.*] Lady Macbeth descends and listens at Duncan's door, and finds all quiet, she then enters. Macbeth and attendant descend, Macbeth discharges him, and moves lightly about. Enter Lady Macbeth. A struggle between her and Macbeth, he being afraid to execute the deed. Lady Macbeth then leaves him. An illusion of a spirit holding a dagger appears, which he endeavours to seize, but it vanishes when he makes the attempt. A bell tolls.

    Macb. Hear not that Duncan; for it is a knell
That summons thee to Heav'n, or to Hell.   *[Exit.*

SCENE VIII.
Grand Bed Chamber.

Duncan in bed—Macbeth throws open the entrance, and listens whether the Grooms of the Chamber are asleep. They stir, he moves fearfully, they are still, and he takes their daggers and approaches the bed, when a spirit sings:
    Sleep no more!
  Macbeth doth murder sleep,
    Sleep no more
Glamis hath murder'd sleep; and therefore Cawdor
Shall sleep no more, Macbeth shall sleep no more.
Macbeth then stabs Duncan, and scene changes.

SCENE IX.
The same as scene seven.

Enter Lady Macbeth, and Macbeth speaks within "who's there? what, ho!" and enters convulsed with horror, two bloody daggers in his hands, and his hands bloody, he looks at them, and remembers he should have laid the daggers by the grooms; (thunder and lightning, the night bird flaps at the window;) he seems averse to return, and Lady Macbeth carries them; she returns, and shows her hands bloody too. A great knocking is heard, which extremely terrifies Macbeth, and he makes his exit, groaning with horror, supported by his wife.

The door is opened, and Macduff and Lenox enter, meeting Macbeth, who returns, having cleansed himself from the blood. Macduff enquires if Duncan is stirring; Macbeth shews him the entrance to Duncan's chamber. Macduff returns and makes known the Murder of the King. A violent alarm ensues, and most of the Characters enter. Malcolm faints. They rush towards the King's Chamber.

92

SCENE X.

The same as scene eight.

All the characters enter. Macbeth stabs the grooms, as if he thought they had committed the murder, the whole stand transfixed at the sight of the murdered king, and the curtain drops.

The end of Act I.

ACT II.

SCENE I.

Mountainous Scene.

The Weird Sisters and Witches enter.

1st Witch. Speak sister, speak—is the deed done?
2nd Witch. Long ago, long ago;
  Above twelve glasses since have run,
  Ill deeds are seldom slow
  Nor single; following crimes on former wait
  The worst of creatures fastest propagate.
Chorus. Many more murders must this one ensue,
  Dread horrors still abound;
  And every place surround,
  As if in death were found
    Propagation too.
1st Witch. He must.
2nd Witch. He shall.
3rd Witch. He will spill much more blood,
  And become worse to make his title good.
Chorus. He must, he will spill much more blood,
  And become worse to make his title good.
1st Witch. Let's dance.
2nd Witch. Agreed.
3rd Witch. Agreed.
Chorus. We shall rejoice when good kings bleed.
  After which a mystical dance of witches, and an introductory *Pas de troix*—Hecate then descends from the clouds with attendants, when one of the weired sisters address her.
1st Witch. Why, how now, Hecate? you look angrily.
Hecate. Have I not reason, beldams as you are,
Saucy and overbold? How did you dare
To trade and traffic with Macbeth,
In riddles and affairs of death;
And I, the mistress of your charms,
The close contriver of all harms,
Was never call'd to bear my part,
Or show the glory of our art?
But make amends now, get you gone,
And at the pit of Acheron
Meet me i'the morning; thither he

Will come to know his destiny,
Upon the corner of the moon.
There hangs a vaporous drop profound:
I'll catch it ere it come to ground:
And that, distill'd by magic slights,
Shall raise such artificial sprights,
As, by the strength of their allusion,
Shall draw him on to his confusion.

     Sprites appear in clouds.

1st Sprite. Hecate, Hecate, Hecate, O come away!
Hecate. Hark, I'm call'd, my little spirit see,
  Sits in a foggy cloud, and waits for me.
2nd Sprite. Hecate, Hecate, Hecate, O come away!
Hecate. I come, I come, with all the speed I may.
  Where's Hadlin?
3rd Sprite. Here.
Hecate. Where Puckle?
4th Sprite. Here.
5th Sprite. And Hippoo too, and Hellwaine too.
6th Sprite. We want but you, we want but you.
Chorus. Come away, make up the court.
Hecate. With new fall'n dew,
  From church-yard yew,
  I will but 'noint, and then I mount.
1st Sprite. Why stay'st so long? I muse.
Hecate. Tell me spirit, what's the news?
2nd Sprite. All goes fair for our delight.
Hecate. Now I'm furnish'd for the flight.

    Hecate ascends the clouds, and—

Hecate. Now I go, now I fly,
  Malkin, my sweet spirit, and I,
  O, what dainty pleasures this,
    To sail in the air,
    While the moon shines fair,
  To sing, to play, to toy, to dance, and kiss,
  Over woods, high rocks, and mountains,
  Over seas, our mistress' fountains,
  Over steeples, towers, turrets,
  We fly by night, 'mongst troops of spirits.
Chorus. We fly by night, 'mongst troops of spirits.

Hecate ascends in the clouds during the chorus, and witches, &c. exeunt.

SCENE II.

Outside of Macbeth's Castle.

    Enter MACDUFF and ROSSE.

Rosse.   Say, Sir, is it known,
By whom this more than bloody deed was done?
  Macd. By these Macbeth hath slain;

Rosse.   Alas the day!
Upon what hopes could their pretensions lay?
Macd. They were suborn'd—Malcolm and Donalbaine
Are stol'n away and fled,
And by their flight awake suspicion of the deed;
And, it is probable, by this unnatural death,
The sovereignty will invest Macbeth.

Huzzaings are heard, and chorus—"Hail Macbeth, King of Scotland, hail!" which Macduff hears with indignation.

Macd. I must hence Cousin and friends, adieu,
Lest our old robes sit easier than our new.

Macduff gives Rosse a letter to convey to his wife.—Banquo and Fleance enter and seem considerably affected.

Enter attendants, one bearing a banner, that "Macbeth ordains a solemn Banquet."—Macbeth enters and invites Banquo, who promises to attend.—Seyton, in the mean time, introduces two murderers.—Banquo and Fleance then depart—the Attendants, &c. Exeunt, leaving Macbeth and two Murderers, with whom he agrees for the murder of Banquo and Fleance, which they promise, and retire.—Macbeth appears satisfied with his success, and exclaims—

Macb. It is concluded:—Banquo, thy soul's flight,
If it find Heaven, must find it out to-night.   [*Exit.*

SCENE III.
Wood, and distant view of a Castle.

The Murderers enter, and agree on slaying Banquo, and take their stations.—Banquo and Fleance enter; the Murderers attack them—they fight—Banquo is wounded.—He says to Fleance—

Banquo. Revenge my death—hence, good Fleance fly,
Thy father bleeds, hence, Oh!—Treachery!

Fleance flies—they fight again—the Murderers kill Banquo by repeated stabs—they congratulate each other on the deed.

SCENE IV.
The same as scene one.

Fleance enters and laments the death of his father, and prays to Heaven for protection, and goes off—the Murderers pass, seemingly in search of Fleance.

SCENE V.
Grand Banquet—a throne erected at the end of the stag, with Macbeth and Lady Macbeth as King and Queen.

Macbeth welcomes his guests—a Murderer half enters and announces the murder of Banquo to him—he appears agitated, and the Murderer retires. He then fills a goblet, and is about to drink, when the ghost of Banquo arises surrounded by clouds—he throws away the goblet and appears convulsed with horror—[*no one is supposed to see but himself*]—Lady Macbeth endeavours to recover him—the ghost descends. He re-joins the feast, is about to drink again, when it re-appears; his agony is repeated till the ghost disappears. In the mean time Lady Macbeth discharges the guests, Macbeth sinks into a chair, when a messenger arrives with information, that "Macduff doth refuse attendance." Macbeth gives orders to surprize his castle and murder his family.

> *Macb.* Come, we'll to sleep: my strange and self-abuse
> Is the initiate fear that wants hard use;
> To-morrow will I the Weird Sisters seek,
> More am I bent to know, more shall they speak.

SCENE VI.

A room in Macduff's castle.

Enter Lady Macduff and her two children; when Rosse enters with a letter, which announces Macduff's flight.

> *L. Macd.* My husband fled! what may I understand?
> What has he done to make him fly the land?
> *Rosse.* You must have patience, Madam,
> *L. Macd.*   he had none—
> His flight was madness, wherefore has he flown?
> To leave his wife, his babes, and titles on the spot,
> From whence himself does fly—he loves us not.
> The most diminutive of birds, the wren,
> Her young ones in her nest will eager strain,
> And against the owl will fight!
> Against all reason is this causeless flight.
> *Rosse.* I must away; here should I longer stay
> It would but disgrace me— I must away.
> [*to the child*] My little coz, may heaven thy slumbers bless—
> *L. Macd.* Father'd he is, and yet is fatherless.
> *Rosse.* Dangers approach, I fear, much too near,
> Take my advice, and do not be found here.
> > > > > > > > > > > [*Exit Rosse.*

> *L. Macd.* Whither should I fly?
> I have done no harm—but I remember still,
> That to do harm is sometimes laudable.
> > > > > > > > > [*a clashing of arms is heard.*
> The Castle is surprized, O! whither shall I fly?
> Flight would be folly—and to stay's to die.
> > > > > *The Murderers enter.*
> *L. Macd.* O, save me from these fierce and cruel men,
> Unless that by their looks my tender babes are slain.

The Murderers each of them savagely seize one of the children, when Lady Macduff gets between them.

> *L. Macd.* Save them, for their tears shall turn to drops of blood.
> > > > [*The Murderers refuse her.*]
> What, refuse me! then to despair I'm driven!
> O, save them! save them, Heaven!

Each of the murderers seize a child and run off with them, Lady Macduff following.

[*They are supposed to be murdered, but very properly off the stage.*]

A *Macbeth* of Few Words

The cave of Acheron—a cauldron in the midst, filled with fire.

1st Witch. Thrice the brindled cat has mewed;
2nd Witch. Thrice; and once the hedge-hog win'd,
3rd Witch. Harper cries:—'Tis time, 'tis time,
1st Witch. Round about the cauldron go;
In the poison'd entrails throw.
Toad, that under coldest stone,
Days and nights hast thirty-one;
Swelter'd venom sleeping got,
Boil thou first in the charm'd pot!
All. Double, double, toil and trouble;
Fire burn; and water bubble.
2nd Witch. Fillet of a fenny snake,
In the cauldron boil and bake;
Eye of newt, and toe of frog,
Wool of bat, and tongue of dog;
Adder's fork, and blind-worm's sting,
Lizard's leg, and Owlet's wing,
For a charm of powerful trouble,
Like a hell-broth boil and bubble.
All. Double, double, toil and trouble,
Fire burn, and cauldron bubble.
3rd Witch. Scale of dragon, tooth of wolf,
Witches mummy, maw and gulf
Of the ravin'd salt-sea shark;
Root of hemlock, digg'd i'the dark;
Liver of blaspheming Jew,
Gall of Goats and slips of yew;
Silver'd in the moon's eclipse,
Nose of Turk and Tartar's lips,
Finger of birth-strangled babe,
Ditch delivered by a drab,
Make the gruel thick and slab;
Add thereto a tiger's chauldron,
For the ingredient of our cauldron.
All. Double, double toil and trouble,
Fire burn, and cauldron bubble.
2nd Witch. Cool it with a baboon's blood,
Then the charm is firm and good.
    Hecate enters, here—and—
    Hecate. O, well done! I commend your pains,
And every one shall share i'the gains.
    Chorus. Black spirits and white,
            Red spirits and grey,
        Mingle, mingle, mingle,
            You that mingle may.
2nd Witch. By the pricking of my thumbs,

Something wicked this way comes;
Open locks, whoever knocks.
                              Macbeth enters.
    Macbeth. How now you secret black and midnight hags!
What is't you do—o'er yon mystic flame?
I conjure you, however hard the task,
I command you, answer what I ask.
    1st Witch. Speak.
    2nd Witch. Demand.
    3rd Witch. We'll answer.
    1st Witch. Say, if thou'dst rather hear it from our mouths, or from
        our master's?
    Macbeth. Let me see them.
    1st Witch. Pour in sow's blood, that hath eaten
Her nine farrow.—Grease that's sweaten
From the murderer's gibbet, throw
Into the flame.
    All. Come, high or low,
Thyself and office swiftly show.
         An apparition appears with an armed head.
    1st Apparition. Macbeth! Macbeth! Macbeth! beware Macduff;
Beware the Thane of Fife.—Dismiss me—enough.
    Macbeth appears to demand more.   [Decends.
    Hecate. He will not be commanded; here's another,
More potent than the former.
         Second apparition, a bloody child rises.
    2nd Apparition. Macbeth! Macbeth! Macbeth!
Be bloody, bold, and resolute: laugh to scorn
The power of man; for none of woman born
Shall harm Macbeth.   [Descends.
    Third apparition, a child crowned, with a tree in his hand.
    3rd Apparition. Be lion hearted, proud; and take no care
Who chafes, who frets, or who conspirer's are;
Macbeth shall never vanquish'd be, until
Great Birnam Wood to high Dunsinane Hill
Shall come against him.   [Descends.
    Macbeth. That will never be;
Who can impress the forest, and bid the tree unfix its earth-bound root?
        yet my heart
Throbs to know one thing more. Instantly impart,
Shall Banquo's issue e'er such interest gain,
That ever in this kingdom they shall reign?
    All. Seek to know no more.
    Macbeth. I will be satisfied; deny me this,
And an eternal curse fall on you.
                  [*Thunder, the cauldron sinks.*

Let me know
Who sinks that cauldron,   [*A groan.*
And what noise is this?

98

1st Witch. Show.
2nd Witch. Show.
3rd Witch. Show.
All. Show his eyes, and grieve his heart,
Come like shadows, so depart.

Apparitions of the eight kings appear, the last with a glass in his hand, and Banquo passes across—during which time Macbeth is much agitated.

Macbeth. What is this so?

1st Witch. Ay, Sir, all this is so; but why
Stands Macbeth thus amazedly?
Come, sisters, cheer we up his sprights,
And show the best of our delights,
I'll charm the air to give a sound,
While you perform the antic round;
That this great king may kindly say,
Our duties did his welcome pay.

A dance of sprites, at which Macbeth gazes with seeming pleasure; the Witches vanish. Lenox arrives with news, that "Macduff has fled to England"—Macbeth appears agitated.

Macbeth. Infernal fiends, infected by the air whereon they ride,
And damn'd all those who in their arts confide.   [*Exeunt.*
End of Act II.

ACT III.

SCENE I.
An apartment in the Palace of King Edward of England.

Macduff and Malcolm—Macduff cheers him; and they show their amity. Rosse arrives, and appears much afflicted, at which Macduff enquires, and after some hesitation, he informs him by a banner: "*Your Castle is surprised, and wife and babes murdered;*" Macduff is deeply penetrated with sorrow, and vows vengeance against the author of the injury he has suffered; they join their swords together, and vow vengeance; when Edward the confessor, King of England enters, with his attendants, to whom they apply for succour.

Edward. Heaven with zeal my bosom warms,
Brave Siward, with ten thousand men in arms
Shall aid you. The English feel blest,
In granting succour to the brave opprest.   [*Exeunt.*

SCENE II.
An apartment in Macbeth's Castle.

A doctor and a gentlewoman enter, and seem to converse respecting Lady Macbeth's illness, and the disorder of her mind.—Lady Macbeth from the back, with a lamp in her hand, asleep—she sets down the lamp, and seems convulsed with horrible recollections; she wrings her hands, thinks they are distained with blood, and utters several groans; she then takes the lamp and retires (during this scene, the doctor and gentlewoman are observing her.)

Macbeth enters, much agitated, though much more desperate than he appears to have been before—he makes enquiries of the doctor after his lady's health, which he finds not mended; he gives him a charge, during which time a messenger arrives with information, that *"Ten thousand English approach;"* his attendants bring his arms, &c. and during the whole time he seems much agitated; and at length says to Seyton and the attendants with his armour—

Macbeth. Bring it after me,—
I will not be afraid of death and bane,
'Till Birnam Forest come to Dunsinane.

SCENE III.

Birnam Wood.

Enter Malcolm, Macduff, Siward, young Siward, &c. &c. with a banner, on which is inscribed, *"Destruction to the Tyrant;"* they congratulate each other, and many join the standard.

Siward. What wood is that I behold?
Lenox. 'Tis Birnam as I am told.
Malcolm. Let every soldier hew him down a bow,
And bear't before him; thereby we shadow
The numbers of our host, and make discovery
E're it report of us—
Quick then your shadows to obtain,
And let us march to'ards Dunsinane.

The characters then lay their arms together in signal of good faith.

[*Exeunt.*

SCENE IV.

Interior of Macbeth's Castle.

Macbeth enters with a picture of his castle, and directs how it is to be defended; a groan is heard, Macbeth starts, when the attendant of Lady Macbeth enters with a confirmation, that *"The Queen is dead;"* he shews a momentary horror, but resumes his firmness again, when a messenger arrives, and repeats *"The wood of Birnam moves towards Dunsinane."*

Macbeth. If this which he avouches does appear,
There is no flying hence, nor tarrying here;
I 'gin to be a-weary of the sun,
And wish the state o'the world were now undone,
Ring the alarum bell; blow, wind! come rack!
At least we'll die with harness on our back.   [*Exeunt.*

SCENE V. *and last.*

An open Country, and Macbeth's Castle on the right, with armed men and banner on the turrets.

Malcolm's army approach with boughs.
Malcolm. Now near enough, your heavy screens throw down.

100

The army enters, and sit down before the castle, some part ordered another way, and various orders, when Macduff exclaims:

Macduff. Make all your trumpets speak; give them all breath,
Those clamerous harbingers of blood and death.

The combatants charge and re-charge, young Siward and Macbeth fight, young Siward is slain.

A grand combat of four takes place for the colours, Malcolm enters and charges the castle; a rally of Macbeth's party, Macduff and Macbeth prepare to fight most furiously, Macduff is slightly wounded.

Macbeth. Swords I smile at, weapons laugh to scorn,
Brandish'd by man that's of a woman born.

Macduff. Despair thy charms, and curse the fiends that urged you to
your doom,
For know, Macduff untimely torn was from his mother's womb.

Macbeth seems inclined not to fight; but being shewed the banner, he summons new courage.

Macbeth. I will not yield to be young Malcolm's scorn,
Though thou oppos'st me, of no woman born!
Yet I will try the last. Lay on Macduff,
And damn'd be him that first cries "Hold, enough!"

Macbeth and Macduff fight, Macbeth falls and dies; the crown is presented to Malcolm by a nobleman on his knee; and the curtain drops amidst a flourish of trumpets.

FINIS.

Theodore Page, Printer, Black Friars Road, London.

THOMAS B. STROUP
Professor of English
University of Kentucky

The Scenes in Shakespearean Plays

HE SCENE OF GREEK TRAGEDY WAS PRETTY GEN-erally confined to the front of a building of some sort, a palace, a temple, a council hall, a house, or a hut, though the play might be enacted before the cave of the Cyclops; and though a change from this basic exterior might be effected to represent an interior, it seems to have been seldom and then awkwardly done. Equally awkward was the introduction of the realm of the gods by the use of the machine. Likewise the action of Greek and Roman comedy was usually confined to the street before or between two houses, though the front of a farmhouse or cave or a public square might be designated. The change of scene within the play was apparently uncalled for. The classical dramatists recognized the three great areas for action and their relationship, the interior and domestic, the exterior and public, and the unseen and spiritual; but they chose to focus upon the middle and set each play in one place.

102

With the rise of the drama anew in the Middle Ages the three areas were quite as well recognized and far more frequently and deliberately represented. The localization of scene was at first quite as well known, even if not stated explicitly, for the events presented and the place of their happening were known of all who saw the mystery plays. The resurrection from Joseph of Aramathea's tomb in Jerusalem, the birth in the stable in Bethlehem, or the crucifixion in Jerusalem needed no scene markings either on stage or in text. The Corpus Christi pageants indicate well enough the place of their representation. The Wakefield Master could with complete confidence in the understanding of his audience place a contemporary shepherd's hut on a Yorkshire moor, as it were, next door to the sacred crèche. The difference lay in the whole. Even in trilogy, the classical plays were discrete. The pageants, though separate in scene, were linked together to form a whole play, whose stage was the world and whose time was all time. The series reached from Eden to Eternity, from Creation till the last syllable of recorded time has brought the dissolution of the great globe itself. Neither heaven nor hell was excluded from the scene, and time future as well as time past was rifled to furnish the required pageant. The history of the race was set forth in memorable scenes.

This history was presented in a quite different way in the morality plays, especially the earlier ones. In them it became the account of the universal pattern of salvation, the history of the individual Mankind as opposed to the race. Thus the scene became cosmic in a very different way. No particular place was required; none under the circumstances was logically possible. Since everyman became Everyman, one man, every place became one place, Everywhere. Thus Mankind, Everyman, Humanum Genus, and the rest played Everywhere, on the stage of the world. To particularize their stage would be to destroy their scene. Even such a set as that of *The Castle of Perseverance*, since it is allegorical, is of cosmic design: we all live in this castle. Later the secular moralities were set in a scene no less broad, as were such interludes as *The Four Elements*.

So it was that the Elizabethan playwrights might follow the

multiple scene practice of the writers of the cyclic plays and also the universalized, or non-indicated, scene practice of the writers of the moralities. From the cycles they probably inherited the idea of history as basic subject matter. They probably saw in it, as Miss E. Catherine Dunn thinks the cyclic dramatists saw, "the unfolding of God's plans for his people."[1] Just so they found in the narrative verse tragedies, whose subjects were from history, models of popular morality and turned them into series of pageants, to tell the life and death of kings. And whether historical or not, the pageantry of history pervaded their tragedies; it also furnished the scheme for much of romantic comedy; and by its variety and movement it even enriched farce and the regular comedy brought from ancient Rome. From the moralities they might follow the single or indefinite scene practice, the setting of action whose place is of no importance without suggestion of place in the dialogue or directions, or perhaps the setting in a generalized place such as a wood or a plain. From whichever heritage, the Elizabethan faced the same paradox the medieval dramatist faced: his theater at once contained the world and was contained by it. Perhaps, however, this is nothing more than one expression of the paradox of all drama— or all art indeed.

Perhaps it was because of this very paradox that the Elizabethan playwright managed to express so well the universal within the particular and the particular within the universal which give his art its supreme worth. He stood between the universal of the past and the partial and particular of the new age, a happy place for the artist to stand. His management of place and scenes, especially their variety, reveals his conscious attempt to make his plays suggest the whole world, if not the cosmos indeed. A brief analysis of the kinds of places represented in some of Shakespeare's plays, with references to others, will serve, I believe, to reveal one aspect of the universalizing method of this drama.[2] One is struck first perhaps with the

1. "The Medieval 'Cycle' as History Play: An Approach to the Wakefield Plays," *Studies in the Renaissance*, VII (1960), 76-89.
2. See Anne Righter, *Shakespeare and the Idea of the Play* (London, 1962), *passim*, for treatment of the relationship of theater imagery in

variety of places allowed by a stage on which scenery was un-
common if not altogether disallowed; and yet the localities for
scenes are repeated again and again, so often indeed as to form
a sort of pattern.[3] Perhaps one can best present these by divid-
ing them into interiors, exteriors, and combinations of the two.

Granted that specific localities for the action are not forthcoming either from dialogue or stage directions, granted that
editors may not always agree upon the place for a given scene,
granted that dramatists did not always intend a particular place,
most of the localities are pretty clear, and most readers agree
about them.[4] At any rate one can usually tell whether a scene
is exterior or interior. Now, many of Shakespeare's scenes are
exteriors, and they furnish greater variety than the interiors.
First among them are the numerous garden, park, and orchard
scenes. The parks, such as that in *Love's Labour's Lost*, are
hardly rural scenes, but places where pavilions are set up, games
played, and dancing done. Likewise, the garden and orchard
scenes represent methodized nature, where ladies and gentlemen disport themselves or take their ease or meditate and phi-
losophize. Not so with the equally numerous forest scenes (the
forest is a place for mix-ups in *Midsummer Night's Dream* and
As You Like It) or the rough country scenes, such as that before
Belarius' cave in *Cymbeline* or perhaps that before Prospero's

---

Shakespeare's plays to the concept of the world as stage. Jean Jacquot (to
whom Miss Righter does not refer) has traced the idea of the world as
stage from its origins into the seventeenth century and has also shown
how it very probably contributed to the technique of the play-within-the-
play. See his " 'Le Théâtre du Monde' de Shakespeare à Calderón," *Revue
de Littérature Comparée*, XXXI (Juillet-Septembre, 1957), 341-72. The
present writer has likewise traced it—entirely independently—and has indicated the basic nature of the concept in the testing motif in Elizabethan
tragedy. See *SEL*, III (Spring, 1963), 175-78 especially.

3. Miss Muriel C. Bradbrook has very briefly pointed out some of
the stock scenes of Elizabethan drama and thus the variety of scenes, as
well as the possible ways for staging them. See her *Themes & Conventions
in Elizabethan Tragedy* (Cambridge, 1960), pp. 10-12. Sir Edmund Chambers did the same, in somewhat more extended fashion, in *The Elizabethan
Stage* (Oxford, 1923), III, 47-154.

4. I have relied upon the traditional scene designations one finds in
such editions as the New Arden Shakespeare and the Kittredge edition
(Boston, 1936), though I have frequently checked the designations by the
internal textual evidence.

cell, or those on the heaths or plains, or in open country. These are either neutral or unkindly disposed toward man and his doings. Actually if we lump together the garden, park, and orchard scenes we find such places represented in at least seventeen of Shakespeare's plays, and this does not count repetitions within a given play: most plays repeated such scenes. Perhaps some of the "fields" should be listed among these, though most are associated with battle scenes, and among the lonely seacoasts and desert country near the sea, such as one finds in *Winter's Tale*. The whole action of *Love's Labour's Lost*, according to the editors, takes place in the King's park, though nothing in the first and several other scenes precludes their being played in the palace halls. However this may be, the public exteriors are more numerous. I speak of streets, roads, "public places," seaports, forums, innyards, courtyards of castles, and all such. Many of these are suggested vaguely and as vaguely marked by the editors. The many battle scenes belong among them. As I reckon them, following the divisions of modern editors, at least forty-two scenes occur on battlefields in thirteen of Shakespeare's plays. Associated with these are the many camp scenes, almost indistinguishable from them. And to round out our lives there are the graveyard scenes, such as those in *Romeo and Juliet, Hamlet,* and *Much Ado.* All are places of human bustle and exchange, places for emphasis on physical activity. Groups and masses of men gather in them for challenges, quarrels, squabbles, fights, marchings and countermarchings, processions, meetings, assignations, the delivery of messages, judgments, warnings, and so on.

Closely allied to these and used for many of the same purposes are the threshold scenes, the scenes "before" a city wall, a gate, a palace, a castle, a house, a manor, a fortification, a shrine, a tent, a prison, a cave, or something else. They resemble those places indicated for the stationary scenes of the classical drama in that they are set "before" something. But whereas all the scenes of the Greek and Roman plays are staged "before" something, the Elizabethan plays are not so restricted; and whereas these "ante scenes" of the classical drama were limited to about half a dozen, they were not thus limited in the

106

Elizabethan. The English dramatist placed his action in this kind of exterior setting before any number of interiors in the background, thus allowing great latitude in the action. The Tower of London, like the walls of a city, allows two levels of action; so does Cleopatra's monument at Alexandria. A street before a shop in London permits action in both exterior and interior, and great speeches are spoken before the gates of a city or a castle, as well as from their walls. In a storm before a hovel on a heath four men's minds are torn to fragments, their souls stripped bare, and their beings reduced to their essential nakedness; and then into the hovel they go. Following a tempest on a savage island before a magician's cell a happy resolution and a just restitution are effected, and out of the cell two happy lovers come. In these scenes one looks from the exterior into the interior, as one so often does when viewing a medieval or Renaissance painting or illumination. The heavens, the earth, and then the covered place for man's use are all accounted for.

If the exteriors and combinations of exteriors and interiors furnish variety, so do the interiors. As with the two former, so with the latter type of scenes: it frequently furnishes neutral acting space, no special kind of interior being necessary. And if one finds more variety among the exteriors, one will probably find the number of interior scenes the greater. Many of them merely call for a room in a house or a palace or a castle, any kind of room. But it is important for us to know whose house or palace or castle it is, or what its name is. For example, the first scene of *I Henry IV* is perhaps a council chamber of the King's palace in London, where Henry meets his barons; so is Scene iii of the first act. But the place is vaguely indicated. Again, the first scene of Act III of *II Henry IV* is merely set in some undesignated room in the Palace at Westminster, into which the sleepless King comes in his nightgown. I count five such vaguely indicated interiors in *Henry V* alone, two in *Coriolanus* (in which play five scenes can be designated no better than with the words "A public place"), and at least seven in *King Lear*. But a great many of the interiors are pretty well signified, and their kind suggested by the text. As every reader knows, numerous scenes of Elizabethan drama take place in the rooms of state, where the king assembles his court and conducts the busines of his realm. Among the best known of these is the second in *Hamlet,* where King Claudius disposes of the business of state. Such scenes are formal, ceremonious, dignified, and colorful in their pageantry. In them trials may take place and judgments be rendered, embassies dispatched or received, declarations made or debates conducted. Next to the rooms of state are the numerous scenes set in the council chamber of the monarch or the duke or the lord of some castle. These are less formal, but are still used for the conduct of official business. The second scene of Act II of *Hamlet* seems to be set in such a room, where Claudius receives Rosencrantz and Guildenstern. Numerous actions also take place in a hall of a castle or palace, or in a gallery. Likewise, the dramatists often placed their scenes in a banquet hall or else placed a banquet in some sort of palace hall. It was a favorite kind of scene. One of these took place, it will be remembered, aboard Pompey's ship in *Antony and Cleopatra,* though it turned out to be a drinking party—and there is evidence that the "banquet" was often thought of as such. Such scenes furnish great opportunity for spectacle as well as the chance to put upon the stage one of the customary activities of humankind. Sometimes the dinner or banquet was represented as going on in the background off-stage, thus giving servants a chance to comment on the action inside as a sort of chorus. The closet, too, was a place of action, such as Gertrude's most private chamber in Elsinore. And scenes are not infrequently placed in a bedroom, the bed very probably being regularly pushed out upon the stage to indicate the place and provide the necessary property. One recalls the final scene in *Othello* as a notable example. Thus another universal activity of humankind is suggested by the place.

But less usual interiors also appear in the plays of Shakespeare and his contemporaries. The Roman Senate House and the Capitol are scenes of action in the Roman plays, and the Parliament House rightfully furnished the place for scenes in the chronicle plays, places for official government acts or debate. To be compared with these are such scenes as those in Westminster Hall, or the well-remembered scene in the Jeru-

salem Chamber at Westminster, where Henry IV lay sick in
state. Churches are likewise called for, such as the brilliant
opening scene of *I Henry VI*, or the Abbey of Bury St. Ed-
munds in the first scene of Act III of *II Henry VI*, or the
church in *Much Ado*, or the chapel in *Winter's Tale*, or the
Temple of Diana in *Pericles*, or that of Apollo in the final
scene of Ben Jonson's *Sejanus*. Thus another customary if not
universal activity of humankind is furnished a place. Associated
with these in function are the friar's cells, such as Friar Lau-
rence's in *Romeo and Juliet* and many another's in other plays
of the period.[5] A few scenes are laid in monasteries and nunner-
ies, such as those in *Measure for Measure*. At least one of Shake-

---

5. It is not within the province of this paper to cover the scenes in
the plays of Shakespeare's contemporaries, but it may lend support to my
work to mention with a few instances the general practice among them.
As far back as *Cambises* (*c.* 1569) one finds in the play the presence chamber or room of state as well as other palace rooms, a banqueting hall, then
a park or orchard or garden and a street. In Marlowe's plays, though the
places of action are only vaguely indicated if at all, one can determine a
good deal about them. In *Tamburlaine*, Part I, some sixteen scenes range
from the familiar camp scenes to a road, a hill, four battlefield scenes, two
palace scenes, the walls of Damascus, and some sort of holy place, a
mosque perhaps. In *Doctor Faustus* they range from Faustus's study to other
rooms within his house, to a grove outside and a field, to an innyard and
its interior, to the Pope's palace and the Emperor's palace, and to a place
before Faust's door. *Edward II*, like the chronicles generally, not only
ranges well over England, but has scenes in France and others suggested
in Ireland, and from a street in Westminster to open country, to various
rooms in various castles to a scene in the Temple and several in the
Royal Palace at Westminster. Jonson, under the influence of Plautus and
Terence, especially in his earlier plays, nevertheless moves from the traditional street inside to give his audience three rooms within Lovewit's
house in the *Alchemist* and three scenes before his house. In *Volpone* the
scenes range from the main room in Volpone's house to passageways and
closets, to rooms in Corvino's and in Sir Politick's house, to the two scenes
in the Senate House and the famous street scenes. In *Bartholomew Fair*
Jonson presents the action first in the room in Littlewit's house, and then,
moving to the Fair, presents at least three areas of it, including the interior of Ursula's booth. The whole Fair is itself a little world. And *The
New Inn* likewise represents a microcosm, wherein the yard must be the
place of at least one scene. *The Devil is an Ass* is a veritable morality
play with the spiritual realm surrounding all. And in *Sejanus*, the historical tragedy, the scenes range conventionally from the room of state in
the palace to private rooms in it, to various private rooms in other private
houses, to the Senate House, to a garden, to the streets of Rome, to a

speare's scenes is played in a witches' cavern (*Macbeth*, IV.i); some few are played on board ship, such as those in *Pericles* and the celebrated ones in *Antony and Cleopatra* and *The Tempest*. More common are the prison scenes, three in *Measure for Measure*, for example. Tavern scenes abound. One scarcely need be reminded of the great ones in *Henry IV*, Parts I and II, and the numerous such scenes in the plays of Shakespeare's contemporaries, especially Heywood. In *Pericles*, moreover, two scenes take place within a brothel at Mytilene. The interiors thus range from a room of state and an abbey church to a brothel, from a council chamber to a tavern. The exteriors range just as widely—from gardens, parks and orchards to lonely heaths to busy and brawling streets. And the combination scenes furnish even more variety. Considering the scenes of the entire corpus of Shakespeare's plays, we must realize that almost every kind of place on the face of the globe is used for action; and of course the Globe furnished a stage for just such purpose. From seacoast and shipboard scenes to wild caves in Wales, from an abbey in Milan to a prison in Vienna, from the Forest

---

space before the Temple of Apollo, and finally to the great scene within the Temple. The areas for men, statesmen, and the gods are accounted for. It is perhaps sufficient to mention the title of *Eastward Ho* to recall the street scenes of Goldsmith's Row, the Blue Anchor Tavern, Cuckold's Haven, the rooms in Touchstone's house, the innyard, and scenes at the Counter. But of all the dramatists of the time perhaps Thomas Heywood is most prodigal of his scenes and their places. He loved especially to present the pageantry of the world, especially in his four plays on the four ages of man. Even in his domestic tragedy, *A Woman Killed with Kindness*, the scene of action moves from various rooms in Frankford's house, to the yard, to the front of the house, then to the open country and a road to a gaol, in which building are two scenes, and the death-bed chamber in the manor house. The action of *The Fair Maid of the West* takes place in streets, fields, on shipboard, in numerous taverns, in a bedroom, and in three splendid rooms of state at the court of Morocco. In *The English Traveller* seven scenes can be indicated merely as rooms, one as some sort of dining room, four as threshold scenes or "before" some kind of house, one as a tavern, one as a street, one as a garden. In *The Rape of Lucrece* one finds more variety: the Senate House in Rome, a temple, rooms in Collatine's house, two bedchambers, two interiors of tents (one with a banquet set out), three camps, a space before a tent, then a bridge, and finally open country on the outskirts of Rome. Most of the interests of most of the classes of human society are suggested by the places.

of Arden to the garden of the Temple in London or an orchard in Verona, from a mere public place of some sort to the room of state in Elsinore or the graveyard nearby—the variety is altogether remarkable. And as we move from play to play, we find it is designedly so.

Similarly, as we look within each play, we find the variety equally remarkable and the design even more apparent. The choice of localities for scenes shows conscious effort to suggest a microcosm for each play and thus to represent by place, within the restrictions imposed by plot, a certain degree of universality. Such practice may be observed rather generally among the dramatists of the Elizabethan period, but especially in Shakespeare, who followed it with care from his earliest plays onward.

In his most Plautean *Comedy of Errors*, for example, one discovers a variety of scene altogether lacking in the *Menaechmi*, its source, just as one discovers far more variety of plot. Whereas in the original the whole action takes place in a street before the houses of Menaechmus and Erotium, in Shakespeare's version it takes place within the Duke's palace, within the house of Antipholus of Ephesus, before his house, then in the market place, then in some public place merely (IV.i), in a street, and in front of a priory. The scenes themselves suggest the orders of society, the ruler, the merchants and tradesmen, and the church: the home of the administrator of the law and public affairs, the home of the merchant, the streets and public places, and the home of the representative of the spiritual body. What is more, Shakespeare's addition to his source suggests the outside area beyond the setting of the play. No scenes are placed in Syracuse, but that city is always present to the mind of the reader and the audience. The action moves implicitly outward beyond the home of Antipholus of Ephesus, to the palace of the ruler, to the city, and to the world beyond. The classical restrictions are removed, and the pattern and variety of scenes at least suggest the world stage.

Similarly in *Two Gentlemen of Verona*, another early play with classical affinities. But here is also insertion from romance, and the scenes are not restricted to one city. The action moves from Verona to Milan and thence to a forest outside that city;

and the places vary from private rooms in Antonio's house and the dukes' palaces to public rooms in their palaces; from a mere open space and a street to a private garden, to a scene under the walls of Milan's palace; from a brief scene, apparently within an abbey, to the forest, where the action is concluded. As in *The Comedy of Errors*, domestic and public interiors and exteriors are represented, as well as combinations of interiors and exteriors. The forest scenes bring in the lawless men and irregular nature, both more just and kind than the more highly civilized and the methodized. And it is through the abbey that Sylvia escapes to the ultimate justice of the forest.[6]

To move from the early comedies to the histories is to move into outright attempts to put on the stage the pageantry of national and world events. The places of the scenes were apparently chosen, or left vague indeed, so as to magnify the peageant-like quality and thus reveal the universal plan of history. In these as well as in other kinds of Elizabethan plays many scenes of course are unlocalized, unidentified in the text. They are merely places where certain characters meet to conduct the necessary business of the action and get on with the story. Yet however vague or however unimportant as a place, almost every scene can be designated and named. The very number and variety given or suggested tend to produce the

6. Much the same practice prevails in the romantic comedies generally, as a few examples will show. The scenes of *Midsummer Night's Dream* are placed within Theseus' palace, perhaps a room of state, in Quince's humble house, and then in various parts of the forest, a fairyland and spirit realm. Those in *Much Ado* are set in various rooms of Leonato's house, both private and public rooms, in his orchard, his garden, a street, a place before his door, a prison and a church; those in *As You Like It*, in an orchard, in various rooms in the Duke's palace, in a space before Oliver's house, and in various places in the Forest of Arden. The scenes of *The Merchant of Venice* are brilliant and varied; they are set in the streets of Venice, rooms in Portia's house at Belmont, rooms in Shylock's house, in a court of justice, and in the garden at Belmont. In the later comedies, *Measure for Measure, Winter's Tale*, and *The Tempest*, the number of scenes and the number of places of action become fewer; the variety is sufficient, however, to suggest the world as the area of action. *Cymbeline*, among the later comedies, indeed moves in some twenty-seven scenes across ancient Britain to Rome and back again, and takes place in caves, on battlefields, and in wild Welsh country, as well as in the King's palace.

effect of the passage of men across the stage of the world itself. To pick at random, *Richard III* has twenty-five scenes, if we accept the usual division. Of these, five are played in the streets of London, six in the King's palace in London and one in front of it, one inside Lord Darby's house, one before Lord Hastings' house, two before and two inside the Tower of London, one at Bayard's castle and one at Pomfret Castle, one in a camp, one on Salisbury Plain, and three on Bosworth Field. The earlier scenes are confined to the King's palace and the streets of London; the central scenes are extended to the Tower and to the castles of the noblemen, and the later ones to camps, open plains, and battlefields. In general, the movement is outward from interior to exterior, from the narrow to the wide and to the vast. In addition to these familiar places, one often finds churchly scenes in the chronicles, an abbey in the background especially, or the splendid opening scene of *I Henry VI* inside Westminster Abbey. Three kinds of places are rather generally indicated in the chronicles as in the other plays—the private or domestic, the public or state, and (less obtrusively) the spiritual or ecclesiastical. Scenes vaguely indicated, or "non-localized," all the more strongly suggest the cosmic extent of the stage.

The point is the more readily realized in *Antony and Cleopatra*, where the pageant of the ancient world sweeps by. The Folio, our only source for the text, gives no act or scene divisions, and rightfully so. But the places of actions do change, some forty-two times according to modern editors; and by their range and multiplicity they help to create the magnitude of the action and the character of the protagonists. The three-pillared world is indeed represented, suggested, or symbolized by the variety of places. The scenes in the rooms of Cleopatra's palace are matched by the scenes in Caesar's house, or by those in Pompey's house or Lepidus' house. The rare banquet scene on board Pompey's galley literally rocked the three pillars of the world; it is balanced by the triumphant procession of Ventidius on a Syrian plain. The various camp scenes at Actium and those before Alexandria in Act IV are preliminaries to the scenes on the fields of battle. And finally the poet gives us the remarkable monument scenes at the end of Acts IV and V, scenes not without their symbolic significance. For high lifted up was Antony in his going and his queen also, as it were in their own memorial. And with all the multiplicity of scenes, even more are implied than are put upon the stage: no one will forget Enobarbus' creation of that upon the barge on the Cydnus, though it was never put upon the stage. The action ranges beyond the compass of the present.

Perhaps two observations should be made about the procession of these numerous scenes, one about their variety and one about their geography. The audience is asked to realize in scene the same variety that it realizes in the character of Cleopatra: here are private rooms and public rooms, rooms of state and a banquet room aboard a ship, street scenes and a scene beside a city wall, a plain and military camps, and then a monument—both its exterior and interior. Public and private places, interiors and exteriors and combinations are called for: the family, the state, and (if we accept the monument as symbolic) the spiritual realm are all suggested. But as time runs out, the geography of the scenes is narrowed. In the last two acts the play does not leave Alexandria, and gradually grows to a point in the monument, being literally reduced to a period. Taken all in all, the world is represented, and the poet throughout consciously contrives the variety of his scenes and deliberately gives them wide geographical spread.

In the great tragedies, plays of somewhat more circumscribed area and more restricted action than the chronicles and the Roman plays, the same cosmic proportions are suggested, and more subtly. In *Hamlet*, for example, the action moves from the vague platform before Elsinore, the very edge of the spiritual world where men and spirits mingle, to the room of state where the King conducts the kingdom's business. Thence it moves to a private room in Polonius' house, then variously to smaller and more private rooms of the palace, to a hall, then to the very boudoir and closet of the Queen. Later it moves outward to a plain with soldiers marching and still later to a churchyard and cemetery, where the funeral procession comes. And scenes not represented are yet described: we wonder after we read whether a shipboard action did not take place on stage,

114

or whether the one anticipated in England might not have, or whether still another did not take place on the skirts of Norway, where Fortinbras sharked up his band. The places of action move outward from the actual to the merely suggested, from the intimate and domestic to the public and national, even to the international, and from these to the eternal beyond. From a meeting with a ghost on the platform before Elsinore Hamlet moves through the cemetery to be carried off in triumph to "the stage" (a very platform), where another meeting may be expected—between two spirits now at rest.

In *King Lear* the scenes spread wide over Britain and reach outward to France, and within the country they vary from the King's presence chamber to the hut on the heath and from Gloucester's castle to open country, from Albany's castle and several scenes before castles or in courtyards to a farmhouse and the fields of battle. And beyond these is one not presented but so vividly described as to be remembered best—the Cliffs of Dover, one way to the world beyond. The highest ranks of humankind and the lowest find places in this play, the highest reduced to the lowliest place. *Macbeth* ranges widely too: from a blasted heath in Scotland to the front of King Edward's palace in England, from Macbeth's castle at Inverness to Macduff's castle, from the palace at Forres to the witches' cavern, and from Dunsinane to the battlefield. Private and public, national and international realms are indicated, and also the mysterious spiritual. *Othello,* with emphasis upon the domestic conflict, suggests less explicitly the spiritual realm than the other great tragedies, unless it be in the crucial garden scene where the protagonist and the villain, the tempted and the tempter, kneel together to swear murder. We dare think it a suggestion of Eden and the Fall. Otherwise, the range of scenes follows the pattern: street scenes, a council chamber, interiors of palaces and castles, a seaport, ante-castle scenes, and the final bedroom; the place of the play moves from Venice to Cyprus.

One might continue indefinitely—and tediously. Enough has been said to show that Shakespeare chose the various scenes for most of his plays with some attention to their power to suggest action of world-wide if not cosmic import, to imply at least their private, public, and spiritual contexts. His contemporaries were equally aware of the contexts, if not always so successful in handling them. It is perhaps notable that Chapman's Bussy d'Ambois, the free and uncommitted bold man, moves from a first exterior scene to interiors, where he becomes increasingly circumscribed in space as he becomes increasingly embroiled in the intrigues of the court and the doings of lesser men until he is destroyed.

Just such change is reflected in the plays of Shakespeare's successors: their scenes moved inside, and their plays suggest less and less the heroic proportions of character and universal import of the action. Not only were there fewer scenes, but fewer scenes were exteriors. Whereas no single play of Shakespeare is without exterior scenes, numbers of the plays of his successors are played wholly within doors. In *The Maid's Tragedy*, for example, only one scene can possibly be an exterior. In five of Ford's plays there are eighty-eight scenes, only fifteen of which are exteriors. Two of his plays are entirely without exteriors, and only his throwback to the chronicle tradition, *Perkin Warbeck*, has the variety to be expected—scenes on the seashore, on Tower hill, before a castle, and on battlefields. His other exteriors are made up of six street scenes, and two garden or grove scenes. The variety has been lost. Rooms of state are used, though not so frequently as by the earlier dramatists; more often the interiors are apartments, bedrooms, or just "rooms." Much the same is true of Shirley. In five of his plays dating from 1628 to 1641 he uses only fifty-six scenes. Of these, nineteen only are exteriors, and six of the nineteen are accounted for by *Hyde Park*, where exteriors are to be expected. *The Lady of Pleasure* has no exterior scene. Or one may see what happens in a slightly different way. In Dekker's early (1599) *Old Fortunatus* some five scenes are exteriors and five are interiors, with one combination interior-exterior. And whereas Part I of *The Honest Whore* (1604) has five exteriors, seven interiors, and three combination scenes, Part II (published in 1630) has only one exterior, two combinations, and ten interiors, a fact which may argue for a later composition of the play than has usually been accepted from the vague entry in the Stationer's Register. One might continue to multiply instances such as these. As time went on, the variety of scene, or place of action, became less and less, and with that lessening the concept of the play as cosmic symbol became less. No longer do scenes provide the degrees of the social order, or regularly for private and public life and for the life beyond. The larger vision is gradually lost.

Variety and patterns aside, the construction of certain scenes, in some cases the scene of the play as a whole indeed, likewise indicates the dramatist's concern for the microcosmic shape of his work. For lack of a better term I shall call it the encompassing action scene plan; and since this phenomenon has elsewhere been discussed with some fullness, though not from my point of view or with my purpose, I need do little more than call attention to it here.[7] It involves the play-within-the-play technique. For the play as a whole the concept is very well illustrated by Peele's *Old Wives' Tale*, wherein the scene within the wood and the cottage encompasses the mythical scenes out of Madge's imagination, which are actually "compassing the wide world round about." Similarly the scene which encompasses the whole *Taming of the Shrew* does not change, though Sly becomes bored and goes to sleep perhaps, the one

7. See Righter and Jacquot as cited above. They find that the shaping force behind the device of the play-within-the-play is the metaphor of the world as a stage, and Miss Righter shows that the device is of wider significance than critics have shown hitherto. She demonstrates very effectively the ramifications of the idea in Shakespeare. One of her most astute observations is that the characters in his plays directly or indirectly indicate that life itself is a very play; it imitates a theater. (See pp. 91-100 especially.) Neither she nor M. Jacquot, however, observes that the variety of scenes and their careful choice may be accounted for by the requirement that the dramatist set his play on the stage of the world. In connection with such scenes as these see W. Creizenach, *Geschichte des neueren Dramas* (Halle, 1909), IV, 303-4, and Hereward T. Price, "Mirror-Scenes in Shakespeare," in *Joseph Quincy Adams Memorial Studies*, ed. James G. McManaway, Giles E. Dawson, and Edwin Willoughby (Washington, 1948), 101-13. Price's extensive treatment shows that many scenes in Shakespeare's plays may be cut without disrupting the movement of the plot but not without loss of symbol in the play, or character revelation, or character presentation. Altogether these scenes extend the scope of the play by making symbol out of incident and giving a "dramatic picture of the character's whole world "(see p. 112).

audience being rightfully forgotten by the other. In a sense, moreover, Machiavel is more than prologue to *The Jew of Malta*: derived from the medieval "presenter," he stands in his own metaphysical realm just outside the physical world of Cyprus, and reveals the action. So it is with Andrea and Revenge in *The Spanish Tragedy*. Their ghostly realm surrounds the main action, and within this main action is set the tragedy of Soliman the Turkish Emperor and the masque, both presented by Hieronimo. More effectively handled, the whole action of *Hamlet* is set within the realm of the Ghost, and within the play proper *The Murder of Gonzago* is produced. So with numerous others: in *A Midsummer Night's Dream* the play of Theseus and Hippolita really encompasses the play of the lovers and the fairies in the forest, and within the play of both these and for their entertainment Quince directs his *Pyramus and Thisbe*. The audience at a London theater is brought directly into the action (or what is represented as the audience) of *The Knight of the Burning Pestle* in the persons of the Citizen and his wife and Rafe. Within the Citizen scene is set the scene of the intended play, *The London Merchant*, and within it are encompassed the exploits of the Knight of the Burning Pestle. Ben Jonson's introductions likewise bridge the same gaps between audience and play. One recalls especially *Cynthia's Revels, Bartholomew Fair, The Staple of News,* and *The Magnetic Lady*. The distinction between illusion and reality is thus also bridged, as it often was in the moralities and earlier Elizabethan plays.

Less obvious are the numerous scenes within scenes. Sometimes they are tiny plays within plays, such as Falstaff and Hal at their pranks in the Boar's Head, reminding us of an earlier exchange of roles between Ralph Simnell and Prince Edward in *Friar Bacon and Friar Bungay*, or such as the scene before the hovel of *King Lear*, where each of the four characters is actually playing a role. The number of such scenes is extensive. Furthermore, a great many scenes are begun and ended by the same character or pair of characters whose task it is to present an inner scene. These characters are not mere choruses; they are integral to the action. Such, for example, is the opening

118

scene of *The Duchess of Malfi*, where Antonio and Delio provide for the introduction of the wiles of the Cardinal and Bosola. An even more brilliant opening is the first scene of *Antony and Cleopatra*. Two Roman gentlemen open and close the scene, showing the audience the whole play in miniature as it were. In the same play Enobarbus opens and closes Scene ii of Act II. Quite a different sort of enclosed scene is that in *Friar Bacon and Friar Bungay*, in which Bacon shows as in a glass the fatal fight between Lambert and Serlsby. Shirley was apparently partial to such scenes. For example, he introduces Aimwell, Fowler, and Clare into the middle of the first scene of *The Witty Fair One*. They break into the scene between Richley, Worthy, and Whibble and speak eight lines; then Richley and Worthy conclude the scene. So it is with the third scene of the same act. Of course, the numerous dumb shows are encompassed actions. And all are basic to the concept of the metaphor of the world as stage. Such scenes suggest quite well what Dryden observed so perceptively—that the structure of the Elizabethan play resembles the movement of the spheres, the main action being the *primum mobile* pulling with it the encircling actions. Indeed one might the better call them spheres of action and think of the basic areas as set one within another, as are the spheres of the Ptolemaic system—the cosmos.

But again, as time went on, the encompassing actions occurred less frequently; the larger design was gradually lost. Relevance of parts to whole was either taken for granted or ignored; that is, the dramatist no longer seems to have felt he was obliged to show that what happened in his play was related to what was happening outside it and to what had happened before it. Fortunately for us the work of Shakespeare and of his contemporaries stands between the two extremes—between his non-restricted but unified and allegorical past and his restricted, fragmented, and particularized future. His characters, and those of his contemporaries, are very persons, but often they stand for much more than a single individual. So with his places for action. His choice of scenes in his plays and frequently his method of framing them enabled him to achieve an effective particularization of his art without sacrificing its universality.

ROBERT A. BRYAN
Associate Professor of English
Assistant Dean, Graduate School
University of Florida

Translatio Concepts in Donne's
The Progress of the Soul

HE REACTIONS TO DONNE'S *The Progress of the Soul* by three centuries of readers are as fragmented, contradictory, and generally inconclusive as the poem itself. A typically puzzling reference to the poem was Richard Hurd's belief that in *The Progress of the Soul* Donne's "good sense brought him out into the freer spaces of nature and daylight."[1] Exactly what Hurd meant by this has never been determined, although presumably he had in mind the large sweep through man's history that Donne had planned for the poem. Alexander Pope once commended it as one of Donne's "best things" but never again gave it any attention.[2] Only Thomas De Quincey stands out as a thoroughgoing admirer of *The Progress of the Soul*: he saw "massy diamonds" in the "very substance" of the poem and found in it "thoughts and

1. *Q. Horatii Flacci epistola ad Agustum. With an English Commentary and Notes* (4th ed.; London, 1766), III, 97.
2. Joseph Spence, *Anecdotes* (London, 1820), p. 144.

120

descriptions which have the fervent and gloomy sublimity of Ezekiel or Aeschylus."[3] Coleridge liked at least parts of the poem,[4] but one of his friends, William Page Wood, thought that aside from one stanza, it "seemed the effusion of a man very drunk or very mad."[5] Edmund Gosse found the poem "extraordinary" but failed to relate with sufficient clarity or detail why he thought it was the "least diffident essay in psychological imagination ever presented to the public."[6] Never, apparently, widely read, Donne's fragment was, as Isaac D'Israeli wrote, "reserved for the few."[7] The targets of the poet's ironic thrusts and the precise strategy of the poem are shrouded by its incompleteness and by a tone at once hopeful in certain stanzas ("I launch at Paradise, and I saile towards home") and darkly cynical in most of the stanzas ("Ther's nothing simply good, nor ill alone,/ Of every quality Comparison/ The onely measure is, and judge, Opinion").

Scholarly attempts to solve the riddles posed by the fragment have been at times helpful and at times misleading. Ben Jonson's remarks to William Drummond have led some students of the poem to focus exclusively on the Pythagorean elements in it and to conclude that the satirical force of the poem was destined to have been directed at one person, Queen Elizabeth. Jonson is recorded as having said that "The conceit of Donne's transformation . . . was that he sought the soule of that Apple which Eva pulled, and thereafter made it the soule of a Bitch, then of a shee wolf and so of a woman. His generall purpose was to have brought in all the bodies of the Hereticks from ye soul of Cain and at last left in the body of Calvin. Of this he never wrote but one sheet, and now since he was made Doctor repenteth highlie and seeketh to destroy all his poems."[8] These remarks, worn smooth by the constant handling of several gen-

3. *The Complete Works of Thomas De Quincey* (Edinburgh, 1863), X, 104.

4. *Biographia Literaria*, ed. J. C. Metcalf (New York, 1926), p. 198.

5. *Coleridge the Talker*, ed. R. W. Armour and R. F. Howes (Ithaca, 1940), p. 239.

6. *The Life and Letters of John Donne* (New York, 1899), I, 140.

7. *Amenities of Literature* (New York, 1848), II, 364.

8. *Works*, ed. C. H. Herford and P. and E. Simpson (Oxford, 1925), I, 136.

erations of scholars, plus the unmistakable allusion to Queen Elizabeth in Stanza VII as the soul's final resting place, have led writers such as Michael F. Maloney to assert that the poem "unquestionably is born of the mood superimposed by the Essex debacle,"[9] and M. M. Mahood to maintain that "this obscure poem probably contains many now unintelligible covert slurs upon the Queen and her ministers."[10] The temptation to see a contemporary political allegory in the poem is great, for it is filled with references to tyranny, treason, and the rise and fall of princes. Yet, as W. A. Murray has pointed out,[11] it is possible to argue that the events of 1601 which culminated in the execution of Essex may simply have moved Donne to a consideration of ethical and historical questions of far more concern to him than the flicker and flare of individual power struggles in Elizabeth's court.

There are those, for instance, like C. M. Coffin who have seen the poem as an incomplete expression of Donne's profound disillusion with the vision of an orderly universe in which "Great Destiny, the Commissary of God," would preserve "the deathlesse soule" without the slightest regard for the value of its habitation.[12] Bredvold was another student of the poem who saw in it a reflection of Donne's contact with a "skeptical and relativist philosophy."[13] Yet Murray has argued that the cynical tone of the poem does not reveal a lack of faith, but reveals instead an "acute . . . realization of the supreme contrast between the decisions made by fallen man and that made by Christ, the infinity of right choice."[14] Maintaining that the Pythagorean doctrine in the poem is "little more than an ingenious device" which enables Donne to move easily from episode to episode, Murray believes that the poem was planned as "an allegory of the development of good and evil in mankind."

While Murray's view of the poem seems to be the richest so

9. *John Donne: His Flight from Medievalism* (Urbana, 1944), p. 26.
10. *Poetry and Humanism* (London, 1950), p. 106.
11. "What Was the Soul of the Apple?" *RES*, n. s., X (1959), 154.
12. *John Donne and the New Philosophy* (New York, 1937), p. 56.
13. "The Naturalism of Donne in Relation to Some Renaissance Traditions," *JEGP*, XXII (1923), 476.
14. Murray, *op. cit.*, p. 154.

far offered by those who have written on it, there remain elements in *The Progress of the Soul* that have not yet been sufficiently analyzed: the concepts of the *translatio emperii* and *translatio studii*, concepts which embody an idea of human history as a westward movement of empire and civilization or humane learning from one epoch and country to another epoch and country, a movement normally originating in the East and moving westward across the globe to Europe.

The richness of the history of these concepts and (as this essay will attempt to demonstrate) their ironical relevance to *The Progress of the Soul* can be suggested by a brief survey of the long series of writers who employed them.[15] Ovid, apparently one of the first to use the concepts, glorifies Rome by giving to it—through the concept of the translation of power and learning—all the virtues of past civilizations, and he prophesies that Rome "shall by changing propagate,/ And give the World an head."[16] In *Cligès*, Chrétien de Troyes used the concepts to establish the glory of France when he argued that the "preeminence in chivalry and learning" which "once belonged to Greece" and "passed to Rome" had now come to France.[17] Tracing the pedigree of empire from Ninus the Assyrian down to the Roman conquest of the world, Dante glorifies his country in his *Monarchia*.[18] In 1405 the concepts appear in Jean Gerson's attempt to trace the translation of man's wisdom and knowledge from Adam through the Egyptians, the Greeks, the Romans down to the French savants in Paris.[19] The concepts had appeal to medieval writers who were developing a historical perspective informed by Christian theology, and the list of such writers who employed the concepts in their works is impressive: Vincent de Beauvais (*Speculum historiale*), Jean de

15. For a detailed account of the *translatio* tradition, see my forthcoming article in *SP*, "Adam's Tragic Vision in *Paradise Lost*."

16. *Ovid's Metamorphosis Englished*, trans. George Sandys (6th. ed.; London, 1669), pp. 305-6.

17. *Cligès*, ed. W. Foerster (Halle, 1884), p. 1.

18. *Monarchy*, ed. and trans. Donald Nicholl (New York, 1954), pp. 48-51.

19. See Etienne Gilson, *La Philosophie au moyen âge* (Payot, 1947), p. 194.

Galles (*Grandes chroniques du royaume de France*), Otto of Freising (*Duae urbes*), Paulus Orosius (*Historiarum libris septem adversus paganos*), and Thomas d'Irlande (*De tribus sensibus sacrae scripturae*).

The concepts seem to have retained their appeal in the Elizabethan period, for at least two of Donne's contemporaries, Spenser and Ralegh, used the concepts in their writings. Spenser's translation of the *Antiquez de Rome*, for instance, carries over Du Bellay's use of the *translatio studii* in the lines where Rome is described as the repository of all that was discovered and known in Egypt, Africa, and Asia. Adopting what may have been a Biblical version of the *translatio emperii* (Daniel vii.4-8), Spenser, in the *Ruines of Time*, pays an extravagant compliment to the House of Dudley as he traces the course of both empire and learning from the "Assyrian Lyoness" to the "Persian Beares" to the "Grecian Libbard" to the "great seven-headed beast" to "Verlame."[20] In the *Faerie Queene*, Book II, Canto IX, Spenser glorifies Queen Elizabeth by using the *translatio* concepts in Britomart's version of what appears to be the history of England.[21] In his history of the world, Ralegh traced "civility" and "magnificence" to their apotheosis in Rome; and, later in this work, dramatically inverting the traditionally honorific intent of the *translatio* concepts, he ironically traced the progress of depravity (he was writing specifically about child sacrifice) from Rhodes to Crete to Carthage, observing that the devil, not being "content to destroy the souls of many nations in Europe, Asia, and Africa," had brought under his "fearful servitude the Mexicans, and other people of America."[22] Except, then, for Ralegh's inversion of the original intent of the *translatio emperii* and the *translatio studii*, it seems that they were used to confer honor and glory upon particular cultures or nations or princes. By the time Donne wrote *The Progress of the Soul* the concepts were rich with honorific associations.

20. *The Works of Edmund Spenser*, ed. Greenlaw *et al.* (Baltimore, 1947), II, 38, 152. 21. Spenser, III, 134-35.
22. *The Works of Sir Walter Ralegh*, ed. Oldys and Birch (Oxford, 1829), II, 221-22; IV, 693. See also his discussion of the translation of "art and civility" from the East "into those parts of neighboring Asia and Judea," III, 187.

The ironic possibilities inherent in an inversion of the *translatio* concepts would have had great appeal to Donne; and, like Ralegh before him, he apparently planned to invert the honorific design of the concepts in order to fashion a keenly satiric commentary on the pretensions of the English court, pretensions whose magnitude became clearer when viewed through the ironic perspective afforded by a knowledge of the *translatio* concepts.[23] The poem traces the progress of a soul from an apple through a series of birds and beasts to Themech, "sister and wife to Caine." The evidence the poem affords indicates that the soul's ultimate destiny is the English court which, according to the terms of the *translatio* concepts, should have been the repository of western civilization. Yet, as the poem makes clear, although the soul ascends biologically—moving from plant to animal to man—it descends spiritually and morally as it progresses; it moves from one host to another carrying all the residue of immorality to which it has been previously exposed.

The progressive diminution of ancient glory—of prowess and *humanitas*—is outlined by Donne in his first stanza in which he announces his purpose to draw the history of the "great world" from "infant morn, through manly noone" to "aged evening," examining, as he progresses, a series of civilizations described as "the gold Chaldee, silver Persian, Greek brasse,"

---

23. Other writers since Donne's time who sensed the ironic possibilities inherent in an inversion of the honorific tradition of the *translatio* concepts were Pierre Davity who, perhaps thinking in terms of a *translatio tyrannidis*, traced in *The Estates, Empires, and Principallities of the World* (trans. E. Grimstone, London, 1615, p. xiii) the course of empire from "mighty Nimrod," the prototype of the tyrant, through "Darius of Media," to Alexander's Greece to Rome; Alexander Pope, who used the concepts both to confer honor on his nation's culture (in the *Essay on Criticism*) and to express his fears that this culture was being debased by a rout of ignorant and insensitive men (see Aubrey Williams, *Pope's Dunciad*, London, 1955, pp. 42-46; and *Pastoral Poetry & An Essay on Criticism*, ed. with E. Audra, London, 1961, pp. 231-32, 320); Matthew Arnold, in much of whose work the concepts seem implicit as he ironically traced nineteenth-century England's rise to power and grandeur; and T. S. Eliot, who gives these concepts intensely ironic expression in "The Wasteland": "Falling towers/ Jerusalem Athens Alexandria/ Vienna London/ Unreal" (*Collected Poems*, New York, 1934, p. 88).

and "Roman iron."[24] The soul, then, is the vehicle by which Donne could sweep through the history of man, and the Pythagorean doctrine embodied in the soul's progress aids him in making the point that the depravity of one host can be transferred to a subsequent host. While he did not write enough of his poem to depict even the "gold Chaldee" civilization, Donne's intentions, as seen in this first stanza seem clear: the "deathlesse soule" carried with it whatever it "saw," and the things it saw were to be chronicled in the poem, a work that Donne claimed would outlast "Seth's pillars." The soul contained all of human experience; it had seen more than the sun; indeed, it "beganne to bee" before the sun. In the first two stanzas and in Stanza VI the scope of this "dark, heavy poem" was established. Donne wrote that he would "launch at paradise" and "saile towards home":

> The course I there began, shall here be staid,
> Sailes hoised there, stroke here, and anchors laid
> In Thames, which were at Tigrys, and Euphrates waide.[25]

In Stanza VII, Donne proceeds directly to tell us that the "crowne and last straine of my song" will be the depiction of the "great soule which here amongst us now/ Doth dwell," a soul which inhabited the bodies of Luther and Mohammed, a soul which had torn and mended "the wracks of Empire, and late Rome," and had lived "when every great change did come." Nowhere in this stanza—a stanza that apparently has misled commentators like Maloney and Mahood—is there an indication that Donne wished in any way to attack Elizabeth herself, that "hand, and tongue, and brow,/ Which, as the Moone the sea, moves us." What does seem apparent is that the soul, having spanned the history of the human race and having seen the rise and fall of many great civilizations, now, with all this knowledge, resides in the body of Elizabeth. Elizabeth is, in this sense, the repository of history; and thus the deeds done in her court are done in the living presence of all that has gone before

24. *The Poems of John Donne*, ed. H. J. C. Grierson (Oxford, 1912), I, 295; hereafter cited as *Poems*.
25. *Poems*, I, 297.

in man's history. And while Donne never got to that point in his poem where he planned to describe either those deeds or that court, there appears to be, in the stanzas he wrote about the progress of the soul from plant to animal to human, persuasive evidence that he planned to attack vigorously both court and courtier.

The soul leaves the apple and inhabits first a blameless, innocent plant which is "short liv'd" because it is plucked to heal a child's fever. Next it enters a sparrow, takes on the lechery of that bird, and dies in three years because of its intemperate pursuit of love. The soul then inhabits a fish which is swallowed up by an arrogant courtier-like swan ("It mov'd with state, as if to looke upon/ Low things it scorn'd"); and leaving the swan, the soul again inhabits the body of a fish. The fish, snatched away by a sea pie, suffers the fate of many who come to court: borne into the sky by the bird, the fish "exalted is," but "to the exalters good,/ As are by great ones, men which lowly stood." It is raised only "to be the Raisers instrument and food." The bird, tired, floats on the sea with its prey and is swallowed by a whale. Donne chose to follow the soul in the fish, and "keeps no calendar" of the bird's soul; it, he claimed, "lives yet in some great officer." In an obvious figure of the court, Donne described the whale who, like "an officer,"

> Stayes in his court, at his owne net, and there
> All suitors of all sorts themselves enthrall;
> So on his backe lyes this whale wantoning,
> And in his gulfe-like throat, sucks every thing
> That passeth neare. Fish chaseth fish, and all,
> Flyer and follower, in this whirlepool fall. . . .[26]

The whale, however, is not indestructible; though now at his "greatest," like mighty empires and great civilizations, the whale is "to destruction nearest; there's no pause at perfection;/ Greatnesse a period hath, but hath no station." His downfall is plotted by the "flaile-finned Thresher," and the "steel-beak'd Swordfish," two natural adversaries, according to popular belief, of the whale. The fight between the whale

26. *Poems*, I, 308.

and his enemies who "conspir'd against him" depicts a typical court intrigue; outflanked and overwhelmed, the whale becomes a "scoff and prey," and beaten back by the thresher shark, the whale is gored from below by the swordfish, and thus "this tyran dies."[27]

Freed from the body of the whale, the soul takes residence in a mouse who, "sent by envy," crawls up the trunk of an elephant into his brain, "gnawed the life cords there," and is crushed by the elephant when it falls. Thus die mighty princes and their insignificant enemies. The soul moves next to the foetus of a wolf which in time becomes an insatiable killer of Abel's sheep. Only Abel's watchdog prevented the wolf from destroying the flock. The wolf, however, "tooke a course, which since, successfully,/ Great men have often taken, to espie/ The counsels, or to breake the plots of foes."[28] He corrupts the shepherd dog by "embracements of love" and is free to slaughter the sheep. Finally the wolf is killed by a trap, "of which some everywhere Abell had plac'd"; and the soul resides for a brief time in the body of the hybrid wolf-dog, the product of the treacherous union of shepherd dog and wolf. The hybrid cannot for long survive; destroying the sheep he was supposed to guard, he fled; and, "like a spie to both sides false, he perished." Thus ends another little parable of court life.

The last animal the soul visits is an ape who aspires to be the lover of Adam's daughter, Siphatecia. Like a love-smitten courtier, the ape could "make love faces," could "doe the valters sombersalts," could "wooe/ With hoiting gambolls, his owne bones to breake/ To make his mistresse merry." Discovered in an attempt to seduce Siphatecia, the ape is killed by the girl's brother, Tethlemite.

In the poem, the soul's last abode is a human being, The-

27. It is interesting to note that Spenser, in his *Visions of the Worlds Vanitie*, depicts in one episode the destruction of a whale by a swordfish; and, in another episode, depicts the destruction of an elephant by an ant who crawls up the elephant's trunk into his head. These struggles of small animals against great ones are found in Aesop, Pliny, medieval bestiaries, and thus were commonplace in the Elizabethan period. See the *Works of Edmund Spenser, op. cit.*, II, 176, 407.

28. *Poems*, I, 311.

128

mech, "sister and wife to Caine." The soul brings with it "some quality of every past shape" it has experienced. The soul that resides in Themech's body has known "treachery, rapine, deceit and lust." Donne is now ready to begin his history of the human race, a history that, as we have noted, he planned to treat in terms of the *translatio emperii* and the *translatio studii.* But at this point the poem breaks off, and "this sullen Writ,/ Which just so much courts thee, as thou dost it," ends abruptly with the observation that there are no absolute values in the world; all is relative. To prove this point, Donne cites the example of Cain and Seth:

> . . . wonder with mee
> Why plowing, building, ruling and the rest
> Or most of those arts, whence our lives are blest,
> By cursed *Cains* race invented be,
> And blest *Seth* vext us with Astronomie.[29]

Seth's pillars, mentioned in the first stanza of the poem, are appropriately referred to again in its last stanza. These pillars—on which is written the record of man's knowledge—stand as mute ironic guardians over the progress of the soul, a progress which brought the soul into man full of error and sin. Had Donne fulfilled the original plan of the poem, the soul would have ended in Elizabeth, who through the operation of the *translatio* concepts would have been an embodiment of all that man had achieved and all that he had lost. Presiding over her proud and glittering court, a court that, in accordance with the *translatio* concepts, should have been the culmination of western culture, Elizabeth, like Seth's pillars, would have become in the poem a brooding presence reminding us that in spite of the great sweep of man's history and his progress through the world, the same story is re-enacted each day, each year, each epoch: man will be man.

29. *Poems,* I, 315-16.

ANTS ORAS
Professor of English
University of Florida

Darkness Visible - Notes on Milton's
Descriptive Procedures in *Paradise Lost*

RITICAL OPINION, EVEN AT ITS LEAST GENEROUS, has been fairly unanimous in acknowledging the broad epic grandeur, the monumental architectonic effect of *Paradise Lost.* "Breadth," "force," "majesty," "heroic dignity" are expressions constantly recurring in treatments of Milton's epic manner, although it seems typical that Eliot's term "magniloquence" tends to be substituted for them with increasing frequency. Powerful simplicity, somewhat at the expense of semantic subtlety, is what, for instance, B. Rajan finds to be the fundamental quality of his epic style.[1] In considering Milton to have used language broadly rather than subtly, for its large outlines rather than for finer shades of meaning, he does not differ very markedly from F. T. Prince, even though the latter in his influential book on *The Italian Element in Milton's Verse* finds historical justification for what

1. *Paradise Lost and the Seventeenth Century Reader* (Cambridge, 1948), pp. 108 ff.

130

he sometimes calls "elegant variation" and sometimes "pleo-nasm."[2] Odd failures of perceptiveness, blurred meaning, inabil-ity to see and formulate things clearly figure among the defects with which T. S. Eliot,[3] even more emphatically seconded by F. R. Leavis,[4] has charged the poet. These accusations have not remained unanswered, but they typify an attitude that still widely persists. None of the above critics—not even Leavis, de-spite the reservations he makes—has denied the effectiveness of Milton's verse as sound, as verbal music, but the tendency to underrate his precision of thought and vision has been marked for several decades.

One of the expressions criticized by T. S. Eliot is the famous oxymoron "darkness visible" in Milton's description of the gloom of Hell.[5] The descriptive appropriateness of this phrase may not be in any need of further defense at this date. Too many critics, ever since the eighteenth century, have done it better justice than the author of "The Waste Land."[6] Even Vol-taire, while admitting that this paradoxical yoking of opposites might shock the French taste of his time, concedes its sublime aptness.[7] It is questionable, however, whether it has been quite

2. Oxford, 1954. See especially pp. 97 and 122-23.
3. "A Note on the Verse of John Milton," *Essays and Studies by Members of the English Association*, XXI (1936), 32 ff.
4. "Milton's Verse," in *Revaluation* (London, 1959), pp. 42 ff.
5. "Milton," *Proceedings of the British Academy*, XXXIII (1947), 75.
6. Not Bentley, of course. The two Richardsons, whose imaginative approach has recently come in for much well-deserved praise, at this point indulge in one of their more erratic surmises. They consider that the figures seen against the dark background may be visible because they per-haps are "Beings of a Luminous Nature," although they may lack the "Necessary Power to disperse Light." (*Explanatory Notes and Remarks on Milton's Paradise Lost*, by J. Richardson, Father and Son, London, 1734; see note on *PL*, I.62). Such eccentricity is exceptional, however. There is more substance in their suggestion that the fire here "was created on Pur-pose, to Torment the Rebel Angels" (*ibid.*). Commentators have noted the parallel with Job x:22: "A land of thick darkness, as darkness itself; a land of the shadow of death, without any order, and where the light is as darkness." This may well have suggested the phrase to Milton, but his presentation of the scene, while keeping the mystery of it, makes it much more acceptable in terms of human vision.
7. "Essay on Epic Poetry"; see p. 43 in Allen and Clark, *Literary Criticism: Pope to Croce* (New York, 1941).

realized how useful a clue this phrase provides for understanding Milton's descriptive method in Book I of *Paradise Lost*.

"No light, but rather darkness visible"—quite obviously not
the light of God, not "holy light, ofspring of Heav'n first-
born," but still a faint source of vision, that which somewhat
later is referred to as a "glimmering of . . . livid flames," "pale
and dreadful," barely sufficient to reveal the extent and depth
of the darkness by permitting the eye to see something, though
none of it distinctly, is of course what Milton here means. This,
far from being a mere verbal flourish, is in fact an exact render-
ing of a visual impression. Satan, from whose point of view
everything is described, casting his "baleful eyes" around at his
new environment, at first, still unaccustomed to the gloom, perceives only a "dismal Situation waste and wilde," with flames
which, though visible themselves, appear to show nothing. But
gradually, as his eyes adjust themselves to the darkness—exactly
in the way one "gets one's night sight"—he sees more: "sights
of woe, Regions of sorrow, doleful shades." The language here,
like the observer's eye, proceeds from the general to the particular. The situation at first glance is merely "dismal"—a word
suggesting a purely emotional reaction; then, more concretely,
it seems "waste and wilde"—an empty wilderness, "a Dungeon
horrible"—apparently of enclosed space. Thereupon some details, however indefinite, begin to emerge: "sights of woe"—a
multiplicity of sights, not just a monotonous expanse of darkness; "regions of sorrow," and within these regions vague suggestions of individual shapes, "doleful shades," a few lines later
identified as "the companions of his fall." Among these Satan
then discerns, and recognizes, the nearest of them, "weltring by
his side," Beëlzebub.

The angle of vision, as so often in Milton, is quite definite
here. We are made to follow the movements of Satan's eye,
first towards the distance, "as far as Angels kenn," then nearer,
until his glance fixes itself on the immediate foreground. The
poet is careful not to show us much. Only a few details are
clearly specified: Satan's eyes, the vast furnace of flames, and, at
the very end of the paragraph, the "weltring" movement of
Beëlzebub. The rest is varying degrees of darkness, with mere

132

ghosts of shapes, much as in a Rembrandt painting. Even the meanings sometimes are ghosts of meanings: "doleful shades" might easily be interpreted as "melancholy shadows," "mournful darkness," although it suggests more than that.[8] It is with the slightest of verbal touches that much of the canvas is filled, but every touch tells. The procedure here is "realistic," if one wants to use the word: this is the way one begins to see at night; yet it also preserves the terror of the unknown, which Milton clearly wishes to evoke. Darkness, by being made only very partly visible, reveals its supernatural vastness: what is being described is the indescribable.

Describing the indescribable is precisely the task Milton has set himself in his portrayal of the nether regions. Any excess of specific detail would have interfered with the atmosphere of mystery, yet enough had to be provided to feed and stimulate the reader's imagination.

In his method of pursuing this aim Milton displays tact and skill. Without showing us much of the actual sights he con-

8. Characteristic examples of the failure to see such niceties in Milton's language occur in Rajan, e.g., pp. 112-13, where the passage "the dire event That with sad overthrow and foul defeat Hath lost us Heav'n" meets with the following comment: "It would make no difference to the meaning if we had 'sad event,' 'foul overthrow,' and 'dire defeat,' or 'foul event,' 'dire overthrow,' and 'sad defeat,' or any of the other possible combinations." There is gradation in the increasing intensity of meaning from "sad overthrow" to "foul defeat"; "foul" is clearly the most intense, as well as psychologically the most significant, of these epithets: it is less the terror than the damage to their pride that affects the chief leaders of the rebels. Note also the precise arrangement of meanings in the nouns. "Event" is a very general term; "overthrow" suggests not only defeat in battle but the actual throwing of the rebel forces over the brink of heaven into the abyss; "foul defeat" sums up the resulting ignominious situation.

The ambivalence of "doleful shades," combining two convergent meanings in impressive concentration, may serve as an instance of what Mrs. MacCaffrey calls "a vocabulary internally cooperative rather than rebellious," serving "a basic simplicity of vision" (*Paradise Lost as "Myth*," Cambridge, Mass., 1959, p. 106). "Subtle simplicity," "subtly shaded unity of vision" would perhaps have been more appropriate definitions of such diction. For some striking examples of such a use of vocabulary see also the present writer's *Notes on Some Miltonic Usages* (Tartu, 1938), especially pp. 26-27. This characteristic places Milton in direct opposition to the "divergent" ambivalences of many meanings in Donne and his followers.

stantly makes us feel that we are seeing or at least sensing them. For the most part he suggests rather than depicts, but at strategic intervals he introduces vivid if minimal sensory detail, until towards the end of Book I we feel we know the scene: a perfect illusion has been created.

What are we told about Satan's appearance? At first only that he is "rowling in the fiery Gulfe," throwing round his "baleful eyes" in the darkness (I.51, 56). Another 145 lines, mostly of dialogue powerfully expressing Satan's state of mind, have to be read before we are shown more of him, and even then a bare minimum in the way of direct description: his head, "up-lift above the waves," his eyes "that sparkling blaz'd,"[9] his "other Parts"—a characteristically unspecific phrase—"Prone on the Flood, extended long and large," "floating many a rood," as huge as the most frightening monsters of ancient and more recent legendry and folklore—these latter enumerated, and partly described, in chronological order. The close relevance of the similes here, as also elsewhere in the epic, the manner in which they help us to add to the picture, has been dealt with by a number of critics, notably by James Whaler.[10] Actually the only

9. One wonders at T. S. Eliot's objections to this phrase. He finds he is "not happy about eyes that both blaze and sparkle, unless Milton meant us to imagine a roaring fire ejecting sparks: and that is too fiery for even supernatural eyes" ("Milton," p. 75). Why "roaring"? By the insidious use of this participle Eliot completely changes the picture, reducing it to an absurdity of which there is no suggestion in Milton.

Eliot regards Milton's blindness as the crucial factor to be considered in examining the nature of his poetry. It is possible to agree with him without drawing the same conclusions. Does blindness, when incurred in later life, necessarily blur one's mental vision, as Eliot seems to assume? Is it not at least equally likely to have the effect of making certain things stand out more definitely while causing others to recede? "Vision recollected in blindness," like Wordsworth's "emotion recollected in tranquillity," might well result in purging one's memory of inessentials, adding to the vividness of matters felt to be important. Light and shade in particular are likely to be remembered with special intensity and to be presented with more than usual distinctness. Anything casual would tend to have faded from the mind. This seems to have happened to Milton, helping, rather than impairing, the strength and monumentality of his epic vision.

10. James Whaler, "The Miltonic Simile," *PMLA*, XLVI (1931), 1034-74. See also the same author's "The Compounding and Distribution

distinctly visualizable feature described here is the appearance of Satan's eyes, those glowing spots in the gloom that were the first detail noted about him; apart from this, all that is explicitly indicated is his position, his floating movement, and his size.

Some thirty lines later we are told a little more. We learn that "Forthwith upright he rears from off the pool His mighty Stature" (221-22);

> Then with expanded wings he stears his flight
> Aloft, incumbent on the dusky Air
> That felt unusual weight, till on dry Land
> He lights. . . .   (225-28)

We hear what he does but the only addition to our knowledge of his physique is that he has wings, which are expanded, and that he is of "unusual weight."

Another 55 lines of dialogue, in the course of which Satan's emotional violence is channeled into incipient military planning, appropriately take us to a passage describing his military equipment, his "ponderous shield Ethereal temper, massy, large and round, Behind him cast," and his enormous spear. This is firm delineation, but it still only forms a point of departure for similes vastly enhancing the impression as well as indirectly contributing to its precision without the poet's committing himself to much explicit statement. A gigantic, warlike figure is emerging, we are beginning to see its outlines, but still only as a looming shape of somber splendor and might. Not until line 589—over 300 lines later—are we given anything like a portrait of the Prince of Darkness, in this instance full face, but here too the concrete visual features are few. He stands "like a Towr," "proudly eminent" above the others, still retaining

---

of Similes in Paradise Lost," *MP*, XXVIII (1931), 1313-27. Also, "Animal Similes in Paradise Lost," *PMLA*, XLVII (1932), 534-53. T. S. Eliot, possibly unaware of Whaler's studies, sees mainly a digression in the last simile of this series: "We *nearly* forget Satan in attending to the story of the whale; Milton recalls us just in time." This is the sort of thing Homer often does; Milton is much more careful in weaving his threads, frequently almost invisible ones, so as in the final result to make our mind form a coherent picture.

some of his "original brightness," but with "th' excess Of Glory obscur'd":

> his face
> Deep scars of Thunder had intrencht, and care
> Sat on his faded cheek, but under Browes
> Of dauntless courage, and considerate Pride
> Waiting revenge: cruel his eye, but cast
> Signs of remorse and passion to behold
> The fellows of his crime. . . .   (600-606)

This is an impressive portrait but largely a psychological rather than a physical one. Again similes clustering around this picture enlarge and intensify the effect but the concrete nucleus directly relating what is seen is slight.

The above are all the physical details concerning Satan that Milton provides in Book I. Trait after trait, never much at a time, although in increasing amounts, and always at points important for the action, has been produced, gradually rounding off the image of Satan until we feel we see him. This feeling—largely illusory, and caused as much by the similes radiating from concrete descriptive centers as by the descriptions themselves—is of course all that was needed for Milton's purposes. With remarkable economy the reader's imagination has been made to work overtime. The nebula of ominous mystery enveloping the concrete core has not been disturbed.

It needs to be stressed that this method is by no means standard procedure with Milton. He has other, far more strictly pictorial ways of portrayal when these suit him, even in some of his later presentations of Satan, where no impression of unearthly, awe-inspiring grandeur is intended, for instance, in the picture he draws of the dread Soldan finding it convenient to disguise himself as a "stripling Cherube" (III.636-44). The "flowing haire" playing in curls on either cheek, the coronet on the curly head, the wings "of many a colourd plume sprinkl'd with Gold," the habit "fit for speed succinct," the silver wand he holds might have come straight from an Italian quattrocentist's painting, providing a sharply ironical contrast to the Michelangelesque awesomeness of the Arch-Enemy as seen previously. Besides, this is a daylight portrait:[11] it is on the sun that Satan meets Uriel who is taken by his disguise. A chiaroscuro technique would have been out of place here.

What are we shown of the appearance of Hell? In Book I, for quite a while, only a few though telling details, again mostly in brief passages affording little more than glimpses. Marjorie Nicolson[12] has demonstrated at some length the close resemblance of the scene, viewed as a whole, to the volcanic area of the Phlegraean fields near Naples, which Milton must have seen during his Italian journey. But while the poet's imagination is certainly not working at random, his method remains a piecemeal one, as in the case of Satan. Right until the orderly march of the infernal forces, after the initial anxiety has somewhat subsided, we get only fragments of description as the action seems to demand them. Similes help all along. Together with other hints here and there, they weave a close net of suggestive associations, but the total effect is one of darkness with only some flickers of dubious light enabling us to envisage something of the background. Like Satan's, our eyesight seems to be working its way through the gloom. Indeed, for some time we see everything through the eyes of Satan: not only in that early passage already dealt with where the stunned leader of the fallen forces tries to survey the place of their fall but also later, when he is beginning to recover from his shock and, still dimly, to form plans for action. It is with Satan that we notice some dry land in the distance:

> Seest thou yon dreary Plain, forlorn and wilde,
> The seat of desolation, voyd of light,
> Save what the glimmering of these livid flames
> Casts pale and dreadful? Thither let us tend
> From off the tossing of these fiery waves. . . .   (180-84)

11. See the carefully differentiated "daylight" and "night" styles in "L'Allegro" and "Il Penseroso": the former abounding in clearly outlined detail, the latter toning visual matters down, often by abstract circumlocution, and only here and there, at well-selected points, enabling the mind's eye to focus. Note also the abandonment of this approach in the early morning section of "Il Penseroso."

12. "Milton's Hell and the Phlegraean Fields," *University of Toronto Quarterly*, VII (1938), 500-513.

The picture seems fuller than before. Actually, it is essentially only a more compact reiteration, in partly different terms, of features presented earlier in the poem, reinforcing impressions already gained. The restless tossing of the fiery lake, the vague light are not new. The only new details are the mention of a dry plain beyond the flaming waves and of the pale, livid coloring of the flames.

As Satan raises himself from the pool of fire, we again are shown what he sees immediately before him—still only the flames, but now in sharp outline, precisely as he would perceive them, forcing his way through the fiery barrier. Before the impact of his flight the flames, driven backwards, "slope their pointing spires, & rowld In billows, leave i' th' midst a horrid Vale" (221-23). As he steps onto the firm ground of the plain, we are presented with a formidable vision of earthquakes and volcanic eruptions but—we are hardly aware of the device—only in a simile, the matter of which is not immediately transferable to the actual scene: the only explicitly stated fact concerning the latter is that the soil burns "with solid, as the Lake with liquid fire" (229). Later on Milton tells us that there is indeed a volcano nearby, but for the time being the simile in fact takes us out of Hell into terrestrial surroundings, providing not the thing itself but its analogue.

Always in connection with some action, item by item, at sizeable intervals, in nearly all instances in a manner suggesting that what is shown is noticed in that particular fashion by the characters of the poem, we learn further that the soil of Hell is of "burning Marle" and brimstone; that Hell is "vaulted with Fire"; that its echoing space is "hollow," covered by a "Cope," a "Concave," and filled with "upper, nether, and surrounding Fires." Moving along with Satan, and at some points with his followers, we quite as gradually as themselves form a notion of what Hell looks like, without in fact seeing much. We explore the darkness as they do, making it yield some of its mysteries, with greater mysteries remaining unseen. Milton here proves himself a master of a "point of view" technique, the slow unfolding of a situation as it presents itself to the eyes and minds of his *dramatis personae*. Assuming their identity, as it were, we see only what they see, and we see what they see in the way they see it.

So far, only visual matters have been discussed. But the other senses, especially the ear, also play an important part in this process of gradual realization. Auditory impressions—less definite and hence more mysterious than visual ones—likewise contribute to our notion of the physical nature of Hell. That Hell has a vault, a concave roof separating it from the rest of the universe and turning it into an immense cavern cannot be established by the eye unable to penetrate far enough into the darkness: its shape is ascertained only by the ear listening to the echoes rebounding from its cope: "He call'd so loud, that all the hollow Deep Of Hell resounded" (314-15); "A shout that tore Hells Concave" (542-43). It goes without saying that Milton's exceptional skill in suggesting aural impressions by the actual phonetic structure of his verse intensifies such perceptions of space through reverberant sound.

The manner in which the followers of Satan are presented shows the same features: the initial vagueness, the gradually sharpening focus, the piecemeal method, the "point of view" approach revealing them as they appear to Satan, the technique of suggestive illusion working through similes. Only "doleful shades" at first, soon identified as "the companions of his fall," they fade out of the field of vision for over 200 lines until their "great Sultan," about to address them in a rousing speech, faces the legions scattered before him in the abyss, "intrans't, Thick as Autumnal Leaves, . . . Abject and lost, . . . covering the Flood Under amazement of their hideous change" (299-313), but at his call springing up "upon the wing," like soldiers who have been forgetful of their duty. Hovering between fires surrounding them from all directions, at his signal "down they light On the firm brimstone, and fill all the Plain" (344-45). The leaders of their units, "squadrons and bands," in which they remain grouped even in their fall, hasten to meet "their great Commander": "Godlike shapes and forms Excelling human, Princely Dignities, And Powers that earst in Heaven sat on Thrones" (358-60).

Such, reduced to its meager core of positive information, is what we are shown of the fallen angels up to this point—astonishingly little if compared with the vividness of the impression we have of them. The next pages, on the other hand, dwell upon them with a wealth of descriptive detail, but of detail applicable to them only as a projection into the future—the carefully elaborated pageant of the heathen deities which they are to become after the fall of Adam and Eve. Perusing this catalogue the mind gets so crowded with absorbing matter that Milton's sleight of hand, his evasion of portraying the routed forces as they are at the moment, for most readers doubtless passes unperceived. When some description of the actual scene follows immediately after, the transition from the future to the present is hardly noticeable.

The similes—an array of them found nowhere else in Milton in such abundance and magnificence—all present matter less foreign to the reader than the, strictly speaking, unimaginable world of Hell. *Parvis componens magna*—a Virgilian phrase which he often inserts in its Englished form—the poet substitutes the more or less describable for that which cannot be fully envisioned. Opening vistas of fable, romance, and distant historical events, he by indirection lends some semblance of familiarity to the totally unfamiliar. Where the similes occur in series, as they frequently do, his prevalent method is to move from the more remote towards that which is nearer in time and space and hence easier to imagine, without, however, discarding the veil of strangeness: here too, then, a movement from the nebulous, dark, and alien towards sharper focus. Note, for instance, the string of similes brought in to illustrate the vastness of Satan. He is likened to the ancient Titans and Giants, first mentioned as mere categories, than as individuals—Briareus and Typhon; and then to the biblical Leviathan: a Leviathan, however, made less remote by being placed in Norwegian waters as a monstrous whale of a sort not infrequently figuring in contemporary sailors' tales. Trying to find analogues for the inconceivable might of the infernal legions, Milton again starts with classical antiquity, to proceed from there to stories of medieval Britain, and from the British Middle Ages to the Renaissance lore of Boiardo's, Ariosto's, and Tasso's Italy, well

140

known to the learned, and also to many of the less learned, of his time. The fascination of these wide and varied perspectives is such that we forget to ask for that which the poem so sparingly supplies, direct description of the matter in hand. Our horizon seems to be widening and filling—with suggestions, allusions, analogues, not with hard facts; but the suggestions and parallels, being apt, converge to create a feeling of full realization of that which is so cunningly shown and not shown: the illusion of our actually witnessing supernatural reality is achieved.

In an essay on "Syntax and Music in 'Paradise Lost' "[13] Donald Davie arrives at the conclusion that Milton's language— in accordance with the general nature of the epic as Davie sees it—mostly lacks that particular quality which makes us ask, "What next?"—in other words, that it lacks suspense. His contentions concerning the language of the poem have, it seems to me, been quite effectively disposed of by Christopher Ricks in his recent study of *Milton's Grand Style*.[14] The more inclusive assertion that Milton's narrative manner as a whole is deficient in suspense can, I believe, be met by considering what has been stated in the present essay. Whatever Milton may be doing elsewhere, in Book I of *Paradise Lost* his descriptive method is of a kind to make us constantly ask precisely the question "What next?" This technique of gradual penetration into a world of darkness, made slowly but never completely visible, of vague, searching beams of light falling fitfully, and always in combination with dramatic action, revealing more and more of the secrets of that world, is in its own way as suspenseful as that of Sophocles in *Oedipus Rex*.

Present-day writers of fiction may not find these methods to be new, but they were by no means generally accepted narrative procedure in Renaissance England, which in its epic technique still remained strongly influenced by Spenser. However greatly Milton may have revered that "better teacher than

13. In *The Living Milton*, ed. F. Kermode, pp. 70-84.
14. (Oxford, 1963); see especially pp. 40 ff. The author could have found much additional support for his statements from Gustav Hübener, *Die stilistische Spannung in "Paradise Lost"* (Halle, 1913).

Aquinas or Scotus," he certainly does not tell his story in quite his way. Indeed, the contrast is glaring. Spenser, almost unaware of the existence of visual perspective, tends to present his descriptions tapestry-fashion, with much detail but seldom with any three-dimensional coordination. The forward pressure is slight. In *The Faerie Queene* we rarely, except at some points of narrative climax, feel induced to ask, "What comes next?" That which is immediately before us is presented *con amore*, usually in a separate stanza or a series of a few stanzas, to be replaced by something else, depicted with equal care and skill to make us linger upon it rather than rush ahead. From this leisurely world the tension of urgent suspense is almost entirely absent. Instead of being stimulated to question and explore we are eased along on waves of two-dimensional vision. Chiaroscuro effects do delight us but there seldom seem to be any darknesses—except sometimes of allegorical meaning—to be anxiously penetrated. Spenser is lavish with only a minimum of dramatic organization, whereas Milton, helped by the irresistible progress of his powerful verse, takes us through areas of deliberately created, tantalizing gloom.

It has already been suggested that this strenuously exploratory attitude is not the only one Milton created in his readers. He is quite capable of full, straightforward description of a more static kind, for instance, in the first picture he draws of Paradise in Book IV. Yet even here we get a definite coordinating point of view, for we see Paradise through the eyes of the intruder as he surveys it, and we see it in the round, as the details of the panorama gradually disclose themselves to the searching eye: at the first glance, the general outlines, then individual features, first the nearer ones, then, point by point, those in the farther distance. This, of course, is daylight scenery, and consequently it is firmly and clearly delineated, but, especially if we compare it with Spenser, we find an element of dramatic suspense in it: the suspense of the observer who is trying to discover a definite objective, in this instance, the exact location of the seat of newly created Man.

In an earlier paper, and in a very different context, I have had occasion to liken Spenser's method of pictorial presentation

142

to that of much medieval art,[15] which, for all its allegorical propensities, still tended to concentrate on the immediate foreground, depicting it meticulously and with loving flourishes, but innocent of perspective. Milton, on the other hand, seemed to me like Rembrandt, illuminating only essentials and leaving the rest in twilight or darkness, perhaps impenetrable but hauntingly alive. I ought to have added that this does not apply to all of Milton's epic poetry, even in *Paradise Lost*. Mario Praz has found Milton to resemble Poussin,[16] and I agree with him that this is frequently true, although the points of resemblance I would emphasize are different, and although I should have preferred to substitute for the name of Poussin that of another contemporary, Claude Lorrain, that master not only of wide, stylized vistas but of mysterious illumination. For all their differences, Rembrandt and Poussin—as well as Claude Lorrain—share a marked insistence on definiteness in the angle of vision they choose. Placing everything in perspective, they love to suggest distance and depth, much as Milton does by the different means of his verbal art. He may never have seen any Poussin, Claude Lorrain, or Rembrandt but the fact of his affinity with these close contemporaries should be difficult to deny. The poet, like the painters, looks beyond the immediate; behind the foreground, there are depths of background to be searched and explored, obscurities to be penetrated, and, sometimes, areas of darkness to be brought to life and made strangely visible.

15. "Spenser and Milton: Some Parallels and Contrasts in the Handling of Sound," in *Sound and Poetry*, ed. N. Frye (New York, 1957); see particularly pp. 131-32.
16. "Milton and Poussin," in *Seventeenth Century Studies Presented to Sir Herbert Grierson* (Oxford, 1938), pp. 192-210.

R. S. CRANE
Professor Emeritus of English
University of Chicago

Notes on the Organization of Locke's *Essay*

N A WELL-KNOWN LETTER TO ANTHONY COL-
lins, Locke congratulated his correspondent
on his "comprehensive knowledge" of the
Essay Concerning Human Understanding.
You do not, he said, "stick in the incidents,
which I find many people do; which whether
true or false make nothing to the main design of the *Essay*; that
lies in a little compass."[1] The "main design of the *Essay*" is my
subject here—or rather a particular aspect of it, of greater interest perhaps to literary than to philosophic students of Locke's
philosophy, which has, so far as I am aware, escaped notice. Specifically, I want, first, to call attention to the character of the
basic analogy—or unifying "metaphor" in the sense recently

1. Quoted by A. C. Fraser in his edition of the *Essay* (2 vols., Oxford,
1894), I, liv. All my references to the *Essay* are to the text of this edition,
which I cite by book, chapter, and section and, in parenthesis, volume
and page.

given to that word by Professor M. H. Abrams[2]—in terms of which Locke appears to conceive of the understanding and its powers and operations and, second, to consider the extent to which this analogy serves to direct the movement of his argument through the four Books into which the *Essay* is divided.

If my conjectures on these points are at all valid, they may perhaps help to implant some doubts about a view of Locke which one still encounters frequently in the writings of literary students of eighteenth- and early nineteenth-century ideas (I confess that I once taught it, undoubtingly, to my classes): namely, that he was typically a philosopher for whom the sources of human knowledge are all external to the mind in sense-experience and the mind itself a passive recipient of impressions from without or at most a mechanical manipulator of the simple ideas it has derived from these. We owe this view in large measure, I suspect, to the propaganda of those Romantic poets and philosophers, including Blake, Coleridge, and Carlyle, who were quite naturally intent on emphasizing the radical contrast between their conceptions of the mind's relation to experience and of the nature and extent of its autonomous activity and the conception they found in Locke; and I should not want to argue that from their point of view they were wrong. The effect, however, has been to blur our eyes to a number of things in the method of the *Essay Concerning Human Understanding*, as Locke himself appears to have conceived it, which an adequate historical interpretation of that work ought surely, it would seem, to take into account.

☆　☆　☆

To admiring contemporaries the explanation of the change which Locke effected in the philosophical fashions of the time seemed simple enough. "Such a Multitude of Reasoners having written the Romance of the Soul," said Voltaire in 1733, "a Sage at last arose, who gave, with an Air of the greatest Modesty, the History of it."[3] The formula, indeed, was one which

2. *The Mirror and the Lamp* (New York, 1953), esp. pp. 48 ff., 57 ff.
3. *Letters Concerning the English Nation* (London, 1733), p. 98. For the French text of 1734, see *Voltaire: Lettres philosophiques*, ed. Gustave Lanson (Paris, 1909), p. 168.

Locke himself had authorized in the *Essay*: his, he declared, was a "historical, plain method";[4] and he characterized the account of simple ideas given in Book II as "a short, and, I think, true *history of the first beginnings of human knowledge;—* whence the mind has its first objects; and by what steps it makes its progress to the laying in and storing up those ideas, out of which is to be framed all the knowledge it is capable of: wherein I must appeal to experience and observation whether I am in the right: the best way to come to truth being to examine things as really they are, and not to conclude they are, as we fancy of ourselves, or have been taught by others to imagine."[5]

The appropriateness of this as a description of one aspect of Locke's method, in opposition to the demonstrative procedures of the seventeenth-century writers against whom he was in revolt, is evident. The *Essay* was clearly a "history" of the soul in the sense that its analysis, unlike that of Descartes, for example, involved a constant preoccupation with temporal sequences. When we look, however, for the reason of this fact, we find, it in a fundamental conception of the subject-matter of his philosophy of which the word "history" gives only a partial idea. The conception rests upon an analogy of the human mind to the world of physical things. As motion is to the body, Locke tells us in the first chapter of his second Book, so is thinking or the perception of ideas to the soul; it is not as the Cartesians have maintained, the essence of the soul, but one of its operations;[6] and as such it is to be understood by means of the same terms we may appropriately use in the consideration of physical activity; motion and thinking being merely the two modes in which the idea of action occurs in our minds.[7] Thus with respect to both motion and thought we may say that they are things which have their existence in succession: both consist in "a continued train of succession"; concerning their diversity, therefore, there can be no question, because "each perishing the moment it begins, they cannot exist in different times, or in different places, as permanent beings can at different times exist

4. Introduction, sec. 2 (I, 27).   5. II.xi.15 (I, 211).
6. II.i.10 (I, 128).   7. II.xxi.4, 8 (I, 311-12, 315).

in distant places; and therefore no motion or thought, considered as at different times, can be the same, each part thereof having a different beginning of existence."[8] Again, with respect to both motion and thought, we may speak of the powers, whether active or passive or both, which are manifest in the changes they either effect or receive;[9] and we may likewise, finally, building on the fundamental idea of powers, consider both motion and thought in terms of the cause and effect relations involved in their production, taking "cause" in this connection as that which makes any other thing begin to be, and "effect" as that which had its beginning from some other thing.[10]

Such is the basic analogy which permits Locke to give a systematic "history" of human knowledge as something that comes to be, in a temporal and causal succession, as a result of the powers with which God has endowed the human mind. But things may come to be, he explains in his chapter on cause and effect relations, in several distinguishable ways. They may come to be by creation, as when "the thing is wholly made new, so that no part thereof did ever exist before; as when a new particle of matter doth begin to exist, *in rerum natura*, which had before no being." Or they may come to be by generation: this occurs when "a thing is made up of particles, which did all of them before exist; but that very thing, so constituted of pre-existing particles, which, considered all together, make up such a collection of simple ideas, had not any existence before, as this man, this egg, rose, or cherry, &c." Or things may come into existence in still a third way: "When the cause is extrinsical, and the effect produced by a sensible separation, or juxtaposition of discernible parts, we call it *making*; and such are all artificial things."[11] Now it requires but a slight acquaintance with the vocabulary of Locke throughout the *Essay* to realize which one, of these three ways by which things may come to be, seemed to him the analogy most proper for an inquiry into the "original" of our knowledge. The mind is invariably represented, in his pages, as behaving like a workman or artist; its

8. II.xxvii.3 (I, 441).   9. II.xxi.2 (I, 309-10).
10. II.xxvi.2 (I, 434).   11. II.xxvi.2 (I, 434-35).

characteristic activities are constantly described by such verbs as "make," "frame," "produce," "fashion," "put parts together," "form," "juxtapose," "combine"; one of his fundamental questions is which of our ideas are, and which are not, "the workmanship of the understanding." And in at least two passages the analogy is given explicit statement in a parallel between the limitations of the mind working with its ideas and the limitations of a workman dealing with material objects: "The dominion of man, in this little world of his own understanding being," in the words of the first passage, "muchwhat the same as it is in the great world of visible things; wherein his power, however managed by art and skill, reaches no farther than to compound and divide the materials that are made to his hand; but can do nothing towards the making the least particle of new matter, or destroying one atom of what is already in being."[12]

In the light of this choice of fundamental analogy we can perhaps more easily understand the traits of Locke's procedure in the *Essay* which seemed most original and important to his contemporaries. If human knowledge is the product of an activity of making, the "extrinsical" cause of the change can be none other than the mind or understanding or reason (in the larger sense of the word) conceived of as a power or collection of powers distinct from the materials with which it operates but limited in its operations by the character of these materials as acquired by it in the process of its activity. The materials, broadly speaking, are "ideas," in the sense of whatever are the objects before the understanding when it is engaged in thinking, and, along with ideas, language as the medium of their expression. Most strictly speaking, the materials out of which the mind fashions its knowledge are ultimately the simple ideas it acquires by experience, the uncompounded appearances, as Locke describes them, which the mind can neither make nor destroy and which have their origin either in sensation, as the effects in the mind of qualities possessed or apparently possessed by external material things, or in reflection, as

12. II.ii.2 (I, 145); cf. II.xii.1 (I, 213-14).

148

the effects of our observation of the activities of our own minds: "These two are the fountains of knowledge, from whence all the ideas we have, or can naturally have, do spring."[13]

The major terms and distinctions by which Locke's account of the "original" of our knowledge is constructed fall into two classes according to the different relations they bear to the central analogy which unifies the *Essay*. In the first place, though it is only by reference to this analogy that we may speak of man's ideas as materials or products in a process of making, nevertheless, once this manner of speaking is adopted, it becomes possible to give to the analysis of ideas and of the acts by which they are brought before the mind as knowledge a certain literal status that permits of sharp and fixed distinctions. Such distinctions appear in the *Essay* whenever it is a question, for example, of the difference which separates simple ideas derived from one sense from those derived from several; or of the difference between simple ideas considered as the primary materials of thought and complex ideas considered as fabrications of them resulting from the no less literally distinguishable processes of combination, comparison, or abstraction; or of the difference between complex ideas of substances on the one hand and of modes and relations on the other; or of the difference between primary qualities and secondary qualities; or between essence and existence; or between simple intuitive propositions and chains of reasoning; or between the province of reason and that of faith. With respect to all these it is possible for Locke to frame definitions that can be kept constant as devices for identifying elements or combinations of elements in thought or discourse no matter in what contexts they may occur.

The *Essay*, however, is not merely an attempt at a literal enumeration of the kinds of ideas men may have or of the psychological operations that may be distinguished in their production or use; it is fundamentally a "history" of human knowledge, and as such it derives its principles of organization and

13. II.i.2 (I, 122).

interpretation from the universal traits of the mind—its powers and its situation—as these are determined by the analogy Locke has set up between the activity of the mind in thinking and the activity of the artist or workman receiving his materials from the world outside him and fashioning them as suits his own desires into objects of use or contemplation. To consider the origin of knowledge in terms of this parallel is inevitably to be led to discover, in each phase of the mind's operations, proportions between what is external in the process and what is internal, between what is passive and what is active; and it is precisely these proportions, applied in context after context throughout the *Essay*, that provide Locke with the general framework, essentially analogical in character, within which his literal treatment of ideas and knowledge is developed.

How important for him, at every step of the analysis, is the ratio of the external to the internal can be seen from even a cursory outline of the contents of his book. There are, he is at great pains to show in Book I, no "innate principles," whether speculative or practical; as with the artist or workman, so with the mind, the materials with which it operates have their origin outside the mind itself; they are ideas to which the understanding is related as an "extrinsical" cause. What is internal here is only man's reason considered at once as a set of powers and as a *tabula rasa* with respect to whatever is knowable in the world. For the mind thus considered ideas are objects, and the fundamental problem, posed at the beginning of Book II, is how they come to be within the mind. The solution, as we have seen, consists in reducing all the thoughts we can have to elements, or simple ideas, derived ultimately from experience. But experience itself is of a twofold character, partly external through the senses, partly internal through the reflection of the mind upon itself. The analysis in each case begins with what is most external to the mind as in some way its object and proceeds to the internal operations by which simple ideas are fashioned into complex and finally made available for knowledge. External in the strictest sense of course are the sensible objects which make up the world outside our minds; introduced into the mind by sensation these become objects in a second sense as

150

simple ideas of sensation related in different ways to the qualities of the real objects they stand for; as ideas within the mind they constitute materials upon which the faculties of the mind may exercise its characteristic operations. But these operations themselves may again be externalized as objects from which by reflection are derived simple ideas of another sort—such as perception, thinking, doubting, willing, and the like—which in turn, as simple ideas of reflection, become materials for the exercise of the mind's internal operations. It is thus that Locke proceeds in organizing his account of the "original" of ideas in the early chapters of Book II: as anything external is to anything internal, so are outward sensible objects to sensation, simple ideas of sensation to the operations of the mind, the operations of the mind to reflection, the simple ideas of reflection to the operations of the mind; and the same proportions serve, later in the Book, to make intelligible the relation of simple ideas of either kind to complex ideas and of complex ideas of substances to complex ideas of modes and relations.

In Book III, which treats of words, the movement is reversed, and the discussion proceeds from "those invisible ideas," of which our thoughts are made up, to the "external sensible signs" by which we can make known the content of our minds to others.[14] In Book IV the proportions continue to run consistently from the inner to the outer as we move from knowledge, which lies entirely in the view we have of our own ideas, to probability or opinion, which involves relations among external things; from knowledge proper to truth, the character of which is that it always involves a joining or disjoining of signs, in mental or verbal propositions, according to the nature of things; from intuitive knowledge to sensitive knowledge; from knowledge of the essences of things expressed in abstract ideas or universal propositions, which are fictions of the mind, to knowledge of their existence; from the character of knowledge as a construction of the mind joining or disjoining its ideas to the character of knowledge as determined not by the mind but by its objects; from reason, finally, as the power of our minds

14. III.ii.1 (II, 8).

to discover and arrange its ideas, to revelation as a source of knowledge external to our natural faculties.

No less important, however, than the contrast of internal to external in the construction of the *Essay* is the contrast which Locke derives from another, though closely related, aspect of the analogy of making. As an artist fabricating the materials he has received from nature is to the same artist viewing or judging what he has made, so is the mind as employed in working up the simple ideas given by experience to the mind assenting, in the way either of knowledge or of probability, to the propositions or arguments it has formed. Though all human thinking, for Locke, is action, yet the powers involved in it—and this is what distinguishes man from God, on the one hand, and from material things, on the other—are powers at once of initiating change and of receiving it;[15] throughout the process both the will and the understanding are at work, the will as the faculty of preferring to attend to this idea rather than that, to pursue this line of investigation rather than some other, the understanding as the faculty of perceiving the ideas present in the mind or the signification of the signs that stand for them or the relation of agreement or disagreement by which they are connected.[16] It is by the cooperation or interaction of these two sets of powers with respect to the materials supplied by experience that all human knowledge, according to Locke, comes to be, and the structure, no less than the doctrine, of the *Essay* is significantly determined by the proportions, running parallel to and overlapping those given by the relation of the mind to its objects, which he endeavors to establish between them. From the reception or awareness of simple ideas, in which, as he insists, the mind is completely passive, to the activity of thought involved in compounding, comparing, abstracting, and naming them; from the passive and involuntary perception of their agreement or disagreement which constitutes intuitive knowledge to the discovery and construction of proofs by the reason and the weighing of evidence and choosing of probabilities: the dialectical rhythm of the treatise is a sucession of mo-

15. II.xxi.2 (I, 309).   16. II.xxi.5-6 (I, 313-15).

ments in which the mind is alternately exhibited as receiving the materials of knowledge and working with them, as contemplating, with a compulsory assent, the products of its making and setting its faculties voluntarily at work to fashion new products or to improve those already in hand.[17]

Nor are the proportions of active and passive, voluntary and involuntary, any less evident when we turn from the larger outline of the *Essay* to the treatment of particular topics. They are, for example, the principles by which, in Book II, Locke orders his account of the faculties of the mind—perception, retention, discerning, etc.—the ideas of which we acquire from reflection. Perception, as the first faculty exercised about our ideas and hence the first and simplest of the ideas we have from reflection, is by some, Locke explains, called "thinking in general." It is important, however, to distinguish between thinking in the proper sense of the word, which signifies in English "that sort of operation in the mind about its ideas, wherein the mind is active; where it, with some degree of voluntary attention, considers anything," and perception in "its bare, naked" form, where the mind is, for the most part, "only passive; and what it perceives, it cannot avoid perceiving."[18] But there is, Locke goes on to show, a "secondary perception," which appears whenever we voluntarily call up or search out the ideas which have been lodged in the memory, and in this "the mind is oftentimes more than barely passive."[19] Both perception and memory are faculties possessed by man in common with the animals; what sets man apart is his power of voluntary activity, limited only by what he can passively perceive and retain, which enables him at once to put together by his wit with quickness and variety such of his ideas as have any resemblance or congruity and to distinguish clearly by his judgment between ideas in which he can perceive a difference, to compare his ideas in respect of extent, degree, time, place, or any other circumstance, to compound his simple ideas more or less freely into complex conceptions, and finally by devising names for his thoughts to provide himself with general or abstract ideas

17. Cf. IV.xiii.1-2 (II, 357-58).
18. II.ix.1 (I, 183).   19. II.x.7 (I, 197-98).

from which all the particularities of his simple perceptions have been voluntarily removed.[20]

It must not be supposed, however, that the freedom of the mind in fabricating its complex and abstract ideas is equal with respect to all the possible kinds of combination. There is something arbitrary in all of them, Locke explains, since they involve an assemblage of simple ideas held together by a name signifying the essence, whether nominal only, as in substances, or both nominal and real, as in modes and relations, of the thing to which the idea refers. But though it is clear that, the real essence of substances being unknown, the only essence we can possess is made by the mind in sorting its simple ideas of things into collections held together by a common name, still the freedom of the mind in fashioning these ideas is restricted both by its perception of the usual character which things have in nature and by its desire to make its ideas intelligible to others. The mind, therefore, "in making its complex ideas of substances, only follows nature; and puts none together which are not supposed to have a union in nature. Nobody joins the voice of a sheep with the shape of a horse; nor the colour of lead with the weight and fixedness of gold, to be the complex ideas of any real substances; unless he has a mind to fill his head with chimeras, and his discourse with unintelligible words. . . . For, though men may make what complex ideas they please, and give what names to them they will; yet, if they will be understood *when they speak of things really existing,* they must in some degree conform their ideas to the things they would speak of. . . ."[21] It is quite otherwise with complex ideas of mixed modes and relations. They are not only made by the mind, but made *"very arbitrarily, made without patterns, or reference to any real existence."* "Nor does the mind, in these of mixed modes, as in the complex idea of substances, examine them by the real existence of things; or verify them by patterns containing such peculiar compositions in nature. To know whether his idea of *adultery* or *incest* be right, will a man seek it anywhere amongst things existing? Or is it true

20. II.xi.1-9 (I, 202-7).   21. III.vi.28 (II, 79).

because any one has been witness to such an action? No: but it suffices here, that men have put together such a collection into one complex idea, that makes the archetype and specifick idea; whether ever any such action were committed *in rerum natura* or no."[22]

The details of the treatment of knowledge and opinion in Book IV exhibit no less clearly the operation of the same fundamental ratios. If demonstration, for example, rests on the discovery of intermediate proofs through the active and voluntary use of the reason, each of its steps nevertheless involves the intuitive and necessary perception of the agreement or disagreement of two ideas immediately conjoined. If reason is active in its search for the ideas the mind needs, it is no less passive in its acquiescence in the successful results of its search, being a faculty capable, like the mind itself, both of making and perception. So, too, the great excellence and use of the judgment, in collecting testimonies and reviewing experience, is in its ability to make "a true estimate of the force and weight of each probability; and then casting them up all right together, [to] choose that side which has the overbalance";[23] but when it has done this, and the proofs are clear, nothing is left for it but a passive and involuntary assent to the propositions it has framed. So again, finally, with the relation of reason and faith: the assent we give to revelation as absolutely determines our minds, and as perfectly excludes all wavering, as our knowledge itself; but it is our privilege, as rational beings, to make our faith in any particular revelation depend upon a previous free and active examination of the proofs upon which its genuineness rests.[24]

It is in terms of this account of the "original" of knowledge, involving as its characteristic devices proportions between the materials of thought and the process, between the process and the product, between what is external to the mind and what is internal, between what is active in thinking and what is passive,

22. III.v.3 (II, 43-44).
23. IV.xvii.16 (II, 409); cf. IV.xvi.6, 9 (II, 375-77); IV.xx.15-16 (II, 454-56).
24. IV.xvii.24 (II, 413-14); IV.xviii.8 (II, 423-24).

that Locke formulates the criteria by which we may determine
the extent and certainty of what we can know, together with
the grounds and degrees of belief, opinion, and assent. There
is apparent in all his reflection on these matters a certain strain
of paradox deriving from the possibility, inherent in his analysis, of considering the problem of knowledge alternately from
two points of view. On the one hand, as he proceeds through
the successive acts of combination, comparison, and abstraction
by which all of our loftiest and most general ideas of things
are brought into being, he may turn his attention backward
to the original materials out of which the construction has been
effected, and when he does this nothing is more evident than
the meagerness and narrow limitations of our knowledge. Of
being in its vast extent we can have only those notions which
can be resolved ultimately into the simple ideas given us by experience: no other conceptions of sensible qualities than what
come from without by the senses, no ideas of the operations of
any thinking substance except those the mind finds in itself
through reflection. "All those sublime thoughts which tower
above the clouds, and reach as high as heaven itself, take their
rise and footing here: in all that great extent wherein the mind
wanders, in those remote speculations it may seem to be elevated with, it stirs not one jot beyond those ideas, which *sense*
or *reflection* have offered for its contemplation."[25] So with the
ideas of infinity or of God, which in earlier philosophers had
been represented as primary and innate: however remote they
may seem from any object of sense or operation of our mind,
it is easy for Locke to show that in the end they are only combinations, fabricated by man in the course of his experience,
out of simple ideas got originally from sensation and reflection.
And indeed the test of the adequacy of any of our complex
ideas lies precisely in a reduction of them to the primary materials out of which they have been composed; when this is
done, it is plain that all the conceptions we have of substances
of whatever kind, since they depend upon a union of simple
ideas we have merely experienced as existing together in nature, can never be more than inadequate copies of their real

25. II.i.24 (I, 142).

originals. From considerations such as these, clearly, we can derive no exalted hopes concerning the possibilities of human knowledge or the ability of the reason to construct sciences possessing any high degree of certitude.

Yet if Locke is thus led to insist on the narrow bounds of a knowledge whose only materials are the simple elements of experience, he is no less inclined, whenever it is a question of the process of knowing or its human goals, to emphasize the extent rather than the limits of what man may achieve. Disproportionate as are our ideas to things themselves, we still have enough light to lead us to knowledge of God and to ensure our virtue and happiness in this world; and though there are many doubts and inquiries concerning the ideas we have which will probably never be resolved, yet it may be confidently said that "human knowledge, under the present circumstances of our beings and constitutions, may be carried much further than it has hitherto been, if men would sincerely, and with freedom of mind, employ all that industry and labour of thought, in improving the means of discovering truth, which they do for the colouring or support of falsehood, to maintain a system, interest or party they are once engaged in."[26] For it is certain that the mind has a great power of varying and multiplying the objects of its thoughts, infinitely beyond what sensation or reflection has furnished it with, and this power, if only properly directed, can give us a body of knowledge, or at least of assured belief, that is entirely adequate for all our human purposes. And the conditions of success are simple and within the reach of our faculties if they are applied to the task with attention and method. Thus, since all knowledge consists essentially in the view the mind has of the ideas it has acquired or fabricated, a primary requisite is obviously that our ideas should be made clear and distinct, or, as Locke prefers to say, determinate, and this is something within our own power. "This, I think, may fitly be called a determinate or determined idea, when such as it is at any time objectively in the mind, and so determined there, it is annexed, and without variation determined, to a

26. IV.iii.6 (II, 192); cf. Introduction, sec. 5 (I, 29-30); II.vii. 10 (I, 164-65); II.xxiii.12 (I, 402-4).

name or articulate sound, which is to be steadily the sign of that very same object of the mind, or determinate idea."[27] With ideas thus made determinate both by the distinctness of our conception of them and the constancy of the words by which they are expressed, we may hope to keep our inquiries and discourses free from the confusion and merely verbal argument which have been the vices of philosophy in the past. And it is likewise within our power to associate our ideas, not merely as we are directed by chance or custom or prejudice, but according to their natural correspondence and connection; to seek systematically for ideas that will establish a connection between those whose relation is yet unclear to us; to test our own experience in the light of the experience of others; to acquire skill in the management of complicated proofs.

The problem of the operations by which we get our ideas, as treated in Books II and III of the *Essay*, is thus for Locke a problem of assessing the relative importance in the process of the passivity of the mind with respect to the simple objects it attends to and of its activity with respect to the products it can make out of the materials it receives from experience; as one or the other of these two factors is uppermost in the analysis, so his emphasis shifts from the limitations to the possibilities of our knowledge. A similar double movement may be observed in Book IV, where the problem is the evaluation of the products of the mind's making in terms, on the one hand, of the certainty they may give us and, on the other, of the uses to which they may be put; only here the statement of limitations and possibilities is complicated by the presence in the analysis not only of the relation of the active to the passive powers of the mind but of the relation of the mind itself both to its ideas and to external things.

27. The Epistle to the Reader (I, 22).

A. A. MURPHREE

Associate Professor of English
University of Florida

Wit & Dryden

 *it*, ONE OF THE MOST PROTEAN OF TERMS IN the vocabulary of John Dryden and other seventeenth or eighteenth century writers, is, next to *Nature*, probably the most elusory of concepts to the student of the neoclassical period. Any reader of Dryden soon realizes not only that he used the word in varying senses but that he sometimes slips from one meaning to another without feeling the need of explanation; in fact, there are occasions when one wonders whether Dryden was aware of his vacillation. The task of determining the exact meaning of the term in every context is, therefore, not an easy one. It is evident too that at times the word is a mere counter term used to express approbation for this or that work or its author. For whatever may be the attitude of later critics toward *wit*, to Dryden it signified, except where it is expressly qualified by some pejorative, a desirable, if not necessary, quality in great works or small.

The apparent confusion in Dryden's usage of the term is likewise patent in that of his contemporaries. Even the philological speculations of a Hobbes or a Locke failed to produce a satisfactory definition that would embrace all its various manifestations. Wit is, after all, a quality so volatile and so multiform that, like poetry, it is perhaps incapable of logical definition.[1] Nevertheless, many besides Hobbes and Locke attempted to define it, Dryden included. Of all the attempts, at least up to the time of Locke, Hobbes' was doubtless the most influential. While Hobbes' pronouncements on the subject are inconsistent, as he equates it variously with fancy or with judgment, yet his general position seems to be that "both fancy and judgment are commonly comprehended under the name of Wit, which semeth a tenuity and agility of spirits, contrary to that restiveness of the spirits supposed in those that are dull."[2] Basically, it is a power of making comparisons, for fancy, according to Hobbes, is a faculty that perceives resemblances in things apparently unlike as judgment discovers differences in things apparently like. Its effect is to surprise and delight. Many Restoration critics accepted these distinctions; but inasmuch as Hobbes had on occasion identified wit with fancy and opposed it to judgment (as had Ben Jonson and others before him), there were many who echoed this antithesis.

Dryden was no doubt influenced by Hobbes' speculations on the subject, but he was no slavish disciple of the philosopher. He is as much indebted to the rhetorical tradition. He seems, for instance, to regard wit as the power of making comparisons, or the result of such a power, when he remarks[3] that

1. As Isaac Barrow intimated in his "Sermon against foolish Talking and Jesting." See Corbyn Morris, *An Essay Towards Fixing the True Standards of Wit, Humour, Raillery, Satire, and Ridicule* (1744), reprinted by the Augustan Reprint Society, Series One, No. 4 (November, 1947), p. vii.
   2. *The Elements of Law*, I, x, 4. Ed. Ferdinand Tönnies (Cambridge, 1928), p. 38.
   3. Preface to *Annus Mirabilis* (wr. 1666) in *Essays of John Dryden*, ed. W. P. Ker (Oxford, 1900), Vol. I, p. 14. (Citations from or to this collection hereafter will be abbreviated as per example: K. I, 14.)

"the proper wit of an Heroic or Historical Poem" consists "in the delightful imaging[4] of persons, actions, passions, or things," or in other words, the representation of such objects by means of images (comparisons, similitudes, tropes) which are conducive to *energia*.[5] In the same context, his first definition and most extended anatomization of wit, he identifies wit, both the faculty and the product, with imagination, although he indicates that the judgment exercises a discretionary power in the operation of that faculty. At other times, as for example in his famous definition of wit as "propriety of thoughts and words,"[6] it is clear that he regards wit as comprehending both fancy and judgment. On yet other occasions, wit is identified with fancy and sharply contrasted with judgment, as when in the Dedication to *Eleonora* (1692) he observes: "I was transported by the multitude and variety of my similitudes; which are generally the product of a luxuriant fancy, and the wantonness of wit. Had I call'd in my judgment to my assistance, I had certainly retrench'd many of them."[7] Never does he equate wit with judgment alone; where it is not used as a synonym for imagination, it is recognized that imagination is an essential ingredient. Dryden seems always to have considered delight of

4. In W. P. Ker's edition of Dryden's essays and in the Scott-Saintsbury edition of his works, the reading is "imagining," but Miss Dorothy Mason of the Folger Shakespeare Library, who many years ago at my request consulted the three issues of *Annus Mirabilis* and their variants, comprising Macdonald 9ai, 9aii, 9aiii, 9b, and 9c (H. Macdonald, *Dryden Bibliography*, Oxford, 1939), kindly informs me that all have "imaging." This is, of course, the reading in *The Works of John Dryden*, ed. E. N. Hooker and H. T. Swedenberg (Los Angeles, 1956).

5. Richard Sherry in *A Treatise of Schemes and Tropes* (1550) defines *energia* as follows: "Energia: Evidence of perspicuitie called also description rethoricall, that is when a thynge is so described that it semeth to the reader or hearer yt he beholdeth it as it were in doying. Of thys figure ben many kyndes." One means of achieving such vividness is by use of comparisons or similitudes, which in some Renaissance rhetorical treatises are referred to by the name of *icon* or *imago* or *image*, a figure included under the generic term *energia*. (See Warren Taylor, *Tudor Figures of Rhetoric*, Chicago, 1937. Cf. Quintilian, *Institutio Oratio*, Loeb Classical Library, VI.ii.28-32; X.vii.15; VIII.iii.88.)

6. K. I, 190.

7. *The Poetical Works of Dryden*, ed. Geo. R. Noyes, Cambridge Edition (Boston, 1950), p. 270. (Hereafter referred to as Noyes.)

some sort as one of its effects; but apparently he did not regard surprise as an invariable concomitant.[8]

Though Dryden essayed three definitions of wit, it was much easier to tell what it is not than to state exactly what it is. Accordingly, he informs us that "the proper wit of an Heroic or Historical Poem" is not

> the jerk or sting of an epigram, nor the seeming contradiction of a poor antithesis (the delight of an ill-judging audience in a play of rhyme), nor the jingle of a more poor paronomasia; neither is it so much the morality of a grave sentence, affected by Lucan, but more sparingly used by Virgil. . . .[9]

In the same essay he adds that

> the proper wit of dialogue or discourse, and consequently of the Drama, where all that is said is supposed to be the effect of sudden thought . . . though it excludes not the quickness of wit in repartees, yet admits not a too curious election of words, too frequent allusions, or use of tropes, or, in fine, anything that shows remoteness of thought, or labour in the writer (K. I, 15).

In both of these statements, as in the discussion that follows concerning the wit of Ovid and Virgil, it ought to be observed, there is an adumbration of his later definition of wit as propriety. Though Dryden later changes his opinion regarding the "wit" of Ovid, he consistently holds to the proscriptions expressed here. Indeed, his objection to the pun, or paronomasia, amounts almost to a mania and doubtless contributed to its low repute among later critics. His antipathy to the epigram and the epigrammatic style, to which he objects in comic as well as in serious poetry—and this antipathy is shared by his

8. As a matter of fact, there is only one passage in which surprise is specifically mentioned in connection with wit. In speaking of Falstaff Dryden remarks: ". . . wherein he is singular is his wit, or those things he says *praeter expectatum*, unexpected by the audience; his quick evasions, when you imagine him surprised, which . . . are extremely diverting of themselves . . ." (*Essay of Dramatic Poesy* (1668), K. I, 84). It may be supposed, however, that Dryden considered surprise an effect of wit in many instances where he does not explicitly refer to it.

9. Preface to *Annus Mirabilis*, K. I, 14-15.

fellow critics—is curious; for the neatly polished and witty epigram was a kind of verse in which neoclassical poets excelled. From the time of Hobbes, who probably was echoing the opinion of Bacon, it was fashionable to hold the "little kinds" of poetry in contempt, or at least not to regard them seriously. Notwithstanding, in one or another of Dryden's works may be found almost every kind of "false" wit he proscribes, including the epigram—and the pun.

Dryden further affirms that "true" wit does not consist of bold metaphors or neologisms (K. I, 51), catachreses like those of Cleveland (K. I, 52), clenches or bombast to which Shakespeare sometimes descended (K. I, 80); nor is it the ridiculous habits and grimaces of a comic actor (K. I, 135), "gross hyperboles" (K. I, 256), "barefaced bawdry" (K. I, 263), "puns" (K. II, 95), "quirks of epigrams" (K. II, 108), "buffoonery" in comedy (SS. XV, 410),[10] "a quibble, a conceit, an epigram" (K. II, 223), "conceits and jingles" (K. II, 256); nor is it, on the other hand, "plain, dull common sense" (SS. III, 381).

Of the three definitions of wit that Dryden formulated, the first, and the most formally elaborated, appeared in his Preface to *Annus Mirabilis* (wr. 1666). It was here that he identified wit, both the faculty and the product, with imagination. (Cf. sense 3a below.) His second definition, wit as "sharpness of conceit," was first enunciated in 1671 in the Preface to *An Evening's Love*"[11] (cf. sense 7 below), though it appears he had used

10. *The Works of John Dryden*, eds. Sir Walter Scott and George Saintsbury (London, 1882-93). Subsequent references to this text will be abbreviated as per example: SS. XV, 410.

11. In this preface Dryden was answering an attack, directed at him and the kind of "witty" comedy he then was engaged in writing, launched by Thomas Shadwell, a Jonson idolator, who took umbrage at Dryden's remark in his *Essay of Dramatic Poesy* (1668) that Jonson was "frugal of wit" (K. I, 81). To this attack Dryden responded that Jonson "needed not the acumen of wit [i.e., imagination] but that of judgment" in writing his humours comedy. If anyone is offended, he continues, by my refusal to allow Jonson's "wit to be extraordinary," he is simply confusing the notions of what is "witty" with what is "pleasant." "That Ben Johnson's [*sic*] plays were pleasant, he must want reason who denies: but that pleasantness was not properly wit, or the *sharpness of conceit*, but the natural imitation of folly; which I confess to be excellent in its kind, but not to be of that kind which they pretend" (K. I, 138-39). Italics mine.

the term in this sense prior to that occasion. After 1672 the phrase "sharpness of conceit," disappears from his critical vocabulary. It may be assumed, nevertheless, that when later he refers to the wit of Congreve or of Wycherley for example, he has in mind "sharpness of conceit." His third definition, wit as "propriety of thoughts and words," which has been so badly misunderstood, first appeared in "The Author's Apology for Heroic Poetry and Poetic License,"[12] prefixed to *The State of Innocense and Fall of Man*, his operatic version of *Paradise Lost*, published in 1677. Adumbrations of this definition may also be found in his earlier application of the term. His conception of wit as propriety continues to the end of his career, though his notion of what constitutes propriety changes with the years, as witness, for example, his varying opinions of the wit of Cowley and Ovid. From first to last, imagination (or fancy) was associated in his mind with wit in all of its literary manifestations.

These three definitions of wit are by no means the only senses in which Dryden uses the word. Following is an enumeration of all the various meanings of the term in so far as I have been able to ascertain them.[13]

I. As a faculty or agency of the mind *wit* had several meanings:

   (1) The mind in general; intelligence; native capacity, aptitude, or genius. These were, of course, common meanings of the word during the Renaissance. Aris-

12. ". . . the definition of Wit (which has so often been attempted, and ever unsuccessfully by many poets) is only this: that it is a propriety of thoughts and words; or, in other terms, thoughts and words elegantly adapted to the subject" (K. I, 190). Isolated from its context, many have regarded this definition as an extreme instance of neoclassic rationalistic thought, in which, as Spingarn puts it, "the element of fancy is eradicated entirely," an opinion that has been echoed by many but rightly rejected by others. *Critical Essays of the Seventeenth Century*, ed. J. E. Spingarn (Oxford, 1908), Vol. I, p. xxxi.

13. This enumeration, suggested obviously by Professor A. O. Lovejoy's well-known study of " 'Nature' as Aesthetic Norm" (*MLN*, XLII [1927], 444-50), is the concluding summary of a longer monograph which is to appear elsewhere and wherein may be found in detail the evidence supporting the following generalizations.

totle's εὐφυΐα was the equivalent of Horace's *ingenium* and both of these terms were sometimes translated in the Renaissance by the native word "wit." It is not surprising, therefore, that Dryden in his emendation of Aristotle should have translated Εὐφυοῦς first by "genius" and then by "a witty man," indicating that to him *wit* and *genius* often signified the same thing.[14] In this example, to be sure, "witty" does not refer to a faculty or agency of the mind but to the person so endowed: see, however, K. I, 180:11; II, 164:21. (See also K. I, 37:25, 147:21, 163:28, 194:1, 196:20, 197:31 ["intelligence"], 243:23, 263:34; II, 22:17, 23:11, 72:32, 84:34.)

(2) Intellectual liveliness, mental acumen, quickness of thought, subtlety of apprehension. Falstaff's "wit" is exemplified in "those things he says *praeter expecta-tum*, unexpected by the audience; his quick evasions when you imagine him surprised . . ." (*An Essay of Dramatic Poesy*, K. I, 84; see also 47:21, 176:19, 187:6).

(3) The poetic or creative agency (K. I, 80:13); or more specifically:

    (a) Imagination, with or without the connotations of (2) above. ". . . wit in the poet . . . is no other than the faculty of imagination in the writer . . ." comprising invention, fancy, and elocution, the attributes of which are quickness, fertility (copiousness), and accuracy (aptness) (Preface to *Annus Mirabilis*, K. I, 14-15; see also 81:31, 138:23, 166:31).

    (b) Imagination and judgment. All references to wit as propriety presuppose the harmonious coopera-

---

14. "They who would justify the madness of Poetry from the authority of Aristotle, have mistaken the text, and consequently the interpretation: I imagine it to be false read, where he says of Poetry, that it is Εὐφυοῦς ἢ μανικοῦ, that it had always somewhat in it either of a genius, or of a madman. 'Tis more probable that the original ran thus, that Poetry was Εὐφυοῦς οὐ μανικοῦ, that it belongs to a witty man, but not a mad man." (Preface to *Troilus and Cressida* (1679), K. I, 221-22.)

tion of these two faculties as the source of the product. (See K. I, 172:25.)

II. As the product of such a faculty or agency *wit* signified (note that the following classifications are not mutually exclusive):

    (4) Loosely, poetry in general, or poetic genius. ". . . our nation can never want in any age such who are able to dispute the empire of wit with any people in the universe" (*An Essay of Dramatic Poesy*, K. I, 88:30; see also 29:29, 80:27, 99:10, 165:15, 238:19; II, 4:33, 23:14, 102:7, 111:32).

    (5) Propriety of thoughts and words or of style. *Wit* in this sense frequently had also the meaning of (6). (K. I, 15:24, ?42:18, cf. line 23, 51:8, 52:19, 172:4, 190:12, 256:8, 270:1; II, 9:16.)

    (6) A figurative representation or style, such as is found, for instance, in Shakespeare's plays. As suggested immediately above, *wit* in this sense might also have the meaning of (5). ". . . the proper wit of an Heroic or Historical Poem . . . consists in the delightful imaging of persons, actions, passions, or things . . . it is some lively and apt description, dressed in such colours of speech, that it sets before your eyes the absent object, as perfectly, and more delightfully than nature" (Preface to *Annus Mirabilis*, K. I, 14-15). In the passage at the top of K. I, 172, where Shakespeare's wit is referred to, the word probably connotes a figurative style, though Dryden is judging it by the norm of propriety. In the Preface to *Tyrannic Love* he declares: "He who creeps after plain, dull, common sense, is safe from committing absurdities, but can never reach any height or excellence of wit" (SS. III, 381). With this passage should be compared his allusion to the "very Leveller in Poetry" whose "poetry neither has wit in it, nor seems to have it. . . . He affects plainness, to cover his want of imagination . . ." (*An Essay of Dramatic Poesy*, K. I, 31-32; see also 100:33, 223:29, 233:35).

(7) "Sharpness of conceit"—acuteness of fancy, the product of (3) with the connotations of (2) above.

    (a) The term "sharpness of conceit," used generally to designate the product of a faculty which might be similarly denominated, occurs only in contexts where Dryden is discoursing of comedy. In these contexts it seems to refer chiefly to the clever, amusing, pointed, sprightly, sparkling dialogue, or repartee, and also perhaps to the gaiety of tone and urbanity which are commonly associated with the comedy of manners. Wit in this application, therefore, has essentially the same meaning one associates with the word when one speaks of the wit of a Congreve comedy.

    (b) Doubtless, however, "sharpness of conceit" had in Dryden's thinking a broader application. Thus, the wit in one of Donne's or Cowley's poems, as distinguished from the less sharp, ingenious, and fanciful manifestations of "wit" in Virgil—for Dryden, be it remembered, attributed wit to him also, cf. sense (6)—might be so described. This was not an uncommon application of the term; thus Edward Phillips remarked: "*John Donne . . . frequented good company, to which the sharpness of his wit, and gaiety of fancy, rendered him not a little grateful: in which state of life he composed his more brisk and youthful poems, which are rather commended for the height of fancy and acuteness of the conceit, than for the smoothness of the verse. . . .*"[15] In this application, of course, the connotation of the term differs somewhat from that of (7a). But in both (a) and (b) there is implied as the source of the product a mind that is sharp, quick, agile, and subtle. (See K. I, 139:32; II, 102:7, ?256:19.)

(8) Repartee. (See 7a.) Since Dryden refers to wit in this sense in contexts where "sharpness of conceit" is not

15. *Theatrum Poetarum* (Geneva, 1824), II, 2-3.

mentioned, this meaning of the word is here listed separately; furthermore, repartee wit might be ex-emplified in serious as well as in comic plays. (See K. I, 15:28, 72:25, 81:10, 140:9, 175:16; II, 142:3.)

(9) Urbanity. (See 7a.) If in the following references wit is not equated exclusively with urbanity, this quality is regarded as an ingredient. (See K. I, 139:21, 174:12, 175:16; II, 75:12.)

(10) Pungent criticism, censure, ridicule, raillery. (See K. II, 84:25, 92:26, 95:1, 103:23.) Cf.: ". . . for to their ignorance all things are wit which are abusive" (Preface to *Religio Laici* (1682), Noyes, p. 161).

(11) Mirth, gaiety, pleasantry. This is, of course, a connotation of many of the senses listed above. (See K. I, 135:23, ?188:10; II, ?27:18, 72:11, ?84:23, 96:7, 107:10, 9:16.) Cf.: ". . . in all courts there are too many who make it their business to ruin wit. . . . These are they, who wanting wit, affect gravity, and go by the name of solid men; and a solid man is, in plain English, a solid, solemn fool" (Dedication to *Aureng-Zebe* (1676), SS. V, 188-89).

(12) Good sense. Cf. sense (1) above.

> Thus Sophocles with Socrates did sit,
> Supreme in wisdom one, and one in wit:
> And wit from wisdom differ'd not in those,
> But as't was sung in verse, or said in prose.
>> Prologue to *Oedipus* (wr. 1678)

III. When applied to persons, it is to be presumed, the term denominated the possessor of such a faculty or agency of mind as defined above. More specifically the word signifies in Dryden's usage (note again that the following are not mutually exclusive):

(13) Loosely, a poet or writer. *An Essay of Dramatic Poesy* proposes to compare "the wits of our nation with those of others" (K. I, 27). In the Preface to *All for Love* Dryden writes: "The death of Anthony and Cleopatra is a subject which has been treated by the greatest wits of our nation . . ." (K. I, 191). In the

Dedication of *Examen Poeticum* he states: Ovid "is certainly more palatable to the reader, than any of the Roman wits; though some of them are more lofty, some more instructive, and others more correct" (K. II, 9; see also K. I, 166:31, 239:18, 253:20; II, 30:20, 255:4, 265:14).

(14) Vaguely, poetic genius. That Dryden sometimes equated wit with genius was remarked above—see sense (2). In the Preface to *Oedipus* he calls Sophocles "not only the greatest wit, but one of the greatest men in Athens . . ." (SS. VI, 131). In the Dedication to *Aureng-Zebe* he declares: "As I am no successor to Homer in his wit, so neither do I desire to be in his poverty" (SS. V, 196). When he acknowledges Jonson to be "the more correct poet, but Shakespeare the greater wit" (K. I, 82), he may be using the term in this sense. It is perhaps unnecessary to add that it is difficult to distinguish between (14) and (13).

(15) A person of quality, well born and properly nurtured. This connotation is derived perhaps from εὐφυής, "which originally meant 'well-grown,' usually included physical perfection, good ancestry, and proper nurture,"[16] a connotation that is often implicit in both (13) and (14). Cf.: "But if I come closer to those who are allowed for witty men, either by the advantage of their quality, or by common fame . . ." (Preface to *All for Love*, K. I, 195); ". . . those noble characters of men of wit and pleasure about the town" ("A Discourse Concerning the Original and Progress of Satire," K. II, 21-2; see also K. I, 26:33, 28:21).

(16) A person of superior mental ability, intelligence, Cf. (1), (12), and (14). "For my own part, if, in treating this subject I sometimes dissent from the opinion of better wits, I declare it not so much to combat their opinions, as to defend my own . . ." (Epistle Dedicatory to *An Essay of Dramatic Poesy*, K. I, 26).

16. W. G. Crane, *Wit and Rhetoric in the Renaissance* (New York, 1937), p. 10.

(17) "A person of lively fancy, who has the faculty of saying smart or brilliant things, now always so as to
amuse" (*OED*). The first use of the word in this sense
as recorded by the *OED* is in 1692. Although one cannot be certain, it appears that Dryden had used the
term, either as noun or as adjective, with this meaning at a much earlier date. See, for instance, Preface
to *All for Love* (1678) K. I, 196:26 and references
under (7) above. Cf.: "I knew a poet, whom out of
respect I will not name, who, being too witty himself,
could draw nothing but wits in a comedy of his; even
his fools were infected with the disease of their
author. They overflowed with smart repartees, and
were only distinguished from the intended wits by
being called coxcombs, though they deserved not so
scandalous a name" (*A Parallel of Poetry and Painting* (1695) K. II, 142). Cf. also: ". . . he [Charles II]
was master of too much good sense to delight in heavy
conversation; and whatever his favorites of state might
be, yet those of his affection were men of wit" (Dedication to *King Arthur* (1691), SS. VIII, 132).

AUBREY L. WILLIAMS
Graduate Research Professor of English
University of Florida

Alexander Pope's "Knack" at Versifying

N THE SPRING OF 1735, EDMUND CURLL, THE infamous and piratical London bookseller, was haled before the House of Lords on charges that, in the publication of a volume of Pope's correspondence containing some letters from noblemen, he had been guilty of a breach of privilege. According to Samuel Johnson, Curll, when he stood at the bar of the House, knew "himself in no great danger," and so "spoke of Pope with very little reverence." Pope, said Curll, "has a knack at versifying, but in prose I think myself a match for him."[1]

Curll's impudence before the lords accords very precisely with that bland and even more "heroic" impudence Pope ascribed to him in Book II of the *Dunciad*, published some seven years before this episode. For all its sauciness, however,

1. *Lives of the English Poets*, ed. G. B. Hill (3 vols., Oxford, 1905), III, 155.

Curll's testimony is echoed a few years later in a statement made by another of Pope's enemies, Lady Mary Wortley Montagu, and recorded by Joseph Spence: "You are very wrong in thinking that Mr. Pope could write blank verse well: he has got a knack, indeed, of writing the other, but was he to attempt blank verse, I dare say he would appear quite contemptible in it."[2] Exactly what Lady Mary may have meant by her use of the word "knack" is perhaps made clear a few pages later in Spence. In a bit of dialogue that seems to take place between her and Spence and which seems originally to have come hard on the heels of her remark above, Lady Mary inquires: "Don't you really think so, Sir?"—[Spence:] I think, madam, that he writes verses very well.—[Lady Mary:] "Yes, he writes verses so well, that he is in danger of bringing even good verse into disrepute! from his all tune and no meaning."[3]

Testimony as to the qualities of Pope's art from such witnesses as these will scarcely be regarded as unbiased, yet if there were those (more especially his enemies) in his own day who could declare the ease and perfection of his art to derive from a mere "knack at versifying" and to signify sheer "tune and no meaning," certainly the world has never since lacked those for whom such declarations have the ring of truth and the force of fact. Are there not many still who would maintain that the poetry of Pope is smooth but empty, easy but insignificant, and that all his artistry is mere clever dexterity and sleight-of-hand, a poetical "knack"?

The reasons for such misconceptions about Pope's art are, no doubt, many and complex, and range from pure unfamiliarity with much of his work (other than what is so often chopped to pieces in anthologies) to a backwash of nineteenth-century attitudes towards his ethical and artistic values. The main reason for the *persistence* of such misconceptions, however, may be the fact that, as Maynard Mack has said, we cannot really be

2. *Anecdotes, Observations, and Characters, of Books and Men*, ed. S. W. Singer (London, 1820), p. 233.
3. *Ibid.*, pp. 236-37. This conversation, separated by two pages from Lady Mary's remark previously quoted, may not concern Pope at all, but the context and sequence of talk do seem to make Pope the most plausible subject of the dialogue.

said to *possess* any of Pope's poems "at the same level of pene-tration that we possess the best of Donne's."[4] And if this be true, if we have not as yet learned to read Pope's verse in the same way that we seem able to read Metaphysical verse, it seems possible, at least, that some part of our failure may result from Pope's very success with a critical principle he both asserted and practiced throughout his poetical career—the principle that the best art is that in which the art is concealed ("ars est celare artem"). Pope was never one to wear his art—or his heart—on his sleeve, and in consequence it has perhaps been easy for us to underestimate the measure of both.

It is perhaps only a coincidence, and a minor irony, of liter-ary history that on several occasions, both before and after Curll's testimony at his trial, Pope himself chose to characterize his poetical talent as a "knack." And casual though such a correspondence in terminology may have been, an exploration of the poet's use of the word may lead us into observations that will serve not only as comment upon such judgments as those by Curll and Lady Mary, but also as comment upon certain essential strategies of Pope's art.

The first two instances of Pope's use of the word "knack" to describe his own art are not crucial, yet even so they serve to illustrate the ironic and self-conscious ways in which he could seem to depreciate his own long labors of the file. Thus in his ironic *Guardian* essay, No. 40 (1713), where he compares his own pastorals to the puerile but then highly esteemed pastorals of Ambrose Philips, he describes himself as that "other Modern (who it must be confessed hath a knack of Versifying)." Again, in the second Moral Essay, *Of the Characters of Women* (1735), the following passage occurs:

> Pictures like these, dear Madam, to design,
> Ask no firm hand, and no unerring line:
> Some wand'ring touch, or some reflected light,
> Some flying stroke alone can hit 'em right:
> For how should equal Colours do the knack?
> Chameleons who can paint in white and black? (ll. 151-56)

4. Review article in *MLN*, LXXVI (December, 1961), p. 870.

The really significant instance, for our purposes, of Pope's use of the word "knack" occurs in a poem published about two years after Curll's trial (since Pope attended the prosecution of Curll, there is of course the possibility that he deliberately and amusedly turns Curll's terminology to his own purposes). This time the word occurs in Pope's "Imitation" of *The Second Epistle of the Second Book of Horace*, and forms part of the climax of a long verse paragraph in which he describes the rigorous self-discipline and craftsmanship practiced by poets who "show no mercy to an empty line," and who

> polish all, with so much life and ease,
> You think 'tis Nature, and a knack to please.   (ll. 176-77)

This couplet is then followed by another, one which serves to make his own conception of his art emphatically clear, and one which (it is important to note) is only a slightly altered version of a couplet that had appeared twenty-five years earlier in *An Essay on Criticism*:

> But Ease in writing flows from Art, not Chance,
> As those move easiest who have learn'd to dance.

We can perhaps best appreciate the precise implications of these couplets by glancing at their Latin counterpart in the Horatian original: there Horace also emphasizes the severe discipline required of the poet, and then says: "ludentis speciem dabit et torquebitur, ut qui/ nunc Satyrum, nunc agrestem Cyclopa movetur." Roughly translated, Horace says that the good poet will give the appearance of playing, yet he will be tortured with effort, like a dancer who now plays a Satyr, and now a clownish Cyclops.

Because Pope's verse so often seems characterized chiefly by an *easiness*, a natural inevitability of thought and movement, there have apparently been many who have concluded that what seems to be so easy cannot really be good or profound, or at the least that such ease as Pope achieved could only be, in the poet's own words, a mere "knack" of pleasing. The irony of all this, of course, is that such is precisely the effect Pope aimed at. At the same time, so innocent a response to Pope's art

174

ignores completely the poet's repeated assertions that the ease he sought in art could be gained only after the most intense effort and the most racking labor. "Ease," he says in *Guardian* No. 15 (1713), is only "to be acquired with the greatest Labour," and to achieve "the Perfection of easie Writing" all "Art will be hid by art." In *An Essay on Criticism* he speaks emphatically in praise of that art which "Works *without Show,* and *without Pomp* presides," and which is *"It self unseen,* but in th' *Effects,* remains." And, as we have already noted, it was in this youthful poem that there appeared the original version of the couplet later to be incorporated into his *Imitation of Horace*:

True Ease in writing comes from Art, not Chance,
As those move easiest who have learn'd to dance.

(ll. 362-63)

Too often, perhaps, we respond to Pope's poetry in the manner of uninformed spectators at the dance; the gestures and movements of his verse may seem so easy and inevitable as to be thought effortless and even meaningless. Yet anyone who studies the manuscripts of Pope's poems will be made extremely sensible of the endless labor exerted by the poet in his effort to achieve that air of graceful inevitability. Equally important, moreover, is the fact that anyone who studies closely the entire body of Pope's work will soon be made aware that his couplet style not only varies widely within individual poems, but that it also is greatly different from poem to poem. The very pace and structure of his couplets are finely adjusted, that is, to the differing moods and subjects of his poems, and thus the couplet patternings of *An Essay on Criticism* are quite different from those of *The Rape of the Lock,* while the diction and couplet patternings in both of these poems are entirely unlike what is to be found in later poems like the *Epistles to Several Persons* and the *Imitations of Horace.* Yet the myth persists that all of Pope's couplets are very much alike, and that they are all to be read in much the same manner.

A short paper scarcely permits persuasive illustration of the ways in which the real artfulness, and the actual significance, of so much of Pope's verse may be subdued to the fine patina of its surface, nor does it permit an examination of the ways in which this verse reaches from the early and more gaudy couplets of *The Rape of the Lock* to the greater simplicity—though perhaps the deeper poignancy—of the couplets in late poems like the *Imitations of Horace*. But at least one may attempt to exemplify briefly the ways in which Pope (to pursue Horace's metaphor) may now move in the mordantly designed awkwardness of a Cyclops, now in the lithe and withering grace of a Satyr.

In one of the *Imitations of Horace*, the subject of which is, among other things, the vice of gluttony, Pope attempts thus to rouse the reader's distaste and aversion:

> The stomach (cram'd from ev'ry dish,
> A Tomb of boil'd, *and* roast, *and* flesh, *and* fish,
> Where Bile, *and* wind, *and* phlegm, *and* acid jar,
> *And* all the Man is one intestine war). . . .[5]

One can hardly read such couplets as these in the sing-song fashion sometimes adopted for Pope's verse, nor can one argue from them that Pope is a slave to polite diction. Instead, the dominating and congestive monosyllabic diction, and the impacted repetition of the word *and* (there are seven *and*'s in three of the lines), force one to chew over the lines in a way that seems to mimic the very act of gluttonous stuffing and cramming Pope is describing.

Effective as the passage undoubtedly is as another illustration of Pope's ability to make the movements of his lines "seem an *Eccho* to the *Sense*," we would be much amiss to leave it at that. For even if we here put aside Pope's use of the image of a tomb to describe a stuffed stomach, we yet must note how these monosyllabic gobs of verse create a raw antagonism among the four elements of bile, wind, phlegm, and acid, and thereby form in their aggregation an emblem of anatomical discord and anarchy. And not merely an emblem of discord and anarchy, but ultimately an emblem of the primal chaos itself. By his use of so momentous a phrase as "intestine war," by his use of

5. *Second Satire of the Second Book*, ll. 69-72. Italics mine.

body juices and gases immediately suggestive of the four elements of earth, air, fire, and water, and by his use of a mono-syllabic technique which surely recalls Milton's more famous use of the same technique in his descriptions of Hell and Chaos,[6] Pope moves us from consideration of a mere vivid instance of personal vice into an awareness of the way in which, in terms of the Renaissance world picture, any instance of individual sin is to be regarded as an assault on the divinely ordained cosmic order, and as an attempt to bring again that disorder and primeval chaos which was thought to be the very product of sin.[7] In this harsh emblem of the dissolution of the four elements within the little world of man, Pope shows once again how much the verse we call "Augustan" is sustained by thought and values to which we apply the term "Elizabethan."[8]

A different and more pliant mode of Popean verse, and also one of the more sad and haunting passages written by the poet, may be illustrated by a paragraph occurring near the end of *Moral Essay II (Of the Characters of Women)*, and particularly by its climactic couplet:

> Pleasures the sex, as children Birds, pursue,
> Still out of reach, yet never out of view,
> Sure, if they catch, to spoil the Toy at most,
> To covet flying, and regret when lost:
> At last, to follies Youth could scarce defend,
> 'Tis half their Age's prudence to pretend;
> Asham'd to own they gave delight before,
> Reduc'd to feign it, when they give no more:
> As Hags hold Sabbaths, less for joy than spight,
> So these their merry, miserable Night;
> Still round and round the Ghosts of Beauty glide,
> And haunt the places where their Honour dy'd. (ll. 231-42)

6. See *Paradise Lost*, II, 621, 948-49.
7. E. M. W. Tillyard, *The Elizabethan World Picture* (London, 1948), p. 18.
8. The passage I have isolated here is closely in touch with the fundamental concerns of the entire poem from which it is taken. The immediately succeeding verse paragraph, for example, gives an instance of blasphemous feeding at clerical feasts, including that of the Eucharist.

The whole paragraph is a fine example of the lightning strike and subsequent reverberation achieved so often by Popean couplets—their combination of straightforward lash and serpentine suggestion. The first line, for instance, evokes an image of charming and childlike innocence of desire, but also, on reflection, suggests that for an adult woman such desire is hopelessly puerile and self-destructive. With its theme of misplaced and unattainable desire thus established, the paragraph then develops from imagery of artless childhood to imagery of a middle—or later—age consumed with spite and affectation, and nears its climax with Pope's use of an alliterative oxymoron—"merry, miserable"—to convey nakedly the gap of anguish that may exist between superannuated desire and fulfillment.

Full appreciation of this paragraph depends, however, on recognition of some rather precise implications of the imagery in its last two couplets. Thus Pope's allusion to the Witches' Sabbat seems, in the highly sexual context of the whole passage, to be something more than a vague charge of blasphemy against the women he is describing; the allusion seems to have the additional aim of recalling the nocturnal sexual orgies engaged in by women who attended the Sabbats, and beyond this to recall the prevalent belief that women who did engage in these orgies found the experience painful and totally distasteful.[9] Only against this background do we fully understand why the nights of these women are described by Pope as being miserable, although "merry."

Additional background to the last couplets of the paragraph is provided of course by the contemporary practice of promenades in the London parks, scenes of many a furtive assignation. Many a lady's honor had there "dy'd," and there seems no reason to deny the sexual implications in Pope's use of the word. The more melancholy implications of the very last couplet in the passage are realized, however, when we recall the superstition that the dead returned to haunt the exact spot of their dying. These eighteenth-century ladies, their beauty faded and

9. For a convenient account of the matter discussed here, see Rossell Hope Robbins, *The Encylopedia of Witchcraft and Demonology* (New York, 1959), especially pp. 423, 466-68.

their honor lost, have become the forlorn ghosts of their former selves, and their return to the place of their "deaths" becomes a circumambulatory parade of restless and tormented shades.

If the very last couplet of this paragraph achieves a haunting sadness, and a memorable perfection of pace, it is because Pope labored for these qualities; the couplet was not, demonstrably, the result of a lucky hit or a happy "knack." We cannot know of all the labor Pope expended on the couplet, but from one of his letters and from various published versions we know that in 1730 its first line at one time read, "Those Ghosts of Beauty wandring here reside," that at another time in the same year it read, "Those Ghosts of Beauty ling'ring there abide," and that in 1732 it read, "Those Ghosts of Beauty ling'ring here reside."[10] It was not until 1735 that the line assumed its final shape in *Of the Characters of Women*, yet who will deny that to this last version the long labor of the file has brought an ease and inevitability of mood and movement not to be matched by any of the former versions:

> Still round and round the Ghosts of Beauty glide,
> And haunt the places where their Honour dy'd.

10. See *The Correspondence of Alexander Pope*, ed. George Sherburn (Oxford, 1956), III, 123, and *The Twickenham Edition of the Poems of Alexander Pope*, III, ii, 67; VI, 316-17.

JOHN T. FAIN
Professor of English
University of Florida

Peacock on the Spirit of the Age (1809-1860)

HOMAS LOVE PEACOCK HAD A QUITE DEFINITE attitude toward the commercialism of his day and toward the natural and social sciences in their role of abettors of that commercialism. However, any attempt, such as the present one, to demonstrate that attitude from the works themselves involves some difficulty. For most of Peacock's ideas here set down can be said to belong to the author only in a special sense. He puts them in the mouths of the characters of his novels and then steps out and lets one whimsey contradict or supplement another, delighting in the way an opinion is expressed rather than in its substance. But he does not entirely step out either, so that one can never be sure when a creature expresses the creator, or just to what degree. This equivocal, ironical half-detachment is one of the elements of Peacockianism, a pattern of humor that depends for its effect chiefly upon a preposterous juxtaposition of

180

words, ideas, stylistic tones; upon a straight-faced, bald over-statement; upon a fantastic caricature of people and their opinions—a humor permeating even those thoughts that come to be recognized by the reader as closest to the author's profound convictions, a humor by which those convictions are toned down, or humanized, rather than obscured.

First let us notice some of Peacock's pertinent statements made before he allowed himself a full expression of his natural satirical vein. In "The Genius of the Thames," published in 1810, he speaks of England as a place

> Where peace, with freedom hand-in-hand,
> Walks forth along the sparkling strand;
> And cheerful toil, and glowing health,
> Proclaim a patriot nation's wealth.[1]

A large part of the credit for England's blessing is due to "sun-crowned science!—child of heaven," who "measures nature's ample plan,/ To hold the light of truth to man" (VI, 142).

These are some of the sentiments for which Shelley criticized Peacock before the two met in 1812. Thomas Hookham, a mutual friend, had sent Shelley copies of "The Genius of the Thames" and "The Philosophy of Melancholy," and Shelley comments in his reply of August 18, 1812:

> The poems abound with a genius, an information, the power and extent of which I admire, in proportion as I lament the object of their application. Mr. Peacock conceives that commerce is prosperity; that the glory of the British flag is the happiness of the British people; that George III, so far from having been a warrior and a tyrant, has been a patriot.[2]

It is probable that Shelley was partly responsible for Peacock's change from serious poetry to prose satire, but not apparently because of such direct criticism. Through contact with Shelley,

1. *The Halliford Edition of the Works of Thomas Love Peacock*, eds. H. F. B. Brett-Smith and C. E. Jones (London, 1924-34), VI, 117. Unless otherwise noted, all references are to this edition of the works.
2. *The Letters of Percy Bysshe Shelley*, ed. Roger Ingpen (London, 1909), I, 359; quoted in part in the Halliford Edition, I, 1-li.

Peacock undoubtedly realized his own minor status as a Romantic poet and was searching for a medium in which he could excel. Therefore, utilizing material close at hand, he discovered in Shelley and his circle a whole set of crotchets and burlesque characters that were ripe for Peacockian satire.[3]

The glorification of science and industry in "The Genius of the Thames" does not mean, however, that Peacock was unaware of the satirical possibilities of his subject. At the same time he was writing the poem he says in his letter of 1809 to Edward Hookham, younger brother of Thomas:

> The Thames is almost as good a subject for a satire as a panegyric.—A satirist might exclaim: The rapacity of Commerce, not content with the immense advantages derived from this river in a course of nearly 300 miles, erects a ponderous engine over the very place of its nativity, to suck up its unborn waters from the bosom of the earth, and pump them into a navigable canal! . . . A panegyrist, on the contrary, after expatiating on the benefits for commercial navigation . . . might say: "And yet this splendid undertaking would be incomplete, through failure of water in the summer months, did not this noble river, this beautiful emblem, and powerful instrument of the commercial greatness of Britain, contribute to that greatness even at the instant of its birth, by supplying this magnificent chain of connection with the means of perpetual utility."[4]

Thus a typical dialogue, which resembles many in the later novels, already lay in Peacock's mind while he was writing his long, humorless panegyrical poem.

Headlong Hall (1816) contains a thorough indictment of the commercial spirit of the age, given by Mr. Escot. At this

3. E. A. Johnson prefers "irony" to designate Peacock's type of humor, apparently because he thinks that Peacock's humor is prevailingly genial and that therefore "satire" is too strong a term. I believe that satire can be genial and also that Peacock's humor is usually sharper and less genial than it is generally considered to be. See Bill Read's comment on Johnson's dissertation in *The Critical Reputation of Thomas Love Peacock* . . . (Ann Arbor, Xerox, 1961), pp. 262-63.

4. VIII, 172-73. This letter was first quoted by Carl Van Doren, *The Life of Thomas Love Peacock* (London, 1911), pp. 39-41, in a somewhat similar argument.

stage of his career Peacock has not yet learned the fusion of speech and speaker which later marks the flowering of his narrative art, so we cannot say that Mr. Escot is even a comic self-portrait. This character does voice the ideas of Rousseau and Monboddo, however, who were favorite authors of Peacock at the time.[5] In the following passage Mr. Escot refutes the advantages which are usually said to counterbalance the evils of England's manufacturing system:

> Profound researches, scientific inventions: to what end? . . . to multiply factitious desires, to stimulate depraved appetites, to invent unnatural wants, to heap up incense on the shrine of luxury, and accumulate expedients of selfish and ruinous profusion. Complicated machinery: behold its blessings. . . . Wherever this boasted machinery is established, the children of the poor are death-doomed from their cradles. . . . Nor is the lot of the parents more enviable. . . . They have neither the corporeal energy of the savage, nor the mental acquisitions of the civilized man. . . . They are mere automata, component parts of the enormous machines which administer to the pampered appetites of the few. . . .   (I, 77-79)

Calidore, an unfinished novel presumably started and abandoned in 1816 (I, lxvii-lxix), is relevant here because in it is Peacock's first satire on paper money. Peacock is himself his most amusing crotcheteer, and his antipathy to paper money is one of his most persistent crotchets. In William Cobbett's *Political Register,* every number of which Peacock apparently read with delight, paper money is always associated with the chicanery of bankers and the victimization of the poor, as it is in Peacock's later works. In this fragment, however, such satire is to be read chiefly between the lines. Calidore has just come from Terra Incognita by means of a small boat which he folds up and puts into his pocket, an incident reminiscent of Peacock's and Shelley's habit of sailing paper boats. He goes to London to get some money:

5. *The Novels of Thomas Love Peacock,* ed. David Garnett (London, 1948), p. 12. I have used this edition for character identifications.

"How would you like to have it, sir?" said a little sharp-
nosed man with a quill behind his ear. "In the circulating
medium of this city," said Calidore. . . . The little man put
into his hand several slips of paper. "Well, sir!" said Calidore, "what am I to do with these?" —"Whatever you
please, sir," said the little man, smiling. "I wish I could say
as much for myself." —"I am much obliged to you," said
Calidore; "and I have no doubt you are an exceedingly
facetious and agreeable person; but, at the same time, if
you would have the goodness to direct me where I can receive my money—" —"Sir," said the little man, "that is your
money." —"This!" —"Certainly, sir, that. What would you
have?" —"Gold coin, to be sure," said Calidore. "Gold coin!
I am afraid, sir, you are a disaffected man and a Jacobin, or
you would not ask for such a thing, when I have given you
the best money in the world. Pray, sir, look at it. . . ." Calidore looked at one of the pieces of paper, and read aloud:
"I promise to pay to Mr. Henry Hare—One Thousand
Pounds—John Figginbotham. —Well, sir; and what have I
to do with John Figginbotham's promise to pay a thousand
pounds to Henry Hare?" —"John Figginbotham, sir, having
made that promise, and put it upon that paper, makes that
paper worth a thousand pounds." —"To Henry Hare," said
Calidore. —"To any one," said the little man. "You over-
look the words: or bearer. Now, sir, you are the bearer."
—"I understand: then John Figginbotham promises to pay
me a thousand pounds." —"Precisely." —"Then, sir, if you
will have the goodness to direct me to John Figginbotham
I will trouble him to pay me directly." —"But, good God,
sir! you mistake the matter."   (VIII, 336-37)

And so on for two more pages. In Peacock it is not enough to
make a point. Peacockian fun really begins after the matter has
been run into the ground.

   Melincourt (1817), the longest of Peacock's novels, is considered by commentators his least successful, the reason being
chiefly that in it Peacock takes his own opinions too seriously.
The censure seems to me a just one as Peacock's genius at its
best is almost wholly comic. The failure of *Melincourt* and its
rationale, however, enhance the argument of the present study
in proportion to the correctness of that censure. A large part of

the book, one of the group happily called by Priestley "novels of talk," is taken up with the conversations of Mr. Forester (based on Shelley) and Mr. Fax (based on Malthus). The former comments as follows on the spirit of the age:

> Insatiable accumulators, overgrown capitalists, fatteners on public spoil, I cannot but consider as excrescences on the body politic, typical of disease and prophetic of decay: yet it is to these . . . that the poet tunes his harp, and the man of science consecrates his labours: it is for them that an enormous portion of the population is condemned to un-healthy manufactories, not less deadly but more lingering than the pestilence. . . . (II, 430-31)

On the constructive side of the argument Peacock reads like a modern social economist. Mr. Forester says:

> I care not in what proportions property is divided . . . pro-vided the rich can be made to know that they are but the stewards of the poor, that they are not to be the monopo-lizers of solitary spoil, but the distributors of general posses-sion; that they are responsible for that distribution to every principle of general justice, to every tie of moral obligation, to every feeling of human sympathy: that they are bound to cultivate simple habits in themselves, and to encourage most such arts of industry and peace, as are most compatible with the health and liberty of others. (II, 269-70)

Actually this point of view, which became many years later the essence of the social criticism of Carlyle, Ruskin, and Morris, is a heritage in Western thought from the church fathers and schoolmen. It is well to point out, however, that Peacock is one of the earliest writers to emphasize its application to the condi-tions of the nineteenth century.

The Misfortunes of Elphin (1829)[6] provides the now mature satirist with one of his best devices, consisting of penetrating glances at the contemporary scene that now and again flash through a mild burlesque of old time. One example will dem-onstrate the method:

6. *Nightmare Abbey* (1818), in which the satire is literary, and *Maid Marian* (1822), in which it is clerical and political, are not included in the present discussion.

As Taliesin grew up, Gwythno instructed him in all the knowledge of the age, which was of course not much, in comparison with ours. . . . The advantages of growing rich by getting into debt and paying interest was altogether unknown. . . . They had no steam-engines, with fires as eternal as those of the nether world, wherein the squalid many, from infancy to age, might be turned into component portions of machinery for the benefit of the purple-faced few. They could neither poison the air with gas, nor the waters with its dregs: in short, they made their money of metal, and breathed pure air, and drank pure water, like unscientific barbarians. (IV, 50-51)

In *Crotchet Castle* (1831) the other aspects of the commercial spirit are not forgotten, but the chief satire of the sort under consideration is directed at the science of economics itself. It may be significant that during this period Peacock was constantly associated in his work at the East India House with James and John Stuart Mill, both, among other things, important economists of the time. Biographers of Peacock seem to be wrong, however, in supposing that Peacock disliked them. On the contrary, he seems to have been a close friend of the father and to have been kind and considerate to the son, who was his subordinate.[7] The following conversation is between Mr. MacQuedy (Q.E.D., representing the Scottish economist McCulloch) and the Reverend Dr. Folliott, an Anglican clergyman. They are at breakfast and Dr. Folliott is praising the fish. Food and drink constitute the most important single topic in Peacock's novels. The passage incidentally illustrates one of Peacock's favorite conversational patterns, rebuttal by means of a remark entirely off the subject, the kind of thing that seems to place Peacock among practitioners of shaggy-dog humor:[8]

7. The evidence for this statement would perhaps lead us too far astray here. It can be found in *The Athenians*, ed. W. S. Scott (London, 1943), p. 61; *New Shelley Letters*, ed. W. S. Scott (London, 1948), pp. 126, 153, 158; and an unpublished letter of Peacock to Lord Broughton (John Cam Hobhouse), British Museum, Add. MS. 47225.

8. Peacock is not mentioned, however, by Eric Partridge in *The 'Shaggy Dog' Story* (London, 1953).

MR. MACQUEDY. Well, sir, and what say you to a fine fresh trout, hot and dry, in a napkin? or a herring out of the water into the frying pan, on the shore of Loch Fyne?

THE REV. DR. FOLLIOTT. Sir, I say every nation has some eximious virtue; and your country is pre-eminent in the glory of fish for breakfast. We have much to learn from you in that line at any rate.

MR. MACQUEDY. And in many others, sir, I believe. Morals and metaphysics, politics and political economy, the way to make the most of all the modifications of smoke; steam, gas, and paper currency; you have all these to learn from us; in short, all the arts and sciences. We are the modern Athenians.

THE REV. DR. FOLLIOTT. I, for one, sir, am content to learn nothing from you but the art and science of fish for breakfast. . . .

MR. MACQUEDY. Then, sir, I presume you set no value on the right principles of rent, profit, wages, and currency?

THE REV. DR. FOLLIOTT. My principles, sir, in these things are, to take as much as I can get, and to pay no more than I can help. These are every man's principles, whether they be the right principles or no. There, sir, is political economy in a nutshell.

MR. MACQUEDY. The principles, sir, which regulate production and consumption, are independent of the will of any individual as to giving or taking, and do not lie in a nutshell by any means.

THE REV. DR. FOLLIOTT. Sir, I will thank you for a leg of that capon.   (IV, 15-17)

Peacock was considered in his day a master of economic theory, and the *Westminster Review*, speaking of his treatment of Mr. MacQuedy, expressed regret that "men are most inclined to satirize that of which they know the most" (I, cli). We have no way of knowing whether Peacock was a master of the orthodox economics of his day since he published no serious treatise on the subject. But there can be no doubt that he was a master of the *criticism* of the orthodox school. In *Crotchet Castle* is the nucleus of all the criticism directed at that school later by Toynbee, Ingram, and Cliffe-Leslie. For instance, Dr. Folliott says:

You have given the name of a science to what is yet an imperfect inquiry; and the upshot of your so-called science is this, that you increase the wealth of a nation by increasing in it the quantity of things which are produced by labour: no matter what they are, no matter how produced, no matter how distributed. . . . Now, I say, if this is so, riches are not the object for a community to aim at. I say, the nation is best off . . . which has the greatest quantity of the common necessaries of life distributed among the greatest number of persons; which has the greatest number of honest hearts and stout arms united in a common interest. . . . The moment you admit that one class of things, without any reference to what they respectively cost, is better worth having than another; that a smaller commercial value, with one mode of distribution, is better than a greater commercial value, with another mode of distribution; the whole of that curious fabric of postulates and dogmas . . . tumbles to pieces. (IV. 127-28)

Gryll Grange (1860), the last of the novels, has all of the elements of the social satire we have noticed in earlier works but for the most part toned down to a mild complacency. One notable exception, however, is his indictment of applied science, in which he has become sharper in proportion to the increased technological development of the three decades since the publication of *Crotchet Castle*. If such sentiments as the following had not been considered the maunderings of a crotchety old man, the learned world would have attacked Peacock as it did Ruskin at about the same time:

Science is an edged tool, with which men play like children, and cut their own fingers. . . . See the complications and refinements of modes of destruction, in revolvers and rifles and shells and rockets and cannon. See collisions and wrecks and every mode of disaster by land and by sea, resulting chiefly from the insanity for speed, in those who for the most part have nothing to do at the end of the race. . . . Look at our scientific drainage, which turns refuse into poison. . . . Look at our scientific machinery, which has destroyed domestic manufacture, which has substituted rottenness for strength in the thing made, and physical degradation in crowded towns for healthy and comfortable country life in the makers. . . . I almost think it is the ultimate destiny of science to exterminate the human race.

(V. 186-87)

In this brief chronological treatment of a segment of Peacock's social criticism, little reference has been made to the sources of the ideas expressed; the implication may therefore be that most of them are to be considered Peacock's own. In fact, they are not. Every age has a characteristic intellectual current felt by many men merely by virtue of their position in the stream of time. In addition to the sources already mentioned, Peacock seems to have got some of the thoughts here recorded from Adam Smith himself, for the father of English economics sowed many seeds that his orthodox followers left undeveloped. The important point here is that Peacock expressed these thoughts in terms of the nineteenth century considerably earlier than did the great Victorian social critics—and better than most of them. Peacock has never seemed to belong anywhere, and one of the reasons why so little is known about him is that historians could never decide where to *put* him. He is not given his just place in commentaries on Romantic writers probably because of the anti-Romantic tendency of his best work. Because his social satire bears a close resemblance to that of many later novelists and essayists, a place might be made for him among the Victorians. He certainly lasted long enough (1866). If those who wish to keep periods unrealistically discrete object that he was born too soon (1785), then so was Landor, who was ten years older, or even Carlyle, who was only ten years younger.[9]

9. Assistance for this and other work on Peacock has been given by the Penrose Fund of the American Philosophical Society.

FREDERICK W. CONNER
Professor of English
Dean, College of Arts and Sciences
University of Alabama

Poe & John Nichol
Notes on a Source of *Eureka*

HE FEAT BY WHICH THE AMAZING DEDUCTIVE powers of M. Dupin are established in "The Murders in the Rue Morgue" is the reconstruction of a chain of associations which has taken place in the mind of his companion as they walk the streets of Paris. The chain begins with a fruiterer and ends with an unsuccessful actor, some of the intervening links being the paving blocks in the street, the art of stonecutting, the atoms of Epicurus, the nebular cosmogony, and the nebula in Orion. The most important link for the purposes of the subject to be discussed here, however, is a "Dr. Nichols," who, as is indicated by the author's use of the name interchangeably with the nebular theory, was John Pringle Nichol, Professor of Practical Astronomy at the University of Glasgow and author of *Views of the Architecture of the Heavens in a Series of Letters to a Lady*, a work which first appeared in 1837 and had gone through several British edi-

tions and one American edition by 1841,[1] when Poe published his story. This book, in which the nebular theory holds a climactic position, was one of the most widely read works of popular science of its day and seems to have made more than a casual impression on Poe even at this early date. Two months after the appearance of "The Murders in the Rue Morgue" he again adverted to the nebular theory in reviewing Macaulay's *Essays*, using it to back up his assertion *contra* Macaulay that astronomers have increased our knowledge of divinity by extending the range of "analogy": "the only irrefutable argument in support of the soul's immortality—or, rather, the only conclusive proof of man's alternate dissolution and rejuvenescence *ad infinitum*—is to be found in analogies deduced from the modern established theory of the nebular cosmogony."[2] Since this kind of use of the nebular theory is prominent in *The Architecture of the Heavens*, it seems reasonable to conclude that Dupin's Scottish astronomer was not taken lightly by Poe.

Between 1841 and the publication of *Eureka* in 1848 I have noted only one other reference by Poe to Nichol.[3] In *Eureka* itself, however, there are a number of allusions to Nichol; he is twice quoted, and *The Architecture of the Heavens* is singled out for an epithet of praise. Moreover, the parallels between the two books, both particular and general, are sufficiently striking to suggest strongly that Poe owed more to Nichol than has hitherto been recognized. That there was a debt of some character was noted at least as early as Woodberry's first biography of Poe,[4] though apparently on the basis of Poe's references alone

1. Said by the *DNB* to have gone through seven editions in seven years. The edition published by Baillere in 1851 is labeled the ninth. The edition used here is the third (Edinburgh, 1839) and will be referred to as *A. of H*. Other works by Nichol, most of which went through several editions, are *Phenomena of the Solar System*, 1838; *Thoughts on the System of the World*, 1846; *The Stellar Universe*, 1847; *The Planet Neptune*, 1848; *The Planetary System*, 1848.

2. *Graham's Magazine*, June, 1841; *The Complete Works of Edgar Allan Poe*, ed. J. A. Harrison (New York, 1902), X, 159. The passage with which Poe was taking issue is in "Ranke's History of the Popes."

3. "Plato Contra Atheos," *Broadway Journal*, June 21, 1845; *Complete Works*, XII, 165.

4. *Edgar Allan Poe* (Boston, 1885), p. 299.

rather than on the parallels. Few people appear to have gone beyond these references to the book itself.[5] Of course, it is no matter for special remark that both men made use of the nebular hypothesis, since this theory had been widely known for nearly half a century. It seems significant, however, that in both *Eureka* and *The Architecture of the Heavens* the point should be prominently made that the "beauty" of this hypothesis is one of its recommendations.[6] Also, though it is not surprising that both books lay great stress on the religious significance of natural phenomena—this was after all the era of the Bridgewater Treatises—it is probably no accident that both books make similar appeals to the principles of unity[7] and analogy,[8] that they deal at least comparably with the questions of the finitude and shape of our firmament,[9] and that they make similar references to Comte[10] and share other details. The most important parallel, however, is in the larger character of the two works, specifically in the fact that both aim more at presenting a history than a blueprint. The principal other works to which Poe is known to have been indebted in *Eureka*—the younger Herschel's *Treatise on Astronomy*, Humboldt's *Kosmos*, and some of the works of Thomas Dick—may truly be said to have presented the "architecture" of the universe in that they were describing its structure and constituents; but both Poe and Nichol, despite the latter's choice of title, were principally bent on describing a process of development. It is a real distinction of both books that they do not, like most astronomies of their

5. Carroll Laverty consulted the work in preparing his excellent dissertation, "Science and Pseudo-Science in the Writings of Edgar Allan Poe" (Duke University, 1951), but he made little use of the parallels.

6. *Complete Works*, XVI, 252; *A. of H.*, p. 186. Interestingly, both statements are made in connection with comments on the retrograde motion of two satellites of Uranus. See also below, pp. 207-8.

7. "The unity of things—their interdependence—their adjusted relationships, are proclaimed by every department of the Universe." *A. of H.*, pp. 174-75. Unity is the central concept of *Eureka*.

8. "The analogy or group of collocated events, is the bud of mighty truth. . . ." *A. of H.*, p. 78.

9. On finitude cf. *Complete Works*, XVI, 200-204, and *A. of H.*, pp. 6-7. On the shape of our galaxy cf. *Complete Works*, XVI, 271-73, and *A. of H.*, pp. 13-19.

10. *Complete Works*, XVI, 260; *A. of H.*, p. 182.

192

time, either ignore the evolutionary aspect of their subject or reserve it for a brief noncommittal chapter, but rather give it a prominent and even dominant position. This fundamental and historically very important parallel will be the main subject of the discussion that follows, where it will be considered first in itself and then in relation to a curious antagonism which Poe seems to have felt for Nichol and which has perhaps diverted previous investigators from the study of his influence.

I

When the history of the popular dissemination of the idea of evolution is finally written, Nichol will certainly receive more credit than has yet been accorded him. The *NED* cites the 1850 edition of *The Architecture of the Heavens* as the earliest instance of the use of the term "evolution" in its astronomical application, though Nichol presented the idea even more strongly in the earlier editions.[11] The first five chapters of the book in its earliest form were largely devoted to supplying necessary preliminary information concerning the present form and mechanics of the universe, but at the beginning of the sixth chapter the climactic theme of the book was introduced in the form of the following question concerning our firmament: "Pondering on the strange outline it now presents in *space*, a new thought slowly arises, regarding its relation to *Time*;—we ask hesitatingly whether these arrangements are *fixed* . . . or whether visible phenomena have not a deeper significancy, and are at once results of a pre-existing state, and germinant of something future."[12] The hesitation in this query turns out to have been merely rhetorical. How much so may be seen by skipping to the perfervid final paragraph of the book, where the "deeper significancy" here tentatively suggested is affirmed in the most sweeping terms. With the air of one brushing aside trifling peripheral difficulties to get at the heart of the matter, the author concedes that even though the nebular cosmogony as a special theory of the process of sidereal evolution might be proved wrong,

11. In the edition of 1850, however, the term is used for the first time as the title of the third and final section.

12. *A. of H.*, p. 129.

This, at least, is established on grounds not to be removed. In the vast Heavens, as well as among phenomena around us, all things are in a state of change and PROGRESS: there too—on the sky—in splendid hieroglyphics the truth is inscribed, that the grandest forms of present Being are only GERMS swelling and bursting with a life to come! . . . —TO COME!—To every Creature these are words of Hope spoken in organ tone; our hearts suggest them, and the stars repeat them, and through the Infinite, Aspiration wings its way, rejoicingly as an eagle following the sun.

Farewell![13]

Poe expressed a similar sentiment in less climactic position in these terms: "It was required, in a word, that the stars should be gathered into visibility from invisible nebulosity—proceed from nebulosity to consolidation—and so grow grey in giving birth and death to unspeakably numerous and complex variations of vitalic development."[14]

Visionary and melodramatic as Nichol was in passages like the one just quoted, he was at most times more cautious than Poe. The bulk of his writing was straightforward professorial exposition, and his more daring speculations were reserved for intermittent purple patches. These passages, however, invariably represented the climax of what he had to say, and in them he developed his evolutionary principle in three ways that are closely paralleled in *Eureka*. Thus, both he and Poe viewed the universal evolution as the accompaniment and result of a universal condensation. Poe describes the history of the universe as the "progressive collapse" of an original irradiation of matter under the influence of the universal attractive force known to us as gravitation. The gigantic clusters of the heavens he looked upon as "colossal atoms" that would one day merge into a final cluster of clusters and then into "one magnificent sun."[15] Nichol's similar conception of the process may be seen in the following passage:

Even the larger forms of the Heavens . . . are congregating towards that nucleus, around which the new order of things

13. *A. of H.*, pp. 210-11.
14. *Complete Works*, XVI, 290-91.
15. *Complete Works*, XVI, 269.

is slowly up-growing, and where the mighty orb, foretold by their progressing aggregation, is preparing to be born. I cannot avoid reverting to the notion of Mr. Coleridge; what is this after all, save a prolongation of the condensing of a Nebula? Already some few of its particles have come together and formed its secondary stage; and now, that secondary stage, which we term a firmament, is passing into a third, where all the dispersed atoms will be gathered together, and lodged at the centre of the mass!

We may venture even one step higher. If the suns of each firmament, which are but the congress of multitudes of atoms originally distinct, are related in this wise—may not some similar system and similar destiny characterize Systems of Firmaments? Perhaps in the meanwhile these are also related, somehow as the stars in each cluster—slowly performing mighty revolutions, whose recurrence constitutes the greatest Annus Magnus of Creation—the highest unit of existing Time.[16]

The phrase "progressive collapse" Poe borrowed from Herschel rather than Nichol, but, as he was aware, Herschel was examining the concept only for the purpose of rejecting it.[17] Nichol, however, was thinking of a real possibility, and in so doing he may have supplied one of the most potent suggestions that went into the making of Poe's wondrous theory.

Nichol and Poe, moreover, did not limit their attention to sidereal evolution, but extended their theories to include the smaller and nearer aspects of universal change. Reasoning from his own peculiar conception of repulsion between bodies as well as from the force of attraction, Poe arrived at the evolutionary principle that "the importance of the development of the terrestrial vitality proceeds equably with the terrestrial condensation," and pointed out that "this is in precise accordance with what we know of the succession of animals on earth."[18] Elsewhere he added that vitality has not only increased in "importance" during the process of condensation but has mani-

16. *A. of H.*, pp. 203-4.
17. *Complete Works*, XVI, 297. See Sir John F. W. Herschel, *Treatise on Astronomy* (London, 1833), pp. 400-401.
18. *Complete Works*, XVI, 259.

fested itself on successively higher levels, first of sensitivity, then of conscious thought and spirit.[19] In making this addition he was in agreement with Nichol, who included biological, psychological, and moral progress in his universal optimism. "What is the intention of such a mass?" Nichol asked in one instance, during a discussion of nebulae,

> Is it to abide for ever in that chaotic condition—void, formless, and diffuse in the midst of order and organization—or is it the germ of more exalted Being—the rudiments of something only yet being arranged? . . . nay, who can tell—who that has looked on those monuments of bygone worlds, the fossil relics which mark the early progress of our own planet—but, this amorphous substance may bear within it, laid up in its dark bosom—the germs, the producing powers of that LIFE, which in coming ages will bud and blossom, and effloresce, into manifold and growing forms, until it becomes fit harbourage and nourishment to every varying degree of intelligence, and every shade of moral sensibility and greatness.[20]

Since Poe was considerably less sanguine in general outlook than Nichol and less interested in geology and biology, he dwelt less lingeringly and lovingly on this subject. In his basic conception, however, he was in agreement with Nichol, and a closer relationship than agreement may be suggested by the fact that in the little that he had to say on geology he followed Nichol in singling out for discussion the question of the fossil remains of tropical life at the poles.[21] It is perhaps also worth noting that the American editions of Nichol's book, dated 1840 and 1842, contained an eight-page appendix on this subject.[22]

Probably the most striking parallel between the two books, however, lies in their highly dramatic conclusions. In keeping with his strong sense of climax Poe saw the cosmic story in

19. *Complete Works*, XVI, 309.
20. *A. of H.*, pp. 137-38.
21. *Complete Works*, XVI, 257-58; *A. of H.*, pp. 121-22. Poe's explanation, however, is more ingenious and far-fetched than Nichol's. For a more extensive consideration of Poe's evolutionism see my *Cosmic Optimism* (Gainesville: University of Florida Press, 1949), Ch. III.
22. The appendix was not written by Nichol but, apparently, by L. D. Chapin.

terms of an end as well as a beginning and a middle, and this end he deduced with amazing logic from his principles of attraction and repulsion. From the major premise that matter is a synthesis of attraction and repulsion and the minor premise that attraction and repulsion can exist only *between* atoms, he drew the conclusion that in the final condensation, when all "betweenness" shall have been squeezed out, matter will cease to exist: "Matter without Attraction and without Repulsion— in other words, Matter without Matter—in other words, again, *Matter no more.*"[23] Nichol enjoyed the benefit of no such ingenious syllogism but his story had a finale no less dramatically eschatological, which he stated in terms which caused even Poe to accord him the epithet "eloquent":[24]

> Still farther;—the system, though strong, is not framed to be EVERLASTING; and our Hypothesis also developes the mode of the certain decay and final dissolution of its arrangements. Remember the effects of the Solar Ether! Although no mark of age has yet been recognised in the planetary paths, as sure as that filmy comet is drawing in its orbit, must they too approach the sun, and, at the destined term of their separate existence, be resumed into his mass. The first indefinite germs of this great organization, provision for its long existence, and finally its shroud, are thus all involved in that master conception from which we can now survey the mechanisms amid which we are! And mark the nature of this decay. It comes, not as Newton though, by accident, derangement, or disease, but through the midst of harmony; it is an easy consequence of the venerable power which first evolved us, infused our scheme with the spirit of life, and gave it structure and strength. . . . So dies Nature's unblemished child—the simple flower! It bursts its seed, buds and blooms; and then in unimpaired obedience draws in its leaves and sinks into the lap of its Mother Earth.[25]

Nor does the story quite end here for either writer. Neither of these scientific melodramatists was willing to let the fair hero-

23. *Complete Works*, XVI, 310-11.
24. *Complete Works*, XVI, 222.
25. *A. of H.*, pp. 193-94.

ine be ground to death under the wheels of time. There was
to be a hairbreadth escape and a happy ending. As in "Ligeia"
and "For Annie," death did not end all. Reaching into his bag
of tricks, Poe drew out "that omniprevalent law of laws, the
law of periodicity" and affirmed that the whole process would
be repeated again and again—"a novel Universe swelling into
existence, and then subsiding into nothingness, at every throb
of the Heart Divine."[26] Nichol, in a passage which followed by
only a few pages a discussion of Lagrange's principle of periodicity, presented a similar conviction:

> The idea of the ultimate dissolution of the solar system,
> has usually been felt as painful, and forcibly resisted by
> philosophers . . . but, after all, why should it be painful?
> Absolute permanence is visible nowhere around us, and the
> fact of change merely intimates, that in the exhaustless
> womb of the future, unevolved wonders are in store. The
> phenomenon referred to would simply point to the close
> of one mighty cycle in the history of the solar orb—the pass-
> ing away of arrangements which have fulfilled their objects
> that they might be transformed into new. Thus is the peri-
> odic death of a plant perhaps the essential of its prolonged
> life, and when the individual dies and disappears, fresh and
> vigorous forms spring from the elements which composed
> it. Mark the Chrysalis! It is the grave of the worm, but the
> cradle of the unborn insect. The broken bowl will yet be
> healed and beautified by the potter, and a Voice of joyful
> note will awaken, one day, even the silence of the Urn![27]

Here, plainly, was the "argument in support of the soul's immortality . . . found in analogies drawn from the modern established theory of the nebular cosmogony" to which Poe appealed
in his review of Macaulay in 1841; and here also may have been
the suggestion for the climax of *Eureka* seven years later.

II

The possibility of indebtedness so strongly suggested by
these parallels—not duplicated so far as I have been able to dis-

26. *Complete Works*, XVI, 311.
27. *A. of H.*, pp. 194-95.

cover in the work of other contemporary writers—adds greatly
to the interest of the fact that at the very same time that Poe
was presenting *Eureka* in preliminary form as a lecture at the
Society Library, Nichol was also lecturing on astronomy at the
Mercantile Library, having come to this country on a lecture
tour a little more than two months earlier. In August of 1847
Emerson had responded to a request that he recommend Nichol
for appointment as a Lowell Institute lecturer, and on November 4, in Liverpool, he was able to render him further aid as he
was about to embark for America. Emerson found him "polished and intelligent," and not only gave him letters of introduction to Theodore Parker and Longfellow but entrusted to
him a letter to Mrs. Emerson. Nichol arrived in Boston on
November 22 and was promptly called upon and entertained
by Longfellow,[28] who, like such other notable readers as the
young Mary Ann Evans and the elder Channing, was impressed
by the way in which *The Architecture of the Heavens* "wafts
one away into infinite depths of space."[29] Nichol's charm, abilities, and fame secured him a warm welcome not only with
Longfellow but at the Harvard and Cincinnati observatories
and enabled him to bring out an American edition of his
Thoughts on the System of the World, the new preface of
which is dated February, 1848, the period of his New York
lectures. He was apparently as well received in New York as
he had been elsewhere. The New York *Tribune* carried only
a brief account of Poe's lecture, but Nichol's series was printed
three times in full stenographic transcript, first in the daily
issues following the individual lectures, then seriatim in the
weekly supplement of February 19, and finally as a separate
publication by the firm of Greeley and McElrath.[30] The daily
reports appeared on January 27 and 31 and February 3, 8, 10,

28. R. L. Rusk (ed.), *Letters of Ralph Waldo Emerson* (New York, 1939), III, 408, 433-34, 436.

29. Samuel Longfellow, *Life of Henry Wadsworth Longfellow* (Boston, 1891), II, 63.

30. *Views of Astronomy: Seven Lectures Delivered before the Mercantile Library Association of New York in the Months of January and February, 1848. Reported for the New York Tribune by Oliver Dyer, Phonographic Writer* (New York: Greeley and McElrath, 1848).

14, and 17. Poe's lecture was delivered on the evening of Thursday, February 3, and it has been said that he finished the manuscript of his book and presented it to Putnam within a few days.[31]

The interest of this coincidence and of Nichol's probably great influence on *Eureka* is further heightened by two facts. The first is that Poe's quotations from Nichol in *Eureka* were not taken from *The Architecture of the Heavens*, where doubtless other students of Poe than I have searched for them in vain, but from the lectures, despite the fact that these were scarcely begun when he gave his own lecture and only half completed when he may have given his manuscript to Putnam. The second fact is that Poe's treatment of Nichol, though it includes some small compliments, is on the whole antagonistic. In the discussion that follows, these two facts will be elaborated, and an attempt will be made to shed some light on Poe's motives in regard to his more successful rival.

The first of the two quotations from Nichol is taken from

31. According to Maunsell B. Field (*Memories of Many Men and Some Women*, q. Mary E. Phillips, *Edgar Allan Poe—The Man*, Philadelphia, 1926, p. 1257) Putnam stated the day after the lecture the "luckless poet presented himself to him with the manuscript of the 'Universe.'" Putnam's son gives two different versions of the occurrence (G. H. Putnam, *George Palmer Putnam, 1814-1872*, I, 234-37, and II, 259-60). In one Poe said only that he had a manuscript which he was bringing to completion and asked for desk, pen, ink, and paper to work on it: "He wrote furiously during the hours of daylight that remained, until the time came for my father to take his boat for Staten Island. The author was then turned over to the care of the book-keeper and remained writing until the book-keeper also had departed for home. The porter had patience for a little time longer and then, more interested in the plans for his own supper than in the secrets of the universe, put the poet out notwithstanding protests. The next day [Saturday the 5th?] the performance was repeated on practically the same lines. On the third day [Monday the 7th?], the completed manuscript was brought by the poet to the publisher's desk and was handed over with most glowing prophecies. . . ." In the other version the poet arrived with the completed manuscript on Saturday afternoon and was promised a decision on Monday. In any case, *Eureka* did not appear until July and was not in proof until May 19. This would have allowed ample time for Poe to make such use as he might wish of the full series of Nichol lectures. For references bearing on the dating of *Eureka* see J. W. Ostrom, *The Letters of Edgar Allan Poe* (Cambridge, 1948), II, 363, 364, 365, 366, 369, 375.

the newspaper report of February 3, the morning of Poe's own lecture, and is presented by Poe as follows:

> Referring to the Newtonian Gravity, Dr. Nichol, the eloquent author of "The Architecture of the Heavens," says:—"In truth we have no reason to suppose this great Law, as now revealed, to be the ultimate or simplest, and therefore the universal and all-comprehensive, form of a great Ordinance. The mode in which its intensity diminishes with the element of distance, has not the aspect of an ultimate *principle*; which always assumes the simplicity and self-evidence of those axioms which constitute the basis of Geometry."[32]

Poe's confused comment on this confused statement is that what are commonly *called* "ultimate principles" do indeed "always assume the simplicity of geometrical axioms," but that these principles are not truly ultimate, since there is but one truly ultimate principle, the Volition of God, and this principle, far from being simple, is the very "consummation of the complex." In being divine it is "unintelligible," and—so the reader is allowed to infer—unintelligibility implies complexity. Quite apart from the fact that Poe has completely ignored the special context in which Nichol's statement was made (he was talking about discrepancies between the observed and calculated paths of Uranus), his comment is at best a quibble, first on the word "principle," confusing it with a power (i.e., the Volition of God), secondly, in equating complexity and divine incomprehensibility. Moreover, Poe's use of the term "principle" here is inconsistent with his usual practice elsewhere in his book. The basic "principle" to which he himself most frequently appeals, that of "oneness," he describes as "the absolute extreme of simplicity," and yet as he uses it, it is also sufficiently "ultimate" to explain the constitution, present phenomena, and inevitable annihilation of "at least the material Universe."[33] Finally, even if we grant to Poe that such a principle ought not to be called ultimate and that Nichol should certainly have rec-

32. *Complete Works*, XVI, 222.
33. *Complete Works*, XVI, 207.

ognized that beyond any such principle lies the will of God, he is blaming Nichol for an error which he did not commit, as he must have known from *The Architecture of the Heavens* and could also have found out in the morning paper of three days before. At the end of his preceding lecture Nichol had asked the question, What is gravity? and had answered in his last sentence that it is the immanent action of God as "the ever present Preserver, Sustainer and Efficient Cause of all phenomena." The best that can be said of Poe's remarks in this case is that they were intended as a device of exposition rather than as responsible criticism.[34]

The second of the quotations from Nichol (from the first lecture, reported on January 27) is handled with the lofty indulgence of the man of genius for the limited vision of the man of mere talent. Nichol had been discussing the patterns of the "nebulae," or, more properly, clusters of stars, and had stated that in many cases these are surrounded by masses of stars "stretching out apparently *as if* they were rushing toward a great central mass in consequence of the action of some great power." Poe commented that Nichol's words were part of the presentation of "quite a different view of the cosmical conditions from any taken in this Discourse" and objected that Nichol had stated only metaphorically what was true in fact, that he had stumbled upon a great truth but lacked the perception to recognize it:

> Were I to describe, in my own words, what must necessarily be the existing condition of each nebula on the hypothesis that all matter is, as I suggest, now returning to its original Unity, I should simply be going over, nearly verbatim, the language here employed by Dr. Nichol, without the faintest suspicion of that stupendous truth which is the key to these nebular phenomena.[35]

34. This is perhaps also the best that can be said of the use which I made of this passage in *Cosmic Optimism*, pp. 68-69. I now know that the connection in which I used the passage was impossible, since the passage was not available to Poe until after he had established the main outlines of his theory and presented them in his lecture.

35. *Complete Works*, XVI, 298. It should be observed that Poe did not regard the "great central mass" as *now* existing. See his footnote.

One reads these words with a good deal of surprise. As we have seen, it is not unlikely that Poe owed the first suggestion of his "stupendous truth" to the very man whom he now dismisses as not having the "faintest suspicion" of it. At the very least he knew that Nichol was thoroughly acquainted with the nebular cosmogony, for in his first reference to Nichol years before he had presented his name as an inevitable association of the theory.

III

What is the explanation of this strange attitude? A part of it may have been haste in composition, combined with the fact that he was using Nichol's statements largely as conveniences for the introduction of ideas of his own. Another and larger part is certainly that Poe and Nichol were rivals in a very precise sense and that Poe was seldom patient or charitable with his rivals. There was a third factor, however, which is more important for our purposes because it tells us more about the intellectual relations of the two men. A real difference had grown up between them. Because of certain changes of opinion that Nichol had undergone in the middle forties, Poe had come to feel at odds with him, more at odds, in fact, than was justified by Nichol's actual position. Thus in another place in *Eureka* Poe criticized Nichol for having "abandoned" the nebular cosmogony. "The most enthusiastic defender," he wrote, "and most eloquent popularizer of the theory, Dr. Nichol, went so far as to 'admit the necessity of abandoning' an idea which had formed the material of his most praiseworthy book." In a footnote he softened his impeachment as follows:

> A letter, purporting to be from Dr. Nichol to a friend in America, went the rounds of our newspapers, about two years ago, I think, admitting "the necessity" to which I refer. In a subsequent Lecture, however, Dr. N. appears in some manner to have gotten the better of the necessity, and does not quite *renounce* the theory, although he seems to wish that he could sneer at it as "a purely hypothetical one."[36]

36. *Complete Works*, XVI, 262-63.

We must take a look at the development of Nichol's views if we are to understand this relationship. In the early editions of *The Architecture of the Heavens* he had been thoroughly convinced of the truth of the nebular cosmogony not only because of its remarkable explanatory power but because of what he regarded as "ocular" proof. Thus, in the first place, it seemed evident to him that true nebulae, that is, "filmy or Nebulous fluid shining of itself,"[37] actually existed in the skies. Such a nebula as that in Orion not only resisted resolution into a mass of stars when examined with the aid of powerful telescopes but even seemed to grow more nebulous in appearance when examined with successively more powerful glasses.[38] In the second place, as the elder Herschel had pointed out long before, the nebulae were in different but nicely graded stages of aggregation and thus seemed to be acting out the process of evolutionary condensation before the very eyes of the astronomer. It was, Herschel had said, as though a botanist had before him successive stages in the growth of a plant.[39] However, the powerful six-foot reflector of Lord Rosse, completed in 1845, had not been long in use before a number of supposed nebulae were resolved into clusters of stars, and this ominous development caused Nichol to insert a cautionary preface in the 1845 edition of *The Architecture of the Heavens* in which he re-examined the logical status of the nebular theory (that is, whether it was a matter of observation or hypothesis) in the light of the possibility that all the so-called nebulae might prove illusory. The test case for him was the nebula in Orion, which had previously so strongly resisted resolution; and thus when on March 19, 1846, Lord Rosse wrote him that there could be "little, if any, doubt as to the resolvability"[40] of this nebula, Nichol definitely and publicly altered his position in respect to the nebular theory: it was a matter of supposition rather than ob-

37. *A. of H.*, p. 135.
38. *A. of H.*, pp. 135-36.
39. *A. of H.*, p. 202.
40. *Thoughts on Some Important Points Relating to the System of the World* (Boston and Cambridge, 1848), p. 94. The resolution of nebulae was front-page scientific news and widely known. See reference by Emerson, *Complete Works*, Centenary Edition, Boston, 1903-4, VII, 8; XI, 391.

servation. It was to be the opinion of Agnes Clerke, the later historian of nineteenth-century astronomy, that he and others like him were too precipitate in their judgment concerning the existence of nebulae,[41] but in *Thoughts on the System of the World*, first published in 1846 and republished in an American edition shortly after the New York lectures, he was ready to say that "every shred of evidence, on the ground of which we previously believed in the reality and diffusion through the Heavens, of masses that are not stellar, is forever and hopelessly destroyed,"[42] and that

> Laplace's story is not only now hypothetical in its foundations, but also *hypothetical throughout*. So long as Herschel's views continued acceptably, the doctrine of the genesis of our System from a Nebula, rested in so far on FACTS—the process of condensation being actually discerned. . . . *Now*, however, we start with what is purely an hypothesis, viz., that the system came into being through the condensation of a nebula; an hypothesis . . . which . . . can commend itself only by the correspondence of its results with the existing arrangements of our System.[43]

The important point to be observed here is that Nichol had not, as Poe said, "abandoned" the nebular cosmogony. The only theory that he had abandoned was that which held that a nebulous fluid now exists in the heavens and that therefore we have ocular evidence of the condensation of nebulae. But in this Nichol was not in disagreement with Poe, whose view was that the period of the existence of nebulae was long past.[44] Moreover, though in his lecture reported on February 10, as in the passage just quoted from the *System of the World*, Nichol admitted emphatically that the theory must for this reason be regarded as hypothetical, he cannot, of all things, be said to have "sneered" at it. On the contrary, he called the process that it attempts to explain "the most sublime in the

41. *History of Astronomy during the Nineteenth Century* (2nd. ed., London, 1887), p. 149.
42. *System of the World*, p. 99.
43. *System of the World*, p. 104.
44. *Complete Works*, XVI, 263-65.

whole range of Astronomy," he devoted nearly half of his lecture to a careful and complimentary exposition of it, and he based his whole passionately optimistic conclusion on it, saying without hesitation or reservation that it "shows us, not only the origin of our system, but carries us onwards to the time when it shall undergo some great organic change . . . immense motions accomplishing majestic purposes—all things rushing on toward some new condition—proclaiming that evolution, ceaseless and irresistible—advancing from the imperfect to the perfect is the Law of the Universe."[45]

There is no evidence that Poe was acquainted with the *System of the World*, and of course if he submitted his completed manuscript on the seventh of February, as has been reported by his publisher's son, he could not have had previous knowledge of a lecture delivered on the ninth and printed on the tenth. There is thus a theoretical possibility that in preparing the text of *Eureka* Poe was simply not adequately informed about Nichol's position and that his footnote was a belated qualification inspired by the lecture of February 9. Since *Eureka* was not published until July and Poe was working on proofs as late as May, this is an unlikely hypothesis, but it is in any case of little moment since there is a more fundamental explanation of Poe's antipathy. For in Nichol's concern for ocular evidence and in his removing the nebular theory to arm's length as "hypothetical throughout," he revealed the hard-shell Baconian which underlay the romantic speculator. Actually Nichol's position was a rather foolish one, since the apparently graded stages of aggregation noted by Herschel had always been more suggestion than evidence; as he himself admitted in the lecture of February 9, in dealing with problems of evolutionary origins "we must begin with hypotheses." An ascetic regard for the limits set by sensory evidence, however, was a badge of respectability in British science at this time and was piously, even

45. It may also be noted that Nichol said in *A. of H.* (p. 210) and repeated in the Preface to the first Edition of the *System of the World* (p. xi) that even if the nebular hypothesis were proved wrong, "This, at least is established on grounds not to be removed: In the vast Heavens, as well as among phenomena around us, all things are in a state of change and PROGRESS. . . ."

206

if not consistently, regarded by Nichol. Poe seems to have recognized this basic loyalty in Nichol as early as 1845 when in condemning the philosophy embodied in a polemical edition of the tenth book of Plato's *Laws* he said that he would prefer even "this noise of Bacon . . . or the nebular star-dust of Nichols [*sic*] to what Dr. Lewis will insist on terming the 'clear, simple, common-sense philosophy of Plato.' "[46] That he had little more admiration for Baconian empiricism than for Greek rationalism is shown in the early pages of *Eureka*, where he lampooned both. Here, no doubt with the scientific fashion of the day in mind, he made known his contempt for the stodgy limitations of the "Hoggian" philosophy and of the "intellectual grovellers" who require "ocular, physical proof,"[47] pledging himself rather to the method of intuition, hypothesis, "guessing"—"Yes! these vital laws Kepler guessed. . . ."[48] So far as Nichol represented Baconianism, it was inevitable that Poe should regard him unsympathetically, and in his treatment of the problem of nebulae Nichol not only stood up for this philosophy but did it on a subject which was essential to Poe's thesis.

The difference between the two men in respect to the nebular cosmogony was in one sense actually very slight. Both held that the theory is a supposition justified by its explanatory power and its inner consistency rather than by ocular evidence. Poe went so far as to concede that the demonstration of the theory does not *prove* it "according to the common understanding of the word 'proof' "[49] and that the theory was, as Nichol said, a hypothesis. The only difference is that to Nichol this characteristic of the theory was a weakness, whereas to Poe it was not. "The common understanding of the word 'proof' " was not Poe's, and thus of the hypothetical character of the theory he had this to say:

46. "Plato Contra Atheos," *Complete Works*, XII, 165. See above, p. 191.
47. *Complete Works*, XVI, 216. See the discussion of the Baconian philosophy, pp. 188-92.
48. *Complete Works*, XVI, 197.
49. *Complete Works*, XVI, 260.

No conviction can be stronger—to *my* mind at least—than that with which I am impressed by an hypothesis that not only reconciles these complex astronomical conditions, with mathematical accuracy, and reduces them into a consistent and intelligible whole, but is, at the same time, the *sole* hypothesis by means of which the human intellect has been ever enabled to account for them *at all*.[50]

The nebular theory, he said, was *"beautifully true . . .* far too beautiful, indeed, not to possess Truth as its essentiality."[51] Nichol had only been willing to say in the parallel passage referred to early in this essay, "The theory is so beautiful and perfect, that perhaps we might have assumed it to be universal. . . ."[52] Poe was presenting a revelation, and it is not to be expected that he would look kindly on the treatment of any essential portion of it as a mere—albeit inspiring—speculation.

50. *Complete Works*, XVI, 261.
51. *Complete Works*, XVI, 252.
52. *A. of H.*, p. 186.

WILLIAM RUFF
Professor of English
University of Florida

Thackeray as Laocoön

NE OF THE AGREEABLE LEGENDS OF NINE-
teenth-century literature is that of the great
writer lamed by the prudery of his time. We
think of Byron, of Shelley, of Flaubert, and
of Baudelaire. William Makepeace Thackeray would like to be of this company, too.
Here is what he has to say, in *The Virginians*, on what *he*
might have written, if he had not been harmed by the squeamishness of his age:

> Suppose we were to describe the doings of such a person as
> Mr. Lovelace, or my Lady Bellaston, or that wonderful
> "Lady of Quality" who lent her memoirs to the author of
> *Peregrine Pickle*. How the pure and outraged Nineteenth
> Century would blush, scream, run out of the room, call
> away the young ladies, and order Mr. Mudie never to send
> one of that odious author's books again! . . . it may be that
> the novelist's art is injured by the restraints put upon him,

209

as many an honest, harmless statue at St. Peter's and the Vatican is spoilt by the tin draperies in which ecclesiastical old women have swaddled the fair limbs of the marble. But in your prudery there is reason. So there is in the state censorship of the Press. The page may contain matter dangerous to *bonos mores*. Out with your scissors, censor, and clip off the prurient paragraph! We have nothing for it but to submit. Society, the despot, has given his imperial decree. We may think the statue had been seen to greater advantage without the tin drapery; we might plead that the moral were better might we recite the whole fable. Away with him—not a word! I never saw the pianofortes in the United States with the frilled muslin trousers on their legs; but, depend on it, the muslin covered some of the notes as well as the mahogany, muffled the music, and stopped the player.[1]

Surely Thackeray means that his own notes were covered, his own music muffled, and he, the player, stopped from writing his best. If he is one of the blighted writers of the nineteenth century his case is tragic. But I wonder how good are his claims.

When critics mention Victorian prudery, they like to quote that terrifyingly true sentence in Thackeray's Preface to *Pendennis*: "Since the author of *Tom Jones* was buried, no writer of fiction among us has been permitted to depict to his utmost power a MAN." He says much the same thing in *The Virginians*: "O the Truthful, O the Beautiful, O Modesty, O Benevolence, O Pudor, O Mores, O Blushing Shame, O Namby Pamby—each with your respective capital letters to your honoured names! O Niminy, O Piminy! how shall I dare for to go for to say that a young man ever was a young man?"[2] When I read so kittenish a denunciation of prudery, I wonder how seriously Thackeray took this matter of free speech. In his own lifetime he had an opportunity to fight censorship had he chosen. What other English novelist of the nineteenth century had so many ways in which he could express himself? Thackeray could draw so well that he might have become a Daumier; he could

1. Chap. XLI. I have used the text of the Oxford *Thackeray* throughout.
2. Chap. XLI.

write fair light verse and admirable prose; he wrote travel sketches, book reviews, parodies, essays, short stories, plays, and, best of all, novels. In his public career he was not only an outstanding novelist, but he was—at various times—a newspaper editor, a contributing editor of *Punch*, and the editor of the *Cornhill Magazine*; he was a widely popular lecturer in the United States and Great Britain, a candidate for Parliament, and a man of the world. In all these activities except one he was successful: alas, what he said in extemporaneous addresses was not what he had meant to say.

A man of Thackeray's influence and powers and audience, a man with such a hatred of prudery, might be expected to praise such outspoken writers of past times as Swift; he might have praised the best satirists of his own day for honesty; he might have fought the prudery of audiences on his lecture tours, or encouraged honest writing when he was an all-powerful editor. And if he wanted the best weapon of all for attacking prudery he had it in a book like *Vanity Fair*.

Exactly what use did he make of all these chances?

I

If Thackeray considered himself a martyr of prudery, he not think much of the other martyrs. He did not care for Byron: "that man *never* wrote from his heart. He got up rapture and enthusiasm with an eye to the public. . . ."[3] Of *The Revolt of Islam* Thackeray wrote his mother: "an odd kind of book containing poetry wh. wd. induce one to read it through, & sentiments wh. might strongly incline one to throw it in the fire."[4] Nor did he care much for the author of *Madame Bovary*: "The book is bad. It is a heartless, cold-blooded study of the downfall and degradation of a woman."[5] But Thackeray was not really interested in free-speaking rebels, as he proved on his lecture tours in America.

3. *From Cornhill to Cairo*, Chap. V.
4. *The Letters and Private Papers of William Makepeace Thackeray*, ed. Gordon N. Ray (Cambridge, Mass., 1945-46), I, 74.
5. H. Sutherland Edwards, *Personal Recollections* (London, 1900), p. 36.

When he went to America in 1852 and in 1855 he did not carry a lily in his right hand, as Oscar Wilde did later, nor lecture in silk knee-breeches to the miners of Colorado, but for all that he was just as much an apostle of culture. He was an even more popular lecturer than Wilde, one whose word was more powerful in recommendation and criticism. And when Thackeray was praising Dickens, for example, what would he say? that Dickens was one of the greatest and most outspoken satirists of his time? No! In 1853, in a lecture called "Charity and Humour," Thackeray recommended Dickens as: "this kind friend, who soothed and charmed so many hours, brought pleasure and sweet laughter to so many homes; made such multitudes of children happy; endowed us with such a sweet store of gracious thoughts, fair fancies, soft sympathies. . . . The atmosphere in which these people live is wholesome to breathe in . . . you come away better for your contact with them. . . . All children ought to love him . . . the kind satirist. . . . What a kind light of benevolence. . . ." This for the author of *Nicholas Nickleby* and *Martin Chuzzlewit*! Though Dickens could have thanked the lecturer for gliding over those satires on the United States in *Martin Chuzzlewit*, still he might have wondered why Thackeray refused to believe that novels could be disagreeably honest or sharp in their criticism, or anything but sweet and written just for boys and girls.

During the same lecture tour in which Thackeray proved that the best books are those which most appeal to children, he told his audiences what books to avoid. He told them to dislike Congreve: "no more feeling in his comedies, than in as many books of Euclid," and to avoid the other playwrights of his time: "That miserable, rouged, tawdry, sparkling, hollow-hearted comedy of the Restoration. . . ."[6] Apparently he could not recommend any outspoken writer of the seventeenth century or of the eighteenth, even Swift: "an awful, an evil spirit . . . as for the moral [of *Gulliver's Travels*] I think it horrible, shameful, unmanly, blasphemous; and giant and great as this Dean is, I say we should hoot him . . . tearing down all shreds of modesty, past all sense of manliness and shame; filthy in word, filthy

6. The lecture "Charity and Humour."

212

in thought, furious, raging, obscene."[7] Of Sterne he was almost as critical: "The coward . . . quoting the Lord's Prayer, with a horrible baseness of blasphemy . . . wretched worn-out old scamp . . . the feeble wretch . . . this man of genius, this actor, this quack . . . he used to blubber perpetually in his study . . . a great jester, not a great humourist . . . Mountebank! . . . There is not a page in Sterne's writings but has something that were better away, a latent corruption—a hint, as of an impure presence. . . . The foul Satyr's eyes. . . ."[8] The modest Americans seemed delighted with these attacks, for not once did Thackeray speak in behalf of a frank writer. There is much about benevolence, and "innocent laughter and the sweet and unsullied page"[9] of Dickens, but of recommendation for the bold writers of the past not one instance. Again Thackeray is trying to limit what books may say.

However, there is one author of the eighteenth century for whom Thackeray has an almost complete regard—Henry Fielding. As early as 1840 Thackeray could recommend Fielding as "one of the honestest, manliest, kindest companions in the world . . . an honest-hearted fellow, with affections as tender and simple as ever dwelt in the bosom of any man. . . . Vice is never to be mistaken for virtue in Fielding's honest downright books; it goes by its name, and invariably gets its punishment." And yet Thackeray must defend the work of Fielding from certain charges: "boys and virgins must read it with caution. . . ." In characteristic fashion Thackeray later ruins his arguments by admitting that Fielding is occasionally outspoken and wrongly so:

> The world does not tolerate now such satire as that of Hogarth and Fielding, and the world no doubt is right in a great part of its squeamishness; for it is right to pretend to the virtue of chastity even though we do not possess it; nay, the very restraint which the hypocrisy lays on a man is not unapt, in some instances, to profit him. . . . It is wise that

7. *The English Humourists of the Eighteenth Century*, "Lecture the First."
8. *Ibid.*, "Lecture the Sixth."
9. *Ibid.*

the public modesty should be as prudish as it is; that writers should be forced to chasten their humour, and when it would play with points of life and character which are essentially immoral, that they should be compelled, by the general outcry of incensed public propriety, to be silent altogether.[10]

So well does Thackeray defend censorship that it is of no use for him to murmur, plaintively, in the same essay, that Cruikshank and Dickens dare not talk of what the elder novelists discussed honestly. Thackeray is much too much an advocate of prudery for his own good or that of contemporary writers.

His best device for narrowing the range of literature is in his lecture "Charity and Humour." That device is to associate the word "humour" with preaching: "our humourous writers, our gay and kind weekday preachers. . . . If the humourous writers claim to be weekday preachers. . . ." And he goes on to say that, "Humour! humour is the mistress of tears . . . the best humour is that which contains most humanity, that which is flavoured throughout with tenderness and kindness." This is an admirable defense of the humor of Goldsmith or Lewis Carroll, but it forbids us to like Swift or Sterne. Thackeray's criticism, in short, is one of exclusion: he would block our reading, our appreciation of anything vigorous or outspoken. He has the tolerance of a librarian in a girls' school.

Later in life, Thackeray had a chance to control the taste of his times even more actively than as a lecturer, for he became editor of a monthly magazine, the *Cornhill*, and took care that nothing displeasing to women and children should appear in its pages. In 1861 he wrote Mrs. Elizabeth Barrett Browning, "In your poem ["Lord Walter's Wife"] you know there is an account of unlawful passion felt by a man for a woman—and though you write pure doctrine and real modesty and pure ethics, I am sure our readers would make an outcry, and so I have not published this poem."[11] When Thackeray read "Mrs. General Talboys" by Anthony Trollope, he rejected the story, even though Trollope snapped back, "I will not allow that I

10. *The Times* (London), Sept. 2, 1840.
11. *Letters*, IV, 227.

am indecent, and profess that squeamishness—in so far as it is squeamishness and not delicacy—should be disregarded by a writer. I of course look back for examples to justify myself in alluding to a man with illegitimate children, and to the existence of a woman not as pure as she should be."[12] Though Thackeray groaned when he had to reject such authors, there is no evidence that he ever relented in his honest, unending fight for prudery, or in his respect for its exemplar, Queen Victoria: "I am sure the future painter of our manners will pay a willing allegiance to that good life, and be loyal to the memory of that unsullied virtue."[13]

This is the conclusion, then, to Thackeray's long career as a leader of public taste. From the time he started writing he did everything in his considerable power to limit the extent of frankness in literature. He limited humor by calling it weekday preaching; he denounced the writers of the Restoration for immorality; he lashed Swift and Sterne for their outspokenness; he scolded his favorite, Fielding, for poor morals; and he praised heaven that he, Thackeray, was not required in the nineteenth century to write as boldly as they. He did not approve of contemporary novels which were frank; as an editor he encouraged censorship; as an essayist he complimented the Victorian public on their good taste; as a lecturer he scolded the eighteenth century as a whole, and held up Victoria as a model of virtue. And when he had to recommend a novelist to the United States he recommended Charles Dickens—as a writer sure to please the children. What more could a public-spirited gentleman and writer do to encourage prudery? If the music of a piano was muffled in the nineteenth century, as Thackeray complains in *The Virginians*, it is Thackeray who helped muffle that music.

II

Perhaps Thackeray as editor and critic and lecturer *did* encourage prudery. Yet he was a novelist above everything else; and if everything in his collected works but *Vanity Fair* and *Henry Esmond* were forgotten he would still be called great. If

12. *Letters*, IV, 206.
13. *The Four Georges*, "George the Fourth."

in fiction he tried to tell the truth as he saw it, if he insisted on having his own way in spite of the objections of critics and readers, then we can forget how he fought for prudery in every other capacity, and remember only that he used the novel as a sword. And here is a crucial point. If Thackeray believed that the novel as a form of art could criticize life, then he is right to complain of Victorian prudery wherever it hampered his fiction. On the other hand, if he thinks that the novel as an art form can never tell the whole truth about life, then he has no business denouncing prudery for harming his novels. If the novel is limited just because it *is* a novel, then prudery has nothing to do with its limitations.

Yet he must surely have prized the art of the novel, for we remember that haunting sentence, "Also, it may be that the novelist's art is injured by the restraints put upon him, as many an honest, harmless statue at St. Peter's and the Vatican is spoilt by the tin draperies. . . ." Unfortunately for his defense of fiction, he followed the quotation above (within a hundred pages) by this: "And here the old lady narrated at length the history which we know already, but in that cynical language which was common in her times, when the finest folks and the most delicate ladies called things and people by names which we never utter in good company nowadays. And so much the better on the whole. We mayn't be more virtuous, but it is something to be more decent: perhaps we are not more pure, but of a surety we are more cleanly."[14] How neatly Thackeray recants!

He always has an odd way of withdrawing his criticisms of Mrs. Grundy, and of apologizing for anything bitter he has said about that ideal reader of his, Lady Squeam. It is as if he cared nothing for fiction as art, as if the novel were not worth a fight. And we remember how casually he interrupts *The Adventures of Philip* to say, "O me! O my beloved congregation! I have preached this stale sermon to you for ever so many years,"[15] or breaks the suspense of *Vanity Fair* to inject, "If Rawdon Crawley had been then and there present, instead of being at the

14. *The Virginians*, Chap. LIV.
15. Chap. II.

216

club nervously drinking claret, the pair might have gone down on their knees before the old spinster, avowed all, and been forgiven in a twinkling. But that good chance was denied to the young couple, doubtless in order that this story might be written."[16] One remembers how lightly he refers to the characters of *Vanity Fair* as puppets and to himself as a puppet master. The quickest way to learn what he felt about this book is to look at an edition illustrated by himself, for he knew how to comment by means of his caricatures on himself, his readers and his characters. In *Vanity Fair* he pictured himself as a clown who tries to preach, and he is also a man piping to one listener, a dog; he is a grinning demon; a broken-nosed, spectacled boy holding a clown's mask and stick; and at the end of the novel, in the chapter "Which Contains Births, Marriages, and Deaths" he is a black-faced schoolmaster about to birch a pupil. Becky is a child building a house of cards, a child flying a kite (when she is trying "to live well on nothing a year"). Amelia is a girl in asses' ears holding a baby, who has inherited similar ones; she is a child hiding behind an umbrella, and when she has discovered the truth about her husband, only a child watching a fire blaze up and burn out. Thackeray made George Osborne a cupid in a cocked hat, an infant struggling with a banner, and when he dies, children in asses' ears march in his funeral. And what of Dobbin the good? He is a boy in a wooden sword and a cocked hat of paper, the manager of a peepshow for two children (Amelia and George), a schoolboy looking at sweets he cannot get. And what is the entire novel according to these pictures? only a collection of dolls that two little girls, typical readers, toss back in their box. A novelist is a fool, says Thackeray, and his characters are children.

If Thackeray laughs at his characters, he is not more respectful towards his readers, whom he calls by a multitude of names. "Dear reader" is his common way of addressing his audience, but there are many other ways. Here are some I have collected from various books: "Jones, fair young reader, my respected reader, polite reader, my dear friend, my esteemed reader, my dear Miss, my good sir, miss, my dear, my dear sir,

16. Chap. XVI.

my worthy friends, my amiable reader, dearly beloved brethren, good reader, young folks, o critic, Madam, the lovely ladies to whom this is addressed, the keen observer of human nature, dear friend, respectable reader, beloved reader, the astute reader, my fair young readers, man of the world, the judicious reader, gentle and unsuspicious readers, young boys and virgins, dear and respected reader, the patriotic reader, my Lord Bishop, the honest English reader, ye Barons and Baronesses of England, brother wearers of motley, Protestant readers." And there are also "Miss Prim, Lady Squeam, Mrs. Downright, Miss Sowerby, and Mrs. Grundy."

Thackeray's names for himself are just as disrespectful. What novelist could be serious who would use such pseudonyms as Goliah Gahagan, Theophile Wagstaffe, Charles James Yellowplush, The Fat Contributor, Michael Angelo Titmarsh, C. Jeames de la Pluche, Esq., Ikey Solomons, Esq. junior, Major G. O'Hagan, H. E. I. C. S., and George Fitz-Boodle?

It is Thackeray's belief in wholeness that dictated this contempt for himself as author, most of his feeling about prudery, and his contempt for fiction. One sample of his belief in wholeness I have already quoted: "Since the author of *Tom Jones* was buried, no writer of fiction among us has been permitted to depict to his utmost power a MAN." In 1840, on finishing *Catherine*, Thackeray wrote: "No one has read that remarkable tale of *Oliver Twist* without being interested in poor Nancy and her murderer; and especially amused and tickled by the gambols of the Artful Dodger and his companions. . . . A most agreeable set of rascals, indeed, who have their virtues, too, but not good company for any man. We had better pass them by in decent silence; for, as no writer can or dare tell the *whole* truth concerning them, and faithfully explain their vices, there is no need to give *ex-parte* statements of their virtues."[17] Once more in the Preface to *Pendennis*, he says, "To describe a real rascal, you must make him so horrible that he would be too hideous to show; and unless the painter paints him fairly, I hold he has no right to show him at all." So the matter is clear: the novel as a form of art is not worth much.

17. "Another Last Chapter." This is the last chapter in *Catherine*.

218

If, therefore, Thackeray is glad his novels are purer than eighteenth century ones, if he laughs at his characters, his plots, the unreal atmosphere of all fiction, and at himself for writing such trash; if he laughs at his readers, and thinks that if one cannot tell the whole truth in fiction, one had better try another form of preaching, what are his conclusions about the art of the novel? For one thing he liked to call novels story-books, or novel-books, or just sentimental writing. In 1861, when he was writing an introduction to the first number of his new magazine, the *Cornhill*, and wished to sum up the experiences of his lifetime as a novelist, he said, "You take the allegory? Novels are sweets. . . . Figs are sweet, but fictions are sweeter. . . . But as surely as the cadet drinks too much pale ale, it will disagree with him; and so surely, dear youth, will too much novels cloy on thee. . . ."[18] And with that he introduced his readers to the first installments of *Denis Duval* and *Framley Parsonage*. I wonder how Trollope liked his novel to be called "jellies, pale ale, sweets, tarts, and ice"? And I also wonder whether a novelist dare complain of limitations on his art, if he says of that art, "You take the allegory? Novels are sweets." This was a public confession, no more bitter than what he said in private. In 1856, for example, he told his good friends, Mrs. Elliot and Kate Perry, "I am frivolous and futile[;] a long course of idleness (wh. novel-writing is) has wasted my intellect. . . ."[19]

When Thackeray wrote, "I never saw the pianofortes in the United States with the frilled muslin trousers on their legs; but, depend on it, the muslin covered some of the notes as well as the mahogany, muffled the music, and stopped the player," he was denouncing prudery and censorship and squeamishness and anything that contracts the power of his art. But he was also saying that the instrument in question was not much of an instrument anyway. He may have felt like Laocoön entangled in the prudery of the nineteenth century, but the snakes were not really harmful, and he had decided early in life that it was not worth his while to struggle.

18. *Roundabout Papers*, "On a Lazy Idle Boy."
19. *Letters*, III, 559.

III

It is true that Thackeray denounced prudery and encouraged it all his life, but there are three excuses for such a contradiction. First, there were personal reasons for his timidity; second, he was the victim of the Victorian Age and its worship of the prim; and third, he had an overpowering sense of responsibility for his readers. Let us take personal reasons first, and recognize that Thackeray was rightly nervous for fear the circulation of the *Cornhill* might fall below its first sales of a hundred thousand, and that consequently he did not dare offend his readers. He needed the money he received as editor to provide an income for his two daughters, his mother, his stepfather, and his insane wife. He knew that death was never far away, and when he went to America on two lecture tours, he had one fear in his mind, that he might die without leaving money for his children. No wonder he wrote little that would displease his audience; no wonder he encouraged them in their stiff opinions; no wonder he refused to offend the subscribers to his novels. And too, there were personal reasons, not much talked about in his biographies, why he should have felt as strongly as George Eliot that one should be on the side of virtue in spite of one's own lapses. Poor Thackeray, forever struggling for a capital, forever watching the sale of his novels fall below that of Dickens, forever extravagant, and so forever forced to compromise. If he had wanted to fight the prudery of his times, there were too many reasons why it would be unsafe.

But as for the second defense, that he was the victim of a prudish age, it is possible to say that he created the taste he moans about. The Victorian Age, especially towards the end of Thackeray's life, was an age of excessive moral standards, of prudery, of squeamishness, simply because there were so many leaders of opinion who shared Thackeray's dislike of Sterne and Swift and tales of illicit love, and like him would not discuss the unpleasant facts of life. The Victorian Age encouraged Lady Squeam and Miss Prim and Mrs. Grundy because Thackeray encouraged them too. He was, in every respect, a creator of the conscience of his age. And so this second excuse, that he lived in the wrong age, is not valid.

220

Perhaps Thackeray did lack courage because he lacked money, and certainly the Victorian Age is moral because it was made up of Victorians like Thackeray, but these are minor reasons for his encouragement of prudery. The best reason for his refusal to fight against squeamishness is his sense of responsibility for anyone who might come across a book of his. He seems to have been born with a sense of responsibility, or to have acquired it very early in life, for his first books were devoted to killing the taste for the rogue novel, "the novel of excitement," and what he called "the Silver Fork School" of fiction. He genuinely wanted to change the type of novels read by most women; he meant every word of it when he said, "I am thankful to live in times when men no longer have the temptation to write so as to call blushes on women's cheeks, and would shame to whisper wicked allusions to honest boys." And when he said, "If the gods would give me the desire of my heart, I should be able to write a story which boys would relish for the next few dozens of centuries,"[20] he meant that too.

To see how responsible he felt towards the common man, look at what he said in his campaign for Parliament in 1857. In the usual manner of election campaigns, his opponents charged him with wicked notions. They said he told his friends at the Mitre Hotel on July 9, "I would not only open the Crystal Palace, the British Museum, and the National Gallery but I would go further, and open the CONCERT ROOM and THEATRES on Sundays."[21] In reply, Thackeray issued a broadside of his own:

I never spoke or thought of opening Theatres on Sunday.—
I would try to multiply the means of procuring peace and harmless pleasure for the people on that day, and know that in many Theatrical Pieces there are jests, and allusions, and situations ill-fitted indeed to any, but especially to the Sacred Day.

I would consent to and encourage good Band-Music, which has been played before our Sovereigns for a hundred years past; but would object to Songs, for the same reason

20. *Roundabout Papers*, "De Juventute."
21. *Letters*, IV, facing p. 382.

that renders me averse to Plays,—because Songs may be made vehicles for jokes and buffoonery, which, on such a day, might justly shock the sense of religious persons.[22]

I believe Thackeray meant this political message, because I believe that if he had wanted to enjoy a pleasure which might harm a fellow being he would instantly have abandoned the pleasure. When he was campaigning for Parliament he could *see* the voters and realize what was good for them. When he was lecturing, he felt so keenly that some of his hearers might be harmed by a careless word or a jest on a serious topic that he took double care to be circumspect. And when he was writing novels, he saw the faces of his readers before him as no other novelist of the century could do, and hence he talks directly to them, his dear readers.

When Thackeray wrote that paragraph previously quoted from *The Virginians* denouncing the prudery of his time, he was old in spirit and tired and sick; he was writing fiction because he was used to writing fiction; spinning out a story that he had really finished long ago. The last ten years of his life he spent writing sequels; a sequel to *Henry Esmond*, a sequel to *Pendennis*, a sequel to *A Shabby Genteel Story*. He often suggested that he hated prudery, but it was something else in his character that made him positively encourage it. He had a natural delicacy of taste; he loathed vulgarity in all forms, hated scenes of low life in fiction, and consistently avoided them in his own; he agreed with every attack on sordid realism in novels; he whole-heartedly agreed that there were some things nobody should tell *his* daughters, and stories they should not be able to read in *his* library. He despised his intellectual inferiors, and his readers were inferiors, yet at the same time he felt he was bound in honor to protect them from harm, to explain to them the differences between good people and bad, and to make up for their lack of brains. He despised the form of the novel, because it would not let him say what he wanted to say. Yet if he had to choose between free speech and the slightest harm to the boys and girls who read his books, he had no hesitation in choosing to be prudishly, helpfully decent. He felt

22. *Letters*, facing p. 383.

that he was not popular, not anyway as Dickens was popular, and yet he felt that Dickens was his inferior, that it was a crime to write as cheaply as Dickens sometimes wrote, as in *Oliver Twist*, for example. How tired Thackeray became of his lecture tours, and his American audiences, and the need to please people he cared nothing for. Yet he felt he had to give the thousands who listened to him not something for their money but something for their souls.

He genuinely felt he was not doing the job of a grown man when he wrote novels, that anyone with his brains should be in a better field. He really felt he had a responsibility to his daughters, and to the daughters of other men, and to the whole world of uninformed, ill-educated readers of novels. Maybe other novelists would pander to their low tastes, but he, Thackeray, would rather not. Nor did he.

GEORGE M. HARPER
Professor & Chairman
Department of English
University of North Carolina

The Reconciliation of Paganism
& Christianity in Yeats' *Unicorn*
from the Stars

HE CANON OF YEATS' WORK REPRESENTS ONE OF the most determined efforts of our time to resuscitate the slowly expiring literary hero. Robbed of his traditional Christian faith in the nobility of man by Tyndall and Huxley, as he wrote in the *Autobiographies*, Yeats turned from one religious and philosophical system to another in his search for a satisfactory substitute. The inevitable result was a kind of contrapuntal religiosity firmly grounded in the conviction that "all religions are one."[1] This basic premise justified, perhaps necessitated, blending, altering, discarding as his mind sought for the answer to what the hero of *Hotel Universe* called "the fundamental problem of the location of Man in the Universe." In the dramas particularly, this mythical quest for man's meaning and place is projected in the protago-

1. Geoffrey Keynes (ed.), *The Complete Writings of William Blake* (London, 1957), p. 98.

nists, and a careful study of changing religious and ethical values of these idealized projections of their creator will certainly help to resolve many apparent ambiguities and paradoxes. I propose to look closely at one—Martin Hearne of *The Unicorn from the Stars*, who is a curious amalgamation of the Christian hero and the Nietzschean superman. For such a study, this play is particularly important because it represents a radical revision, both structural and ideological, of the most obviously Nietzschean of all Yeats' works, *Where There Is Nothing*.

Some time after 1900, Yeats became seriously disillusioned with the artistic image he had created in the strongly pastoral heroes and landscapes of his early work, and he concluded ironically that "Man knows himself by action only, by thought never."[2] His quest for a more satisfactory hero coincides remarkably with his discovery of Nietzsche, whom he was reading in 1902 while composing *Where There Is Nothing*.[3] From this time on his heroes are primarily men of action, who function, in Nietzsche's words, "beyond terror and pity, *to realize in fact* the eternal delight of becoming, that delight which even involves in itself the *joy* of annihilating."[4] Like Yeats, Nietzsche was convinced that "every argument carries us backward to some religious conception,"[5] and he projected his idea by means of Apollo and Dionysus as symbolic representatives of two radically opposed visions of the world. "In order to bring these two tendencies within closer range," he wrote in *The Birth of Tragedy*, "let us conceive them first of all as separate art—worlds of *dreamland* and *drunkenness*; between which physiological phenomena a contrast may be observed analogous to that existing between the Apollonian and the Dionysian."[6] Yeats accepted this distinction, as passages in the letters and essays indicate, but not without modification. Paul Ruttledge, the hero of *Where There Is Nothing*, is the first exploration in

2. Yeats quotes Goethe, *A Vision* (New York, 1961), p. 145.
3. Allan Wade (ed.), *The Letters of W. B. Yeats* (New York, 1955), p. 379.
4. Friedrich Nietzsche, *The Complete Works*, ed. Oscar Levy (Edinburgh and London, 1909-13), I, 193.
5. W. B. Yeats, *Plays and Controversies* (London, 1923), p. 99.
6. *Works*, I, 22.

depth. As the play opens he is, in Nietzsche's words, "an Apollonian, an artist in dreams."[7] Languid, lonely, misunderstood, and ineffectual, he is completely apathetic until excited into becoming "a Dionysus, an artist in ecstasies,"[8] by the appearance of a band of tinkers. Seized with an urge to wander the roads of the world, Paul searches for ecstasy first in drunken abandonment and then in violent destruction of the old social order. He finds his theme in what Yeats described to Lady Gregory as the play's Latin text, a line from the Twenty-third Psalm, "Et calix meus inebrians quam praeclarus est," which Paul translates as "How splendid is the cup of my drunkenness."[9] This doctrinally convenient variation of the familiar "My cup runneth over" foreshadows the whole of Yeats' ironic intent. Essentially the first half of the play is devoted to an exploration of the search for joy in the life of the beggar-man of the world. But this is not the answer, and the tinkers finally leave Paul, exhausted and despairing, at the doorway of a monastery.

The beggar-man becomes a saint, and the search for truth continues. The remainder of the play is Yeats' attempt at "the reconciliation of Paganism and Christianity,"[10] of Dionysus and Christ, of Nietzsche and Blake, those men of *antithetical wisdom*"[11] who grew from "the same roots."[12] The primary object of *Where There Is Nothing* as well as *The Unicorn from the Stars* is to demonstrate that there is no essential difference: as archetypal heroes Dionysus and Christ spring from the same subconscious racial urge, a conception that was to haunt him the rest of his life.[13]

The chief inspiration for Paul Ruttledge is Nietzsche's

7. *Works*, I, 28.   8. *Works*, I, 28.
9. W. B. Yeats, *Where There Is Nothing: Being Volume One of Plays for an Irish Theatre* (London, 1903), p. 7.
10. *A Vision*, p. 291.   11. *A Vision*, p. 299.
12. *Letters*, p. 379.
13. Years later, in a letter to Olivia Shakespear, Yeats referred cryptically to the "resurrection of Christ and Dionysus" as "the slain god, the risen god." In still another letter he discussed a plan to write "a play about Christ meeting the worshippers of Dionysus on the mountain side" (*Letters*, pp. 826, 715), an idea later incorporated somewhat obscurely in a little poem called "Images," which was never published. (Quoted in Richard Ellman, *Yeats: The Man and the Masks*, New York, 1948, p. 269.)

iconoclastic character sketch of the Apostle Paul included in Thomas Common's collection of Nietzsche's gems, which Yeats owned and annotated.[14] Although such minor details as the visionary trances and the insistence that "Brother Paul . . . get up and preach"[15] need not be traced to a source, Paul's climactic sermon, which contains the doctrinal heart of the play, is surely directly indebted to a sermon in Common's collection, especially in two striking themes: (1) that man is lost unless he returns to the joy of the green earth, and (2) that ecstatic joy proper to the human race can be realized only *after* or *in* the destruction of Law and Number—that is, Church and State.[16] Not only is the romantic paradox that destruction and creation are inseparable contraries most likely indebted to Nietzsche, the title was probably suggested by a sentence from Nietzsche. Paul's dying injunction to "remember always where there is nothing there is God"[17] seems too close for chance to the phraseology in *Beyond Good and Evil*: "Where there is nothing more to see or to grasp, there is also nothing more for men to do."[18] And the verbal echoes in *The Unicorn from the Stars* are even closer. Martin's speech which concludes with "where there is nothing—there is God" also declares that "we shall not come to that joy, that battle, till we have put out the senses, everything that can be seen and handled."[19] That is, to recall Nietzsche's phrase, "more to see or to grasp." If indeed this is the source of Yeats' title, his substitution of "there is God" for Nietzsche's "there is also nothing more for men to do" suggests a conscious imposition of the Christian level on Nietzsche's thinking.

But Yeats was not long satisfied with the vision of the world projected by Paul Ruttledge, who was, I think, too Dionysian

14. Thomas Common (ed.), *Nietzsche as Critic, Philosopher, Poet and Prophet: Choice Selections from His Works* (New York and London, 1901).
15. *Where There Is Nothing*, pp. 87-88.
16. *Ibid.*, pp. 93-99. As Paul concludes his heretical sermon and is about to be driven from the monastery, he declares that his thoughts have come "from Jesus Christ, who made a terrible joy, and set it to overturn governments, and all settled order."
17. *Ibid.*, p. 129.   18. *Works*, XII, 22.
19. W. B. Yeats, *The Collected Plays* (London, 1952), pp. 381-82. Hereafter cited in the text as Y and followed by the page numbers.

for Yeats. Some six months after he had written an excited letter to Lady Gregory commenting in succeeding paragraphs
upon "Nietzsche, that strong enchanter" and the "Latin text"
for Paul's sermon, a letter to John Quinn about the American
publication of *Where There Is Nothing* expresses the beginning of a retraction or partial disillusionment: "I have always
felt that the soul has two movements primarily: one to tran-
scend forms, and the other to create forms. Nietzsche . . . calls
these the Dionysiac and the Apollonic, respectively. I think I
have to some extent got weary of that wild God Dionysus, and
I am hoping that the Far-Darter will come in his place."[20] It is
not surprising, of course, that Yeats' enthusiasm should have
been tempered: he had already drunk too deeply from the pastoral springs of Shelley, Spenser, and Blake.

At any rate, he was unhappy with his enthusiastic attempt
to fuse Dionysus with St. Paul and Christ, though he had not
lost faith in the dramatic possibilities of the reconciliation
theme; and he continued to search for a more satisfactory structure. The result is the greatly altered version which appeared
six years later as *The Unicorn from the Stars*. The commit-
ment to Nietzsche is still obvious, but the changes, especially in
the ethics of the hero, are equally striking. From the beginning
this time, Yeats has made it clear that Christ is the model for
Martin Hearne. His very name reminds us that to Yeats, as to
Dylan Thomas, the herne is a symbolic fisher-bird grieving in
the "weeded verge" of the water of generation "for the sake of
the souls of the slain birds sailing."[21] And the Christian names
of the other chief characters (Thomas, Andrew, and John) also
are suggestive, as is the setting and the fact that no mention is

20. *Letters*, p. 403.
21. From "Over Sir John's Hill." Both the name Martin Hearne and
his chief characteristics are no doubt indebted to Yeats' unfinished and
unpublished autobiographical novel *The Speckled Bird*, originally entitled
Michael Hearne. The later title comes from the Bible (Jeremiah xii:9),
though Yeats most likely was prompted to choose it from a reference in
Lady Gregory's *Poets and Dreamers* which suggests that Jeremiah's utter-
ance is "the thought of the idealist of all time" (p. 78). Like Jeremiah, certainly Martin might have cried, "Mine heritage is unto me as a speckled
bird; the birds round about are against her." This is obviously Yeats'
conception of the dilemma of the poet-prophet in society.

ever made of Martin's parents. Martin is a kind of assistant car-
penter in a coachbuilder's shop. As the play opens, he is in a
visionary trance, which is compared to the trances of another
"poor tradesman," Jacob Boehme, who was also searching for
the "supreme truth" (Y329). Doubting Thomas, his uncle, has
no faith in visions or trances because they are unprofitable and
unreal, devices people use "to make the world wonder the time
they think well to rise up." It is more likely, Andrew says, that
Martin has the falling sickness, a punishment cast "on the un-
believing Jews" (Y335). It is Thomas' plan to make of Martin
a "good hardy tradesman . . . that will live quiet and rear a
family" (he married a woman of the roads in the earlier version), so he will not go "against the Government" (Y331). But
women have no place in Martin's thinking.

The strangely diverse doctrinal elements in the play are
illustrated in Martin's description of what he saw in his vision.
The Dionysiac rites are suggested in the reference to the sight
of "grapes in bunches" and the smell of the wine as unicorns
"began trampling the grapes and breaking them" (Y337). Father
John (like the Baptist, a preacher from the wilderness) gives us
the key to another level of the play's religious symbolism in
a comment upon Martin's vision: "That is strange, that is
strange. What is it that brings to mind? I heard it in some
place, *monoceros de astris*, the unicorn from the stars" (Y337).
Since this reference is to the Order of the Golden Dawn, whose
members were sworn to secrecy, Yeats would not reveal the
meaning of his title. Thirteen years after the play was finished,
he wrote to his sister Lolly: "The truth is that it is a private
symbol belonging to my mystical order and nobody knows what
it comes from. It is the soul."[22] Actually, it is a mystic title
which Yeats took for himself at the end of the third grade or
stage up the ladder of the Golden Dawn,[23] and the symbolic
referents of both the lion and the unicorn on Martin's coach
as well as the gold they were to be gilded with may be traced

22. *Letters*, p. 662.
23. See Virginia Moore, *The Unicorn: William Butler Yeats' Search
for Reality* (New York, 1954), p. 146. The titles he assumed for the first
two stages may also have some relevance to the purpose of the play: at the

to an early seventeenth-century book, *The Chymical Marriage of Christian Rosencreutz*, which Yeats no doubt read in A. E. Waite's *The Real History of the Rosicruscians* (1887).[24] Of course, the unicorns had been in *Where There Is Nothing*, but Yeats evidently wanted to increase their symbolic burden. One other notable symbol from the Golden Dawn is the Mountain of Abiegnos, upon which grow the vineyards of Eden to which Martin insists with his last breath that he "must go" (Y382). Abiegnos was no doubt the scene Yeats had in mind for "a play about Christ meeting the worshippers of Dionysus on the mountain side,"[25] and most likely the setting for *At the Hawk's Well*.[26] The ritual of the Golden Dawn points out carefully the religious significance of the holy mountain: "This is the symbolic Mountain of God in the centre of the Universe, the sacred Rosicrucian Mountain of Initiation, the Mystic Mountain of Abiegnus." "The meaning of this title," we are told, is "Mountain of the Lamb of the Father, and the Strength of our Race."[27] It is perhaps significant to observe that Yeats concluded an anonymous pamphlet about the Order of the Golden Dawn with these words: "Signed D. E. D. I. In the Mountain of Abiegnus."[28]

Martin was roused from his trance without comprehending the significance of his vision, and much of the play's ironic in-

---

end of the first *Periclinus de Faustis* or "Wanderer in the Wilderness"; at the end of the second *Poraios de Rejectis*, "Brought from Among the Rejected." In fact, it may well be that Yeats conceived his revised play as one step further along the mystic way to truth than its original. *Where There Is Nothing* is divided structurally into two parts: in the first, when Paul joins a band of tinkers and takes to the roads in the search for truth, he describes himself as a Homeric Wanderer and calls the roads the symbol of eternity; in the second, he and a small band of disciples are rejected by the Father Superior of a monastery. In *The Unicorn from the Stars* Yeats may have felt that he was projecting symbolically the third rung of the Cabalistic ladder of spiritual truth.

24. See especially p. 133.
25. *Letters*, p. 715.
26. See F. A. C. Wilson, *Yeats' Iconography* (London, 1960), Chap. II.
27. Israel Regardie, *The Golden Dawn* (Chicago, 1937-40), II, 237, 202.
28. "Is the Order of the R. R. & A. C. to Remain a Magical Order?" (London, 1901), p. 30.

tent lies in his subsequent misunderstanding of a great command he recalled imperfectly from his dream. The chance words of a beggar entering his house remind Martin of his command: "Destroy, destroy, destruction is the life-giver! destroy!" (Y346). The remainder of the play is devoted to a resolution of the ironic paradox inherent in destruction as a life-giver. As Martin explains it to Father John, "I am to destroy. . . . To bring back the old disturbed exalted life, the old splendour" (Y349). And Father John recognizes this as the fundamental motivation of the revolutionist: ". . . now it is all work, business, how to live a long time. Ah, if one could change it all in a minute, even by war and violence!" (Y350). From this stage on, the play contains a fairly obvious level of political allegory, and it may well be a kind of warning to Yeats' own contemporaries who insisted upon changing Ireland by fire and sword rather than by intellectual battle.[29] It is, of course, the horns of the dilemma Yeats spent much of his life struggling with, represented most dramatically in his failure to agree with or perhaps understand Maud Gonne; it is Yeats' attempt to project the irreconcilable differences between the visionary response of the artist and the expository method of the sociologist; it is, in effect, the difference between poetry and prose, art and nature. Just as Father John warns Martin that "we must have patience" (Y350), Andrew comes in with the news that he is bringing back "the old disturbed exalted life" with "the juice of the grey barley" (Y351).

The radical change in the treatment of the hero's clerical friend in the two plays is surely significant: Father Jerome, of *Where There Is Nothing,* is at times almost a comic butt, whereas Father John, of *The Unicorn from the Stars,* is always sympathetically portrayed, and he is often profoundly moving in his inability to comprehend the ethical vision of Martin Hearne. This, in itself, is perhaps indicative of Yeats' reaction from extreme Nietzscheanism: in the shift from Eleusinian fanaticism to Christian moderation, always with Rosicrucian overtones; or, to use Nietzsche's own symbolic pair, from

29. See especially Johnny's speech and song to the effect that "the pikes will be up and the traders will go down" (Y364).

Dionysian excess to a reconciliation with its Apollonian opposite. Although Nietzsche had argued for the necessity of his
ideal fusion and had in fact insisted that the Greek drama had
achieved it, his emphasis is certainly upon Dionysian drunkenness rather than Apollonian dreams.

Martin's disillusionment and subsequent enlightenment
perhaps represents this reconciliation on several levels—political, religious, and aesthetic—which Yeats, like his master Blake,
would not have attempted to discriminate. The wrangling and
complete self-interest of the people of the roads is indeed de-
moralizing to the idealistic revolutionary, and the absence of
the romantic aura surrounding the tinkers of the early play is
surely significant. Instead of searching for the supreme truth on
the roads of the world, these beggars plan to plunder the big
houses. Mistaking Martin for the exiled revolutionist Johnny
Gibbons, they encourage him to lead them in their fight. To
them Martin's lion is the symbol of Britain, and the unicorn
stands for "the league that will fight and destroy the power of
England and King George" (Y356). The confusion of politics
and vision continues. When Martin asks if they "can see anything or hear anything that is beyond the world" (Y357), the
answer is painfully obvious, but he is still eager to "begin the
destruction" (Y357), though he is "full of uncertainty" (Y358)
as he asks himself what he is to begin with in order to "bring
men once more to the wildness of the clean green earth" (Y358).
The first step in the return to the ancient "exaltation of the
heart" must be the destruction of the Law, for it was "the
first sin, the first mouthful of the apple" (Y359). That the Law
represents science or false knowledge is clearer from Paul's
ironic speech in the early version: "I am one of those who think
sin and death came into the world the day Newton eat [sic] the
apple."[30] The next goal must be the Church. Again the peasants

---

30. *Where There Is Nothing*, p. 25. This, of course, is a commonplace in Blake, who described the world as a "Newtonian Void," and Wal-
lace Stevens manages a magnificent symbolic reference to the common
experience of Eve and Newton with the apple, extended ironically by an
allusion to Poor Yorick's skull, in Stanza IV of "Le Monocle de Mon
Oncle."

confuse metaphysics with politics: to them destroying the Law and the Church means overturning England and the Protestants; Martin's Nietzschean insistence that life must be a "dance bred of the secret frenzy of their hearts, or a battle where the sword made a sound that was like laughter" and that "events that are not begotten in joy are misbegotten" (Y362) is, of course, beyond their comprehension.

As the third act opens, the peasants and Martin have sacked and burned two of the big houses; he is unconscious, and Johnny Bocach moans that there must be "some malice or some venom in the air, that is striking down one after another the whole of the heroes of the Gael" (Y368). Martin is now in another trance, and many of the references from this stage on are reminiscent of Christ's last hours. Johnny remarks that "the spirit went from him about the middle hour of the night" (Y372). The analogy to the resurrection is even more obvious: "He will have great wonders to tell out, the time he will rise up from the ground. It is a pity he not to waken at this time and to lead us on to overcome the troop of the English. Sure, those that are in a trance get strength that they can walk on water" (Y373). Like the Jewish masses who misconstrued Christ's function, the Irish rabble insist that the great leader should get on with "the business he has started . . . here and now" (Y374). As Paudeen gloats, "We'll be marching to attack Dublin itself within a week. The horn will blow for him, and all good men will gather to him" (Y373). "The country [is] waiting for him to awake!" (Y376). And when Martin dies Johnny insists upon bringing the body "away to the quarry" because he "will not leave that body to the Law to be buried with a dog's burial or brought away and maybe hanged upon a tree" (Y382-83).

But the awakened Martin has heard the "high joyous music" (Y376) of Paradise, and he realizes that destruction of property "was not the work I was sent to do" (Y377). "It was but a frenzy, that going out to burn and destroy. What have I to do with the foreign army? What I have to pierce is the wild heart of time." "I was mistaken," he continues, "when I set out to destroy Church and Law. The battle we have to fight is fought out in our own mind" (Y377-78). Like Blake's apocalyptic hero, he perceives that he must "form the golden armour of science for intellectual War."[31] Dionysian destruction is not the solution. The way of the "wild God," the way of revolution, is the easy way, but does it get at the truth? "My business," Martin said, "is not reformation but revelation." The way of Apollo, the pastoral divinity, is not action but contemplation, not politics but art; and the return to "radical innocence" can be achieved only through the "long climb to the vineyards of Eden" (Y382), not through annihilation, which surely leads to anarchy. In the moment of vision Paul understands that

> Unorganiz'd Innocence [is] An Impossibility.
> Innocence dwells with Wisdom, but never with Ignorance.[32]

Whereas Paul Ruttledge expires in "the rapture of the Dionysian state,"[33] crying out to be plunged "into the wine barrel of God,"[34] Martin Hearne falls among the rocks, haunted by the Apollonian vision of Edenic bliss on "the Mountain of Abiegnos" (Y382). According to the ritual of the Golden Dawn, "the ascent of the Mountain is by the Spiral Path of the Serpent of Wisdom," and Abiegnos contains the body of Christian Rosencreutz in a symbolic heptagonal tomb representing the "Seven Lower Sephiroth" or grades in the ascent to wisdom.[35]

On one level Yeats' two plays project variations of the artist's problem in an unsympathetic society. They represent the poet's self-scrutiny of his "mission in Ireland," to use Yeats' own phrase.[36] Citing Thomas Moore and Clarence Mangan as evidence, he once concluded that "Irish national literature . . . has never produced an artistic personality in the modern sense of the word."[37] Although he insisted that he was "just as strenuous a Nationalist as ever" and that he thought of "Ireland as a

31. Blake, p. 379.
32. Blake, p. 380.
33. Nietzsche, *Works*, I, 61.
34. *Where There Is Nothing*, p. 35.
35. Regardie, II, 237, 201.
36. *Letters*, p. 352.
37. *Letters*, p. 447.

sacred land,"[38] he found that he must "express these things all differently."[39]

The years from 1902 to 1908 were also crucial in the stylistic development of Yeats. As he tried to alter the image of the languid young dreamer he recognized in himself, he sought for a style fitted to the cold hardness of the "astringent joy" which characterized the new heroic ideal. Paul Ruttledge and Martin Hearne are images of their creator, not so much what he was as what he wanted to be. In the search for a philosophic ideal which would enable him to blend the worlds of dreamland and drunkenness, Yeats first leaned toward the Dionysian, and Paul is a strange mixture of Dionysian satyr and Pauline saint. In the six years during which Martin evolved from Paul, however, the pendulum swung toward the Apollonian. The model is now Christ rather than Saint Paul, but Yeats' Christ is not the humble wraith of Victorian Sunday School art. He is the Christ of "the Middle Ages and the Renaissance," a brother, in Yeats' thought, to "some classic hero[,] Saint Francis and Caesar Borgia [who] made themselves overmastering, creative persons by turning from the mirror to meditation upon a mask."[40] He is the Christ of Blake's *Everlasting Gospel* who insists that

> Good & Evil are no more!
> Sinai's trumpets, cease to roar![41]

He is one who, in Nietzsche's words, "would have disavowed his doctrine if he had attained my age; he was noble enough to disavow!"[42]

By 1902, Yeats was convinced that "Nietzsche completes Blake and has the same roots."[43] Thirty-five years later, Nietzsche symbolizes "the greatest possible belief in all values created by personality," and his phase is "before all else the phase of the hero, of the man who overcomes himself, and so no longer

38. *Letters*, p. 407.
39. *Letters*, p. 432.
40. W. B. Yeats, *Mythologies* (London, 1959), pp. 333-34.
41. Blake, p. 754.
42. Common, p. 13.
43. *Letters*, p. 379.

needs . . . the submission of others, or . . . conviction of others to prove his victory."[44] It was just such heady wine which led to the creation of Martin Hearne as the heroic ideal of *"antithetical* wisdom,"[45] representing Yeats' reconciliation of Nietzsche's paganism to Blake's Christianity in the conviction that "Greek and Roman antiquity were as sacred as that of Judea, and like it 'a vestibule of Christianity' "[46] because "all religions are one."[47] In blending the Homeric wanderer, the Christian visionary, and the Dionysian satyr, Yeats may well have been attempting that union of "stoicism, asceticism and ecstasy" which his friend J. M. Synge once told him was yet to be achieved.

44. *A Vision*, p. 127.
45. *A Vision*, p. 299. Such as Blake, Patmore, and Nietzsche.
46. *A Vision*, p. 291. This "reconciliation of Paganism and Christianity" which Yeats credits to Pope Julius is surely his own.
47. Blake, p. 98.

HERMAN E. SPIVEY
Professor of English & American Literature
Vice President
University of Tennessee

The Mind & Creative Habits
of Elizabeth Madox Roberts

LIZABETH MADOX ROBERTS (1881-1941) DE-
served and deserves more readers than she
had or has for her twelve books: seven novels, two volumes of short stories, and three
volumes of poetry.[1] Only two of these twelve
were well received, and a third fairly well:
The Time of Man, The Great Meadow, and *Under the Tree.*
Readers now are better able to understand and appreciate her
nine volumes of fiction, not only because of the illuminating
books of Campbell and Foster, Rovit, and McDowell,[2] but also

1. *In the Great Steep's Garden* (poems, 1913), *Under the Tree* (poems,
1922), *The Time of Man* (a novel, 1925), *My Heart and My Flesh* (a
novel, 1927), *Jingling in the Wind* (a satirical fantasy, 1928), *The Great
Meadow* (a historical novel, 1930), *A Buried Treasure* (a novel, 1931), *The
Haunted Mirror* (stories, 1931), *He Sent Forth a Raven* (a novel, 1935),
Black Is My True Love's Hair (a novel, 1938), *Song in the Meadow*
(poems, 1940), and *Not by Strange Gods* (stories, 1941).
2. Harry M. Campbell and Ruel E. Foster, *Elizabeth Madox Roberts,
American Novelist,* Norman, University of Oklahoma Press, 1956; Earl H.

because the vogue of the novel of violence and of the staccato style, so noticeable in the 1920's through the 1950's, is passing. Although her achievements were greater than was realized by her contemporary readers, her handicaps as literary artist were probably greater than she understood or was able to overcome.

It is the purpose of this essay to suggest a few of the strengths and weaknesses which justify this judgment. The briefest way to do this, perhaps, is to take a close look at her second novel, *My Heart and My Flesh* ["crieth out for the living God," Psalms lxxxiv:2], on which Miss Roberts worked for sixteen months and about which she wrote her publisher (Viking) thirty-seven letters, only a few of which have been published. For the most part, the novel was composed on two water fronts: three-fourths of it by the Pacific in Santa Monica in the winter of 1926-1927 and the rest in Chicago in the spring and early summer of 1927. The last major parts to be rewritten before sending the manuscript away were the long symbolic prologue (which, to the uninitiated reader, is an unfortunately bewildering and mysterious introduction to the novel) and the passages dealing with music, one of the major motifs of the novel.[3]

Although *My Heart and My Flesh* is not extraordinarily subtle, to the first readers the profoundly significant theme and philosophic implications were not fully clear or impressive.

Rovit, *Herald to Chaos: The Novels of Elizabeth Madox Roberts*, Lexington, University of Kentucky Press, 1960; and Frederick P. W. McDowell, *Elizabeth Madox Roberts*, New York, Twayne Publishers, Inc., 1963.

3. While composing much of the novel she listened to Beethoven's Ninth Symphony as atmospheric reinforcement (her favorite Beethoven works were the Fifth, Seventh, and Ninth Symphonies). E. M. Roberts to Grant C. Knight of Lexington, Ky., May 17, 1930, Grant C. Knight Manuscript Collection, University of Kentucky Library. In a note she left with her manuscripts, she says about her symbolic use of music in *My Heart and My Flesh*: "In my dark moments when Voice said to me, 'You have no business writing about a violinist since you are not one,' I have always replied that neither am I a tobacco grower." E. M. Roberts Collection (seventeen boxes), Manuscript Division, Library of Congress. Dr. Woodbridge Spears, in an illuminating dissertation "Elizabeth Madox Roberts, a Biographical and Critical Study," 1953, University of Kentucky Library, gives much information about the growth of her interest in music.

One reason is the vagueness of the long symbolic prologue, better omitted or read last even by the later reader;[4] and another reason is the relatively small amount of external conflict and action in the narrative. Yet the close reader of 1927, particularly if he remembered *The Time of Man*, perceived that this second novel continued the theme of spiritual death and rebirth, but with the material circumstances of the leading character and the sequence of happenings reversed. In this respect *My Heart and My Flesh* is complementary to *The Time of Man*, with contrasting social class, tempo, and direction of movements, as Miss Roberts points out in a note left among her manuscripts.

The Time of Man is organized around the age-old journey motif, or, more noticeably, employs the American motif of extreme mobility, especially the Southern rural tradition of the wandering individual with a hungry heart, "down one road and up another and down again," "aways a-looken at everything in the world and expecting to see something more," "on and on, without end, going, day and night and day and rain and windy weather, and sun and then rain again, wanting things and then having things and then wanting," the eye never satisfied with seeing nor the ear filled with hearing. This first novel, featuring the peasant class, but only as poetic symbol, is a story of irregular additions, Ellen Chesser beginning with scarcely anything more than the breath of life and slowly adding, to quote a manuscript note of the author, "minute particle by minute particle . . . sounds, sights, friends, lovers, material possessions, memories, intuitions, defeat followed by renewal."

In contrast, her second novel, *My Heart and My Flesh*, though set in the same rural area, was designed as an experiment in reverse. It is as if she were now writing a novel, not about poor whites but about the patrician landowners mentioned in the first novel, the Wakefields and the MacMurtries, as she notes in a fragmentary letter written while she was just

4. McDowell (p. 125) defends the prologue but admits that it could serve as well as epilogue: "These opening pages should be read as prologue and as epilogue much as the prologue or first section of a Faulkner novel should be reread in light of the work as a whole."

getting under way with the novel.[5] But these landowners are now conceived of as in gentle decay, again symbolic of a great Southern social change of the nineteenth century. The accent is not on social change, however, but on individual character as affected by the way she reacts to drastic reverses. *My Heart and My Flesh* is a story of *subtraction*, the central character (Theodosia Bell) beginning with family prestige and property but already headed toward relentless loss until she is left with scarcely more than the breath of life, and she tries to destroy even that before she is resurrected. Among her notes Miss Roberts left an undated, revealing comment to herself about her method and intent in this second novel:

> The method here was a steady taking away until there was nothing left but the bare breath of the throat and the simplified spirit. The work begins with a being who has been reared in plenty and security. She has the pride of family, of wealth (as such goes in the South of our country), a pride in being the honored and petted child of parents, a pride in personal charm and in popularity with friends and associates, and finally a pride in musical skill and in a boundless ambition to play the fiddle well. All these gentle conceits are gathered into the person of Theodosia.

> One by one these things are taken from her to the upbuilding of her understanding and the growth of tolerance and wisdom through suffering. Each of these is lost and more. Lover, pride in ambition and the fiddle hand, pride in family, and at length the house in which her family had dwelt—all of these go from her. Friends are lost. Stability is lost and she gives herself in loveless passion. Food is taken from her and health goes. Finally half crazed or more by her condition she lives a brief hell of confusion and despair, warmed and fed by only the stupid lover and his passions. Sunk to the degradation of the nether hell, she lived thus for a winter.

> It is the story of a woman who went to hell and returned to walk among you.

> Out of the icy waters of the frozen pond where she had

5. November 28, 1926, E. M. Roberts Collection, Library of Congress, Manuscript Division.

gone in spirit and determination, being ready to make the last dash from the door that would sweep her into the water to drown, she experienced a resurrection. Spirit asserted itself over the necessities of death. She prepared an orderly departure from her hell, informed by judgment or the knowing and thinking, the associative entity of her being. She went from the aunt's farm and let chance find a way for her again among living men. In the end is the rare lover, the maker of fine cows, the adoring voice among the distant barns singing, or the hand that led her about over the pasture to show her the cattle and the mind to offer her companionship and a shared living among these excellent things.[6]

These contrasting terms, "addition" as applied to *The Time of Man* and "subtraction" as applied to *My Heart and My Flesh*, like all opposites, are relative and reciprocal terms. Neither one has meaning except as it is related to the other. Both Ellen in the first novel and Theodosia in the second lost; both gained. Both reacted to their experiences in such a manner as to gain strength and wisdom. This is the main point the novelist keeps making: the significance is not the precise thing which happened to the characters but how they reacted to what happened to them. Throughout her writing career Miss Roberts kept suggesting the polarities of experience (as did one of her favorite writers, Jules Laforgue), the cooperation of opposites, life's contradictions, the dualism between election and damnation which is a part of the American Puritan tradition.[7]

My Heart and My Flesh introduces several related themes. It may be considered a study in the decay of gentility, the fall of the House of Bell, miscegenation and incest, the transformation of adolescence into maturity, the mysteriousness of memories, the presentness of the past, the capacity to prevail through endurance as if man's first duty were to live, the effects upon character of various reactions to suffering where there is not the

6. Roberts Collection, Library of Congress.
7. Richard Chase, *The American Novel and Its Tradition*, New York, 1957, suggests that the American novel, more than the English, emphasizes life's contradictions and irreconcilables, reflecting the American passion for extremes, life's disunities.

will to suffer (as there is in some Hemingway novels), or cathar-
sis achieved through suffering when aided by sensitivity to phe-
nomenal nature and responsiveness to simple human affection—
all themes which were to recur often in her eight remaining
books. Two other parallel themes, however, seem nearer the
central intent of the author. One is a longing for the identification of spirit, or a yearning to discover a reality beyond fact
(what life essentially is, so elusive, so bewildering), an intense
search for the permanent underlying so much change.[8] Like
Ellen in her first novel, Theodosia is "aways a-looken at everything in the world and expecting to see something more."
Theodosia was always "looking more deeply within, parting
thought and thought, parting the semi-dark which lies between," to use the author's words. The title of the novel features this search: "My heart and my flesh crieth out for the
living God." This is the theme stressed in the first half of the
book, and it is made appealing by the haunting pathos of
Theodosia's absolute aloneness, her mother dead, her father a
lecherous and conscienceless reprobate, her grandfather im-
poverished and defeated by the decay of the world he loved,
one lover jilting her and another burned up accidentally. This
near-desperate search for the meaning of life is dramatized for
the reader about a third of the way through the novel by an
image of lonely Theodosia before a waning fire in the bedroom
of her dying grandfather: "When all the subtractions were
made, the naked man was left. . . . There should be a soul
there somewhere, she thought, and she searched into the with-
ered leavings of crippled body and quavering voice. When she
had found this entity in her grandfather she would, she
thought, be able to identify it within herself."[9] This haunting
search is intensified by Theodosia's primary mode of self-
expression (the violin) and also by the associative imagery of
the highly symbolic prologue, about which more will be said
shortly. Theodosia is in somewhat the same mood as Pascal

8. ". . . each of her heroines is sent on an odyssey of self-discovery
only to learn there is no self to be discovered; there is rather a self in
process of creation." (Rovit, p. 154.)
9. *My Heart and My Flesh*, p. 102.

was three hundred years before: "When I consider the brief span of my life, swallowed up in the eternity before and behind it, the small space that I fill, or even see, engulfed in the infinite immensity of spaces which I know not, and which know not me, I am afraid, and wonder to see myself here rather than there, for there is no reason why I should be here rather than there, now rather than then."[10] The more clearly central theme, however, as has been mentioned, is the age-old one of withdrawal and return, or death and rebirth, which was to be a recurring theme in her later writing and the central one in her seventh novel, *Black Is My True Love's Hair*. Professors Campbell and Foster comment on the frequent recurrence of this theme in Miss Roberts' books and also its prominence in the Old Testament, one of the strong influences on Miss Roberts: in the stories of Noah, for instance, Jonah, Joseph, and especially Job.[11] Theodosia dies and is recreated. She answered affirmatively Job's echoing question: "If a man die, shall he live again?"[12] None of the American naturalists (Crane, Norris, or Dreiser) would have depicted this new birth, even if they could understand it, because they did not believe in being born again. Theodosia survives, not because of her physical fitness or accident or luck, but because of her moral progress in working toward the will to live as a dignified and divine human being. The two simple but great influences in effecting this therapy, in bringing about this resurrection, are sensitivity to rural nature and responsiveness to unsophisticated true love, the ego having established a working relationship with the non-ego. From a letter which Miss Roberts wrote to Louise McElroy in Springfield, Kentucky, when she was just getting a good start on this novel, we know that these two themes (search for a reality beyond fact, and death and rebirth) were at the heart of her intention: "I have tried to develop some essence," she wrote her friend, "such as we may call 'the human spirit.' . . . It is a story of a woman . . . who went to hell and came back,

10. *Pensées*, trans. W. F. Trotter, New York, Modern Library, pp. 74-75.
11. *Op. cit.*, pp. 159-60.
12. Job xiv:14.

who was impaled on the very topmost and last and most ex-
cruciating pinprick of suffering and privation. By moving all
accessories I hope to make live a spirit, a most inner essence, a
will-to-live. It is a large problem, a difficult undertaking perhaps, but necessary."[13]

Miss Roberts mistakenly thought she could help communi-
cate this double theme by experimenting with an ambitious
narrative technique in the prologue, beyond her full mastery,
but interesting; and now with the benefit of her notes clear
enough. This thirty-three-page, over-subtle prologue is a fantasy
employing associative imagery, and the cosmic consciousness
of Luce (symbolically "light"), ranging over time past, time
present, and hinting at time to come. This long stream-of-con-
sciousness introduction is supposed to represent timelessness and
omniscience, as the main part of the novel, coming to us
through Theodosia, represents transiency. As she wrote to
Harriet Monroe, she intended this symbolic prologue to serve
as the introduction to a whole cycle of novels she had already
in mind, and indeed her fourth novel, *The Great Meadow*,
does serve as an introduction to the House of Bell, here in her
second novel falling.[14] Luce lives in Mome[15] (which represents
Covington, Kentucky, where Miss Roberts went to high school),
whereas the world of Theodosia is probably in Washington
County, Kentucky. Among the Library of Congress papers is a
long manuscript called "The Book of Luce," showing Miss
Roberts' lifelong fascination with this method of treating symbolically whole cycles of time. Professors Campbell and Foster
aptly compare this intriguing prologue in her second novel to
the prelude of a symphony.[16] By the time the reader gets to the
end of the prologue he has left the infinite consciousness of
Luce and is supposed to be entering the finite, sensitive consciousness of Theodosia. In a note, Miss Roberts says of her
technique: "The mind here to be entered is the mind of the

13. Roberts Collection, Library of Congress.
14. E. M. Roberts to Harriet Monroe, Monroe Collection, University
of Chicago.
15. Rovit (p. 29) suggests that Mome may stand for "my home."
16. *Op. cit.*, p. 166.

woman, Theodosia. The process begins with a Knower, an Observer, Luce, a sensitive onlooker. The narrative moves slowly into Theodosia's mind, beginning in the mind of Luce, seeing Theodosia first from the outside, moving more closely and intently into her experience until it becomes identical with her consciousness."[17]

Other interesting characteristics of Miss Roberts' style here and elsewhere are her abundant use of symbolism, her use of music as a major motif, her strange attraction to dreams as a means of deepening meaning (not immediately clear to the hasty reader of *My Heart and My Flesh*), surrealistic dialogue,[18] her large use of appropriate folklore, and her lyric prose. Her use of symbols throughout her writing, influenced by her liking for Laforgue, Corbière, and Virginia Woolf, is too pervasive for treatment here. Three years before her first novel she had written a note of advice to herself which might be taken as the aptest possible motto for all her work: Cultivate, she says, "the way of symbolism working through poetic realism."[19]

The symbolic use of dreams is illustrated vividly in this novel by Theodosia's four blurred and prescient dreams on the night her lover burned up, and more suggestively by the dream on pages 177-78 which her publisher objected to and got her to modify a little: one she has in a moment of nodding as she is becoming nauseated at her repulsive father's recollections of lechery; she saw a parade of vague haggard women in the midst of whom her naked father appeared, blown up into a gigantic symbol of excessive sexual vitality.

As with her symbolism, Miss Roberts' large use of appropriate folklore can only be suggested here. It pervades all her books and provides the title of her most elusive book, *Black Is My True Love's Hair*. In the novel we are discussing she uses folk speech, Negro work songs, proverbial sayings ("See them there hens out eaten grass in the rain? When you see hens out in the morning eaten grass in the rain, that's a sure sign hit'll rain all day," page 265), folk health practices (like drinking

17. Roberts Collection, Library of Congress.
18. Rovit, p. 29.
19. Roberts Collection, Library of Congress.

hog's blood), and folk songs on pages 31, 32, 33, 268, 271, and 284.

Characteristically, Miss Roberts couldn't find a title conveying precisely the right thematic implication. Some of the titles she considered before settling on "My Heart and My Flesh" are: "L'Abondante," "The Abundant Woman," "Plenitude," "Behind Green Pastures," "Field Lovers," "Proud Fields," "Without a Name," "The Glittering Sword" (from Job), "The Sparks Fly Upward" ("Man is born unto trouble as the sparks fly upward," Job), "The Chronicle," "The Season's Return," and "Full Circle." No subject occurs so often in her thirty-seven letters to her publishers about this novel. These are fascinating letters because they tell so much about her intent as literary artist. There is room here for only a third of one of these letters, addressed to Mr. Huebsch of Viking and now in the publisher's files:

August 7, 1927

Dear Mr. Huebsch:
I have worked on titles all week and have written three full pages of them only to scratch most of them out after a little. The difficulty is this. A title throws an emphasis somewhere and this book is already complete in itself. I see it lie out before me continually as a complete design. There are only a few ideas that I seem willing to stress. One is the person, the woman involved. Another is the land.

Many thanks for the suggestion, "As the Sparks Fly Upward." It is indeed all the things you say of it. It throws an emphasis on the idea of trouble, however, and seems to me to throw the design out of plumb a little. It is good, though, and I lean toward it. My ideal title would center to the woman and her abundance as a sensitive body and mind. It would be such a word as the French adjective *abondante* used as a noun *L'abondante*, and I have cast about to try to find an English equivalent, but there is not any. "The Abundant Woman" and all such are rejected. "The Time of Man" gets in the way of any title with "woman" in it. Such an idea as this word would convey is exactly what I want. It would cover the abundance of the woman's trouble or sorrow and her discipline. It would include her as a lover and a living spirit. It is a great title and I wish the book might go into French so that it might be used. . . .

I wish I had the musician's privilege of merely numbering my work. A title is an impertinence. . . .

Though not popular, *My Heart and My Flesh* is a significant novel, as is most of Miss Roberts' fiction. Why, then, was it (is it) not more popular? Here are half a dozen suggested reasons.

1. Miss Roberts was too much concerned with man in general and too little with individual man. After her first novel, she let a veil come between herself and the coarse-grained world.[20] Because of her unmarried, somewhat shy, and solitary nature, she lived and wrote as one removed from life in action. Like one of her favorite writers, Virginia Woolf, she lived in an ambiance of ideality, to borrow a phrase coined by Elizabeth Bowen.[21] Rovit considers her second novel more like a case history than the presentation of a struggling individual.[22]

2. In most of her fiction there is too little external action and possibly too little internal tension, especially physical tension. The internal action is probably intense, but more like a severe and unremitting headache and heartache than a shock, and readers in her day wanted to be shocked. Theodosia, for instance, suffers acutely, but she is an enduring sufferer rather than a defiant one; until the end, she *undergoes* rather than acts. The reader misses the appeal of overt, urgent struggle.

3. Like most of her other fiction, *My Heart and My Flesh* is a novel of erosion and rebuilding in an age when we were experiencing an epidemic of violence, whether in international war, labor disputes, or gangsterdom, and when the novel of violence was understandably in vogue. *My Heart and My Flesh* is devoid of overt violence. In fact, there is in it too much humble acceptance and too little rebellion, ranting, and disillusionment for the American public of the 1920's. As in the novel of violence, Miss Roberts reveals our animality, but un-

20. Clifton Fadiman, reviewing her last book in the *New Yorker*, March 29, 1941, p. 68, suggests something like this.
21. *New York Times Book Review*, June 26, 1949, p. 21.
22. *Op. cit.*, p. 47.

like most specialists in this genre she also reveals the human capacity for self-sacrifice and love. A novel like *My Heart and My Flesh* takes time to show the process of the *development* of character, whereas the novels we preferred when Miss Roberts was writing are those beginning near the climax (like a short story or drama) and featuring strenuous and dangerous action, not growth. As Professor Frohock points out, the plot of the novel of violence is like that of a drama more than the conventional novel: it is concerned with mounting tension, climax, and then resolution of tension.

4. McDowell thinks the chief weakness of her second novel is the lack of forceful "subsidiary characters and setting" to reinforce the theme.[23]

5. The carefully modulated sentences, her poetic diction and imagery, and her successful attempt at symbolism through poetic realism were out of harmony with the staccato style of the Hemingway school and also the rhetorical exuberance and vehemence of Faulkner. This, let us hope, will come to be to her honor and glory. *My Heart and My Flesh* is poetic in a period when the content and the mood of the strenuous novels we bought were not suited to poetry.[24]

6. Miss Roberts' unmastered technical experiments (especially in this her second novel, in the fantasy *Jingling in the Wind*, and in *Black Is My True Love's Hair*) hindered public understanding. Without a little help, the average reader does not fully comprehend her aims in most of her novels, except *The Time of Man* and *The Great Meadow*. With only a small amount of help, however, provided by recent studies, her rich experimentation can be understood and appreciated.

One could mention half a dozen commendable features equally compelling. Miss Roberts deserves, and probably will come to receive, more favorable attention than she experienced when living. She is better than our literary historians have discovered yet.

23. *Op. cit.*, p. 127.
24. For a discussion of the American novel of violence, see W. M. Frohock, *The Novel of Violence in America, 1920-1950*, Dallas, Texas, Southern Methodist University, 1950.